8 - 20 - 21 F

11 33 PM

Prisoners of War in American Conflicts

Harry P. Riconda

The Scarecrow Press, Inc.
Lanham, Maryland, and Oxford
2003

SCARECROW PRESS, INC.

Published in the United States of America
by Scarecrow Press, Inc.
A Member of the Rowman & Littlefield Publishing Group
4501 Forbes Boulevard, Suite 200
Lanham, Maryland 20706
www.scarecrowpress.com

PO Box 317
Oxford
OX2 9RU, UK

British Library Cataloguing in Publication Information Available

Library of Congress Cataloging-in-Publication Data

Riconda, Harry P.
    Prisoners of war in American conflicts / Harry P. Riconda.
      p. cm.
    Includes bibliographical references (p.).
    ISBN 0-8108-4765-5 (alk. paper)
      1. United States—History, Military. 2. Prisoners of war—United States—
History. 3. Prisoners of war—History. I. Title.
    E181.R53 20030
    355'.00973—dc21   2003001289

To prisoners of war who returned
and those who did not
Especially Lieutenant Colonal Donald Cook,
United States Marine Corps Winner of
the Congressional Medal of Honor

Contents

Preface

From the beginning of time to the present day prisoners of war have been captured, but their status and treatment have radically changed throughout the centuries. When I was in high school from 1941 to 1945, I avidly read books on war, and throughout college I was fascinated by stories of prisoners in books and films.

Perhaps the most famous for me were *The Great Escape, Von Ryan's Express*, and *Target Unknown*. The film *Target Unknown* was shown at the air force intelligence officers school at Lowry Air Force Base in Denver. In it the Germans try to trick the Americans to reveal information about their units and missions without realizing they are doing it. This particular technique was corroborated by one of my air force ROTC instructors at Fordham College who had been a prisoner of war. Little did I know at that time that I would be involved to some extent at a later date with anti-Communist prisoners of war in Korea.

These prisoners interested me greatly, and I thought that someday I would like to write about POWs. After my discharge, I settled down to teaching history and English in high school. After I retired I turned to writing, as well as teaching as an English adjunct in a community college.

In this book I provide a historical overview of prisoners of war, emphasizing official and unofficial wars in which the United States has participated. I consider the subject from all sides whenever possible.

The topics I address include treatment of prisoners, housing, food, clothing, medical care, and employment of prisoners, as well as retaliation, ransom, parole, and repatriation, which I define in chapter 1.

After a brief consideration of early historical times, I discuss the American Revolution. The remaining topics, which are listed in the table of contents, end with the Gulf War and the current war on terrorism.

An extensive bibliography of all works consulted appears at the end of the book.

1

Primitive Times to Early Modern History

In primitive times there weren't many prisoners of war because victors eventually killed their captives. Will Durant defines "primitive" tribes as those that make "little or no provision for unproductive days, and little or no use of writing."[1] He further states, "It was a great moral improvement when men ceased to kill or eat their fellowmen, and merely made them slaves."[2] Thus another way to dispose of prisoners was by cannibalism, which eliminated any need to feed and care for them.

HOSTAGE STAGE

Sometimes the conquering leaders or members of their families were held as hostages to guarantee no further difficulties. This period probably came later as more societal groups or tribes combined into small nations, although the custom followed by the victors was, generally speaking, to slay the captives and to take no prisoners. Durant also states that cannibalism was "universal . . . in nearly all primitive tribes."[3] Students of English literature recall the irony of Jonathan Swift's "Modest Proposal" in which he lays down a plan for getting rid of the unnecessary children in Ireland in the 1700s. For Swift, this was a biting satire; for primitive peoples, it was a reality.

1

Did the cannibalism stage precede the killing stage? Or vice versa? We have no set answer, but it probably varied from area to area and might even have been simultaneous in some areas.

The term "prisoner of war" is not mentioned in the indexes of many books on ancient history, which tends to support the case for there not being many prisoners of war. The term "slave" occurs often and generally the slave is a prisoner of war, but the two terms cannot be equated universally.

The Bible gives some examples of leaders who did not spare prisoners. Cruelty and savagery seemed to be the norm for dealing with them, not justice or mercy or compassion. The rise of agriculture, which led to the availability of more land and the realization that a live captive could provide practical services, suggested to conquerors that pressing prisoners into slavery was better than killing them. Thus the institution of slavery grew and became profitable. The rulers of Egypt sent many of their captives to the gold mines and used their Hebrew captives and many others as slaves to build the pyramids and other structures.

The Assyrians were particularly cruel to their prisoners, beheading many of them. The Romans subjected prisoners to crucifixion and target practice, made them gladiators, and tortured them for entertainment. As time progressed, slaves were used as a source of cheap labor on Roman farms, and Greek slaves became servants for wealthy Roman families and even tutors for their children. Thus Greeks became "the teachers of Rome."

The Roman Senate outlawed the killing of Roman slaves, and the spread of Christianity improved the conditions of prisoners. Early Christianity, of course, had been a thorn in the side of the Romans. When the wars between Carthage and Rome ended, many captives from Carthage, Spain, Gaul, Macedonia, Greece, and Asia Minor came under the control of Rome and were sold as slaves. Breasted tells us, "The coast of the Adriatic opposite Italy alone yielded one hundred and fifty thousand captives."[4] In Greece, slave labor played an important role in the lives of its citizens. But when Greek victors deemed prisoners of war of no use to them, or if the Greeks thought that the death of prisoners would serve as a warning to enemies, they did not hesitate to kill many and sell the rest into slavery.

TRIBUTE

Tribute is money paid to a hostile foreign nation to leave the payee country alone—protection money. The Phoenicians, who wanted to exercise a commercial monopoly of the Mediterranean Sea, paid off the Assyrian king Shalmaneser to leave them alone.[5] The Egyptian Thutmose I invaded Syria and put it under tribute,[6] and supposedly he received tribute money from the Babylonians and the Hittites. Tribute was the main reason for the war between the Barbary pirates and the United States, which is discussed in chapter 4.

In the Middle Ages, Christianity promoted the code of chivalry, which tried to eliminate killing for the sake of killing among the knights whose main pastime was fighting. The Church promulgated the Peace of God and the Truce of God decrees. The Truce of God prohibited fighting and warfare on certain days of the week and on special holidays, while the Peace of God protected women, children, clergy, and other noncombatants.

THE CRUSADES

The Crusades offered an opportunity to fight for a good cause, but often the Crusaders were intolerant and cruel to their Islamic enemies. The Fourth Crusade was denounced by the pope on account of greed. It served no true religious purpose.

The followers of Islam rarely showed mercy to their prisoners, and both sides exacted cruelties from each other. Both Islam and Christianity failed in terms of justice and religion. Christopher Marlowe's *The Jew of Malta* and Shakespeare's *The Merchant of Venice* are literary pieces that demonstrate these failures. The severity and cruelty of Islamic leaders were relieved only in circumstances that involved valor and gallantry demonstrated by losers. Christian leaders, both lay and religious, burned alleged witches and heretics.

Those who promoted humanitarian principles had an excellent role model in the person of Hugo Grotius, a Dutch lawyer and philosopher, who had been a prisoner of war. He created a set of rules for warring nations to follow for a release in a manner prescribed by agreement of the representatives involved. The next year, 1659, the Treaty of the Pyrenees was settled between the king of France and the king of Spain. Provisions of this treaty dictated that all prisoners be freed when they covered their expenses and paid what they owed. If they didn't pay ransom, provision was made for such a contingency. All other prisoners and subjects of the lords and kings were to be set at liberty without delay. All French soldiers and prisoners in places held by his Catholic Majesty on the African coast were to be freed without paying ransom or expense.

Many subsequent European treaties provided for release of prisoners after wars. The Treaty of Paris, February 10, 1763, concluded the French and Indian War. The European colonists of America had not yet received their independence. Though they were fighting for Britain they felt they had won the war on their own. In this treaty all prisoners on both sides captured on land and sea, as well as hostages, were restored without ransom. This war was called the Seven Years War in Europe. As a result of the treaty, Britain took possession of French Canada and all French territory east of the Mississippi with the exception of New Orleans, which was ceded to Spain.

These territories, of course, figured prominently in the Revolutionary War, as a result of which the United States became an independent nation. American colonists gained a great deal of confidence as a result of fighting valiantly in the French and Indian War, which prepared them for the next war.

NOTES

1. Will Durant, *Our Oriental Heritage: The Story of Civilization: Part 1* (New York: Simon and Schuster, 1954), 5

2. Durant, *Our Oriental Heritage*, 20.

3. Durant, *Our Oriental Heritage*, 10.

4. James Henry Breasted, *The Conquest of Civilization* (New York: Harper, 1926), 561.

5. A. T. Olmstead, *History of Assyria* (Chicago: University of Chicago Press, 1951), 125.

6. Durant, *Our Oriental Heritage*, 153.

2

The American Revolution

By 1763 the French and Indian War came to a close. This had been a war between France and Britain in which the American colonists, the British, and some Indian tribes fought against the French and other Indian tribes. The Treaty of Paris of 1763, signed in February, officially ended the conflict and gave to Britain a great deal of land and resources. Britain felt strongly that it had not received sufficient help from the colonists, whereas American colonists felt they had done most of the fighting and won the contest without much aid from the mother country.

With the newly acquired land and its wealth in resources, however, came new problems of finance. These necessitated a radical change from Britain's previous policy of salutary neglect to an imperialistic policy of economics with emphasis on enforcement. Such measures as the Quartering Act of 1765, the Townshend Acts of 1767, the Sugar Tax of 1774, the Stamp Act of 1776, and the Coercive Acts (also called the Intolerable Acts) of 1774, as well as certain events such as the so-called Boston Massacre of 1770 and the Boston Tea Party of 1773, were generating tension and suggested that rebellion was just around the corner.

When did the actual revolution start? With the measures and events mentioned above? With the first shots fired at Lexington? Or did it start in the minds of the colonists, as some historians have theorized, even before? The fact is that the first shot was fired at Lexington, as

Ralph Waldo Emerson later commented, "Here once the embattled farmers stood and fired the shot heard around the world."

THE DECLARATION OF INDEPENDENCE

The Declaration of Independence represented "the crossing of the Rubicon." Americans could not turn back and would have to fight for their independence. There would be a war, and people on both sides would be killed, wounded, and captured. Those taken captive would raise, for the first time in the history of the newly proclaimed nation, the problem of prisoners of war.[1]

BRITISH TREATMENT OF AMERICAN PRISONERS

Britain looked on the colonists as traitors in a civil war and thus refused to accord prisoner of war status to captive soldiers. Britain, with its experience in previous wars, was fully aware of problems associated with the seizure of prisoners, but for the United States it was a different story.

American prisoners were allowed only two-thirds of the daily rations that British soldiers received, and only minimal medical care, clothing, and quarters. Two very good reasons for returning POWs included the necessity of manpower and the burden of feeding so many men. The British army was not anxious to talk about terms of agreement, since doing so would represent a recognition of American independence. There would be other problems in housing and caring for POWs, such as granting paroles that avoided retaliatory measures.

In July 1776, twenty-seven men were captured at Bunker Hill and confined at Lexington, according to Lowell. His book (as well as those written by Dandridge and Charles Metzger) on Revolutionary War prisoners provides many details.

Another group of Americans taken prisoner was sent to Boston from Virginia. By early 1776 about 300 young Americans who had invaded Quebec in late 1775 were being confined in the seminary of the Jesuit college in Quebec.[2] Among the earliest locations for POWs were Quebec and Halifax, Nova Scotia. Soldiers captured in New York were brought to Quebec but finally sent to Boston and exchanged in early 1776. Reports of POWs in Halifax began in early 1776 and continued until the end of the war. Most of those captured in Quebec and Halifax were remnants of the invasion of Canada in 1775–1776 led by Benedict Arnold and Richard Montgomery, were captured in Indian raids into New York, Pennsylvania, and New England, or were POWs taken during John Burgoyne's invasion of the Hudson River Valley in 1777.

A few unfortunate American soldiers were confined in prisons on other continents. In January 1777 sixteen Americans were transferred from Quebec to Senegal. Benjamin Franklin vainly protested this move. Some men were sent to Antigua in the West Indies and about 400 to England from South Carolina.[3] These moves, restricted to the early years of the war, were bitterly resented by military and political leaders. New York City and Long Island became the center of the entire British prison complex organized during the revolution.[4]

The very first POWs seized by the Americans at Concord and Lexington were put into the custody of the Committee of Safety, and the Massachusetts Provincial Congress immediately took measures to exchange them for Americans in British custody. At Charleston, Massachusetts, on June 17, 1775, the first POW exchange was consummated. In the summer of 1776, local commanding officers were granted the authority to deal in direct negotiations for POW exchanges. This set a precedent for subsequent exchanges, but cartels in 1779–1780 were difficult to effect because the British continued to consider Americans traitors. It was much easier to deal at the local level. Another problem was that there was no single executive under the Articles of Confederation, a problem later rectified by the federal Constitution. There was no general cartel exchange throughout the war.

Housing for prisoners was a serious problem for both sides. The British utilized churches, sugarhouses, and jails, but the worst conditions were endured by men confined in the British prison ships, for whom George Washington expressed great concern. On June 6, 1777, he appointed Elias Boudinot as commissary general to help them, but this was chiefly for captured soldiers and not private sailors who were beyond the scope of his authority.[5] Boudinot, however, resigned April 20, 1778.

On June 23, 1777, seventeen days after Boudinot's appointment, Congress directed that all present and future POWs be delivered to the commissary general or his deputies. In the summation of Boudinot's duties there was no mention of POW exchanges, but he willingly accepted this responsibility. Charles Metzger, in *The Prisoners of the American Revolution*,[6] devoted chapter 13 to the functions of the commissary. The first concern was housing and then provisioning. Rations were subjected to a variety of contingencies—transportation, weather, naval encounters, and the efficiency of supply departments. Another problem was the wives and children of POWs. Fuel and clothing (depending on weather) were important considerations. In chapter 6 Metzger deals with prisoner treatment and in chapter 8 with parole and its advantages over exchange, which could be slow and complex. Later in the revolution the final responsibility for exchange rested on the Continental Congress.

Since few British seamen were held as POWs, Washington didn't really have a good retaliatory possibility at his disposal. New York City Loyalists seemed to be concerned about soldiers confined near them but not about conditions of sailors. They considered the sailors captured as being involved for profit purposes and thus deserving of no sympathy. These were the risks they were taking.[7]

On May 12, 1780, Charleston surrendered and 5,400 surrendered to the British. On August 13, 1780, diplomat Henry Laurens was sent to the Netherlands by the Continental Congress.[8] He left Philadelphia aboard the brigantine *Mercury,* which was captured on September 3, 1780. Laurens was then taken to St. John's, Newfoundland, and later to another ship that brought him to England. He was then confined in the Tower of London from October 6, 1780, to December 31, 1780. He wasn't mistreated and was finally exchanged for Lord Cornwallis, captured at Yorktown in 1781, and permitted to go to Paris. The defeat of Cornwallis in 1781 at Yorktown marked a turning point in the war after which the number of POW exchanges rose.

Men held on prison ships were in crowded conditions below decks without adequate clothing, razors, soap, or vegetables, and they were required to perform labor on the ships. Only seamen, not soldiers, were on the ship *Jersey.* The Hessians took better care of seamen POWs than the British had, but more than 1,000 men died. Being confined on such ships was almost a death sentence. Metzger labels the prison ships of the revolution "floating hells."

Paullin contains some interesting sidelights. Congress ordered the Agent of the Marines on April 15, 1783, to free all naval enemy POWs since it was rapidly getting out of the naval business by terminating the war at sea.[9] When American seamen held as POWs became numerous, they had to be released but only on a parole basis. With the end of the war there were still many Americans in English prisons.[10]

Not everybody was enamored with the illustrious George Washington. General Charles Lee, a hero in the revolution, wrote his friend General Horatio Gates, "Entre nous, a certain great man is most damnably deficient." The same day he wrote the letter, Friday, December 13, 1776, he was captured by the British. In 1775 he had been made a major general, third in command of the Continental Army. At Charleston he prevented the British from taking the town, and he became second in command on the retirement of Artemus Ward. But afterward he seemed "to drag his feet, even to disobey his commander's orders." Then Lee made the mistake of staying too long in a tavern in Basking Ridge, New Jersey, and was captured by the enemy.

Having Lee out of the picture as a POW for sixteen months worked to Washington's advantage because he didn't have a rival under him and was successful in future battles. When Lee was repatriated, he showed his true colors and disobeyed orders, for which he was court-martialed and convicted.[11] Kelly states that, according to documents found 100 years later, "during his captivity, Lee submitted to the British a plan of his own for subduing the rebellious Colonies!"

George III of Britain wanted to treat American captives according to British law and hang Americans seized on land for the crime of treason and to consider as pirates those seized at sea. He would never have approved of the early exchanges of the war made at the local level, but 3,000 miles separated him from America. The British government hired about 30,000 Hessian mercenaries during the American Revolution. Hessian chasseurs and grenadiers under Colonel von Donap and an advanced British guard under Sir Henry Clinton crossed the Narrows to Long Island. Many Hessians were taken prisoner, but the Hessians themselves took about 500 prisoners, two of whom were General Sterling and one other general. According to Lowell, since the Hessians had no horses, some American prisoners were harnessed in front of the cannon[12] and then put aboard the ships of war. Lowell's book clearly outlines the activities and roles played by the Hessians.

A conflict appears between an official report of Sir William Howe who maintained that the American losses consisted of about 3,300 Americans killed, wounded, taken prisoner, and drowned, and an inquiry based on a Washington report stating that the British report exaggerated and the American losses were not more than 1,000 of whom three-quarters were prisoners.

American commanders behaved courteously toward Hessian officers, and General Sterling, who had been exchanged after his capture on Long Island, attested to the fact that he had been well treated and would in turn treat Hessian prisoners similarly.

BRITISH AND HESSIAN PRISONERS

From 1776 to 1783 German mercenaries in the British service in America averaged 20,000 strong, and of the 12,554 who remained, some had been killed in battle or died from their wounds or sickness. There had also been desertions.[13] At the end of the war many chose not to be repatriated. In fact, many of their governments didn't want them back.

When George Washington attacked the Hessians quartered at Trenton, he divided his army into three different units so that one could not help the others—a poor tactical move. Perret, however, points out that this disadvantage was offset by the fact that the Hessian colonel did not use sentries. Consequently, a third of the Hessians escaped, but Americans captured 948 prisoners.[14]

General Burgoyne, after consultation with his generals at Saratoga in upstate New York, surrendered his entire army. Included in the agreement was a provision that his men would return to Britain if they promised not to fight again. In other words, a parole was granted to all of them. But the terms of the agreement were not carried out because General Howe delayed sending transport ships to Boston. Consequently, the Continental Congress had the soldiers marched to Virginia, where they were held as POWs. The number of POWs was rising quickly, including more than 5,000 enemy troops as a result of the Battle of Saratoga. When Lord Cornwallis's army surrendered on October 19, 1781, four years after Saratoga, more British and German soldiers became captives.

After 1782 and the American victory at Yorktown, parole was made much easier to get, even for privates. Parole was always easier to obtain than exchange. From the very beginning of the war the Continental Congress opposed the ransom of prisoners. The only

mention of ransom made during the war occurred when commanding officers of ships were forbidden to make it.

During the revolution soldiers were easier to come by than seamen. On land there were the state militias and volunteer soldiers, but
getting seamen to serve in a fighting capacity on vessels was a real
problem. The press gang approach, which Britain used, was not
adopted. Literature offers many stories of people acquired for sea
duty that way.

According to journals of the Continental Congress, the Congress,
the states, the marine committee, naval boards, and vessel commanders tried many different methods of getting personnel. Attempts were made to put embargoes on privateers who were making
good money, and inducements were offered to captives to change
sides and enter the American services early in the war. Different
public newspapers, the Connecticut *Gazette* in 1777 and the Providence *Gazette* in 1778, cooperated in this effort. Unfortunately, they
admitted to some impressments, but no details were given. What
chiefly worked against some of these efforts was the allure of priva-
teering, which was very profitable and safer than fighting ships, despite the risks of being taken prisoner and experiencing untold hardships aboard prison ships in New York harbor or Plymouth, England.

PRISON SHIPS

Ethan Allen, a military land fighter who had been the hero of Ticonderoga, was held as a POW aboard a prison ship and later moved to
an English jail. Others confined on such vessels were Thomas Andros and Captain Thomas Dring, who wrote of their experiences,
and Philip Frenau, perhaps the most famous prisoner (a passenger
on an armed ship) who was the poet of the American Revolution.
Prison ships and naval prisons of the enemy in New York, Canada,
and the West Indies were overflowing with Americans captured at
sea and on land, and the conditions under which they lived (and so

many died) were absolutely intolerable. Ethan Allen particularly attested to this fact.

Colonel Ethan Allen was captured in Montreal in 1775 in an engagement with General Carleton, betrayed by a spy who escaped from Allen's guard. Allen and his men (40 regulars and some Canadians, Englishmen, and Indians) were outnumbered and had no opportunity to escape. Allen surrendered with the proviso that he would be treated with honor and his men guaranteed humanitarian treatment. Apparently he didn't trust the British, whose treatment of prisoners was somewhat cruel.

An Indian approached Allen and almost killed him. An Irishman with a fixed bayonet came to Allen's aid and Allen commented that his escape from such a terrible fate made even imprisonment look much better, but he had no idea what was to come. He was presented to General Prescott, who called him names and nearly hit him with a cane. The British officer there, Captain McCloud, came to Allen's defense and proclaimed that it would be a dishonorable act for a British officer to hit a prisoner.

General Prescott then ordered some of Allen's Canadians to be executed. Allen threw himself in front of them, maintaining that he was the cause for their taking up arms. General Prescott decided against the execution but had Allen shipped to England with his hands and feet in irons; he was relegated to the lowest and worst part of the ship.

One British officer gave Allen food from his own table and supplied him daily with some grog. Allen, who had treated well the prisoners he captured at Ticonderoga, was permitted to write to General Prescott to tell him about this. Allen was confined in the ship *Gasper* for about six weeks and later transferred to an armed vessel under the command of Captain McCloud, who had treated him properly and transferred Allen to another ship, but this time without the irons. The next ship took Allen to England. Conditions for him and his fellow prisoners were extremely bad—dirty dungeon, little food, and a forty-day voyage to Falmouth. He was considered a rebel and not entitled to better conditions. He fared no better in an English prison. He was returned to America and near the end of November in New York he was admitted to parole with other American officers. He returned to a ship in New York harbor on which he ate with General Campbell and other British officers. The next day he was exchanged for Colonel Campbell and thus Allen's ordeal was over. He had survived. He committed himself to write of his experiences, and his personal narrative is one of the best primary sources for the cruelties perpetrated on prisoners of war on British prison ships.

Captain Thomas Dring also wrote of his recollections in *Recollections of the Jersey Prison Ship.* Poor conditions were vividly described and were quite different from conditions endured by men captured by British soldiers. More than 10,000 died on the *Jersey* and the hospital ships *Scorpion, Strombolo*, and *Hunter*. Conditions in the ships' dungeons were so bad that confinement in any one of them seemed almost tantamount to a sentence of death, as already noted.

Captain Dring was held on a prison ship at two different times. He managed an escape to the Jersey shore but was recaptured and then escaped again. Dring's recollections were reported by Albert Green. At the end of the war in 1783, prisoners were set free. Because of all the deaths aboard the ship, it might well be considered the "Andersonville of the Revolutionary War," according to Green.

The prison ship *Jersey* was located in Wallabout Bay, later the site of the Brooklyn Navy Yard. Although the British started the poor treatment of prisoners, Americans retaliated whenever possible with prison ships such as that in the Thames River near New London, Connecticut. In addition, Americans held captives in the copper mines near East Granby, Connecticut.[15]

Captain Dring's recollections differed from those of soldiers seized by the British. The American navy was in its infancy and depended considerably on armed private vessels operating under letters of marque. Their task was to patrol the coasts and harass enemy ships. There were no cartels in agreements for exchange of unofficial belligerents; consequently, captured British seamen were disposed of by local authorities and not the Continental Congress. General Washington and military authorities were not willing to grant the enemy an advantage by exchanging British Redcoats or Hessians for imprisoned private sailors from American ships. Those who went to sea and ran afoul of a British ship, therefore, would become prisoners in New York harbor British ships for the duration of the war.

Thomas Andros wrote of his experiences in the *Old Jersey*. He was captured August 17, 1781, and placed on the British prison ship moored in New York waters on the Long Island shore. This ship held both diseased and healthy people. When Andros was first on the ship, there were about 400 prisoners there, but this number grew to almost 1,200. Andros estimated that almost 100 Americans died on the ship and felt that if he had remained on it, he would not have survived. He managed to escape before a cartel ship arrived. He had secured permission to go ashore to help get water and confessed that he violated the principle of honor in his escape. He made his way to the east end of Long Island, traveling at night through apple orchards and farms and staying in barns until he arrived at Sag Harbor. After being captured by a privateer near Plumb Island, he escaped, crossed Long Island Sound, and ultimately arrived at Plainfield, Connecticut. Andros likened the prison ship to the Black Hole of Calcutta.

One prime purpose of American ships cruising in European water as was to capture Englishmen and exchange them for American naval prisoners,[16] many of whom had been taken to England, as in the case of Ethan Allen. Paullin further states that 947 Americans were held in Mill Prison in Plymouth. Only one year before the end of the revolution in April 1782, about 1,100 Americans were held in English and Irish jails for the crime of high treason. Some were persuaded to enlist in the British navy and some made successful escapes. Captain Conyngh and sixty prisoners escaped Mill Prison in November 1779.

Benjamin Franklin, as a diplomatic agent on the scene in France, tried to make a deal whereby Britishers who were jailed in France could be exchanged for an equal number of American seamen in British jails. There was extensive correspondence on this issue between Franklin and British officials. Thus, in March 1779, the first exchange of 100 Americans from Mill Prison at Plymouth was sent to France by cartel ships, and in the late summer a second successful exchange was accomplished.

Then suddenly a new problem arose: a requirement that American POWs first be brought to France. Franklin was reluctant to agree with the demand and further difficulties that arose affected the release of British POWs from France. The problem intensified as time progressed, and since so many prisoners were held on American ships, they were released. According to a parole agreement, those released, on their return to Britain, would report to British authorities as released on parole; British authorities were expected to act similarly with American prisoners. Unfortunately, the British were not quite ready to honor this agreement, which resulted in many Americans being held in English prisons at the end of the war.

WOMEN IN THE REVOLUTIONARY WAR

Walter Blumenthal in *Women Camp Followers of the American Revolution* reveals many interesting facts. American women supported many POWs held by the British, as well as fighting troops. British and Hessian women accompanying their men also supported them. The services they gave prevented men on both sides from dying from poor and insufficient food. They also did mending, washed clothes, cooked, and cared for the sick.[17]

Among American militia and soldiers in the Continental Army there were far fewer camp wives and other women than there were with the enemy. George Washington's orders tried to limit the number of camp followers for fear of an inundation of bad women among his soldiers. At the end of May 1778 commanding officers near Valley Forge attempted to persuade women to serve as nurses.

NATHAN HALE

Two soldiers who were not given POW status (and rightly so because they confessed to being spies) were Nathan Hale, an American lieutenant, and Major André, who was in the service of the British. The root of the problem for Major André was the turncoat Benedict Arnold, who did not share the fate of the two spies, Hale and André.

Nathan Hale at the age of sixteen entered Yale, where he was an excellent student and athlete. Among his classmates was Benjamin Talmadge, a colonel of the Revolutionary Army in charge of Major André during his imprisonment. William Patridge wrote a brief biography of Hale, which includes personal information.[18]

The battle of Long Island proved the poor condition of the American forces. The situation seemed hopeless and George Washington asked Colonel Knowlton to call together some officers to try to get a volunteer spy to enter enemy country and ascertain details of enemy communications and movements. Nathan Hale volunteered, but whether or not he was able to secure any information before his capture and transmit it to his superiors is unknown.

Hale spent two weeks behind enemy lines. He made drawings of General Howe's fortifications and estimated the strength and numbers of the enemy. When he was captured and taken aboard the ship *Halifax*, he was well treated but refused any bribery attempts. He confessed his mission fully. Thus General Howe had to order his execution just as George Washington had to do in the later case of Major André, but Howe was thoroughly ruthless in his approach. Washington didn't specifically know about the mission given to Hale until he learned about Hale's death from General Howe's aide, Captain John Montresor. It had been Colonel Knowlton who had secured the services of Hale.

Captain Montresor had been allowed to enter American lines under a flag of truce to make arrangements for a prisoner exchange on the evening of September 22, the day after Hale was captured as a spy.

BENEDICT ARNOLD AND MAJOR ANDRÉ

When Benedict Arnold was assigned as a commandant in Philadelphia, he was dedicated to the American cause, but his fall from grace started there. He was wealthy and used his own money for some of his expeditions, which perhaps was his weak excuse for engaging in speculation on certain items in Philadelphia. There he was charged with profiteering, of which he clearly was guilty. His court-martial sentencing was turned over to George Washington, who simply chided him. Arnold felt insulted about being admonished for his deeds and started negotiating with the enemy to change sides. He made contact with Major John André as his go-between. Ironically, the dashing André (then a captain) had spent his winter courting the lovely Peggy Shippen, daughter of a wealthy Philadelphian, who later married Benedict Arnold.

Arnold was to give the plans for West Point, a strategic geographical site commanding the Hudson River, to Major André. General Henry Clinton didn't have any idea that he was actually corresponding with Arnold, so he sent Major André, his aide-de-camp and chief intelligence officer, to meet behind the lines to arrange for the surrender of the fort. John Miller in his book *The Triumph of Freedom* clearly indicates that André was Clinton's right-hand man and quotes a British officer who said, "By God, Sir Harry Clinton is a mere old woman without André."[19]

On the British ship *Vulture* André sailed up the Hudson and went ashore to deal with Arnold. During their conversation, American batteries opened fire on the ship, which slipped anchor and went down the river. This had the unfortunate result of preventing André from retreating to British lines by water. His only choice was to travel by land. General Clinton had ordered André to wear his uniform and not to have on his person any papers that might compromise the plan. Unfortunately, Arnold strongly suggested that André use a disguise on his return, which he did. This was a serious blunder. Major André (not in uniform) was captured by three militiamen and the papers on him were examined carefully.

At a board consisting of eight brigadier generals and six major generals (one of whom was President Nathaniel Greene), André was court-martialed and sentenced to death with the reluctant approval of George Washington. When André was being led to the court-martial proceedings, Major Benjamin Tallmadge (later a colonel) accompanied the escort and made it a point to sit next to André. In the conversation between the two, Tallmadge revealed the details of Hale's mission as a spy. André recalled that Hale was hanged as a spy and said, "He was hanged as a spy, but you surely do not consider his case and mine alike." Tallmadge replied, "Precisely similar, and similar will be your fate."[20]

Major André's execution was very dignified. He helped the hangman fix the rope around his neck and tie the handkerchief over his eyes. He died in full regimental uniform.

Nathan Hale died on the gallows and made his famous farewell pronouncing his willingness to die for his country. He had not been offered a trial. Sir William Howe gave orders for his immediate execution without benefit of trial. Hale was even refused his request for a clergyman and a Bible by his jailer. According to Commager and Morris in *The Spirit of '76*, Hale was permitted to write letters to his mother and a brother officer.[21]

Major André openly admitted he was a spy and had the honorable distinction of refusing to name his fellow conspirator. Benedict Arnold, about two months later, wearing a British uniform, revealed to the British authorities the name of all American spies in New York. It was quite understandable that many Americans thought the wrong man had been executed and that Benedict Arnold was the one who deserved death.

Washington felt bad about approving André's death sentence, but he had no alternative, just as the British had none in Nathan Hale's case. Both André and Hale were heroes but died for different causes. André, unlike Hale, had a trial. Benedict Arnold, who remained unscathed, received no punishment at all.

SIR HENRY CLINTON

By 1780 the war was in its fifth year and Sir Henry Clinton decided that if he could not conquer the North, perhaps he could at least secure the South for Britain. He decided on Charleston where previously he had failed. With about 100 ships and 6,000 regulars, he arrived at Charleston on February 11. His second in command was Lord Cornwallis. Clinton's delay proved to be a godsend to his opponent, General Benjamin Lincoln, who had only half the forces of Clinton.

Clinton moved to cut off all communications by sea and land. He called for Lincoln to surrender, but Lincoln refused. Clinton's batteries were very effective and they started ripping apart the city of Charleston; on May 12 Lincoln surrendered his army. Clinton returned to New York while Lord Cornwallis tried to wrap things up. The dreadful defeat represented a great loss for the American rebels and the greatest number of POWs taken until Bataan fell in World War II. The Tories were yelling for rebel blood, but Clinton bitterly disappointed them when he granted many pardons and paroles.

Then came a truly crushing blow from Colonel Banastre Tarleton, a bold and brutal cavalry leader who had already routed a small force of American horse and militia in Clinton's plan to sever communications by land. On May 29, Tarleton caught the Virginians on flat ground and his band of mounted Tories soundly beat the American cavalry under Colonel Abraham Buford. When a white flag was put up, Tarleton tore it down, and his men fell on the soldiers with swords and bayonets. Thus the term "Tarleton's quarter" evolved, meaning "take no prisoners." Clinton placed Cornwallis in charge when he returned to New York. The patriots were driven underground into the swamp with their leaders, Francis Marion (the Swamp Fox) and Thomas Sumter.

GENERAL HORATIO GATES

George Washington opposed the appointment of General Gates in South Carolina. Gates's first target was Camden, South Carolina. The ascetic Baron de Kalb tried to rally the scattered Americans, but as a foreigner he had no friends in Congress. Washington preferred Nathaniel Greene as overall commander in the South, but Congress chose General Horatio Gates. Gates took over from de Kalb. Gates went against the advice given him and spent two weeks traveling 120 miles; his forces were desperate for food and supplies. When Cornwallis heard of the advancing troops, he went forward to meet them. The clash came on the evening of August 15 with disastrous results for the Americans. About 2,500 men ran away as well as their illustrious leader, General Gates, who fled 240 miles. This probably vindicated Washington's initial opposition to the appointment of Gates. At this point the hope of the South depended on the so-called partisans.

After the British victories at Charleston and Camden, many northerners started to switch sides. Cornwallis moved inland and north. The partisan leader, General Thomas Sumter, had raised his own guerrilla army. Francis Marion, another partisan leader, and his phantom army never camped more than two nights on one site. Cornwallis sent for Tarleton to track down Marion, but Tarleton couldn't accomplish the mission. Tarleton did, however, defeat General Sumter. Thus, toward the end of 1780, things looked bleak for the South; in both the North and the South, 1780 came to be known as the Dark Days. That year also saw the fiasco of General Benedict Arnold.

THE BATTLE OF KING'S MOUNTAIN

At the Battle of King's Mountain, however, things started looking up. Before Cornwallis left for North Carolina, he detached Major Patrick Ferguson to take care of his inland flank. His ravaging of the Carolinas had not enamored a number of sturdy Scots-Irish frontiersmen living west of the mountains in what is now Tennessee. These people were not rebels but hated Ferguson, who told them to cease their opposition or he would destroy them. Such an ultimatum fired them up enough to confront Ferguson directly. Their numbers increased with people from Virginia and the Carolinas, and they caught up with Major Ferguson at King's Mountain.

All Ferguson's forces were Tories whose advance was met by the American sharpshooters in the trees, and in a short while the Tory position was hopeless. Ferguson would not surrender and twice cut down white flags. The rebels turned to butchery and yelled "Tarleton's quarter" and then proceeded to "take no prisoners." Colonel Campbell, the frontiersmen's unofficial leader, rode among them, telling them that to continue would be murder. The men finally stopped before their victory at King's Mountain became a shameful slaughter. When Cornwallis heard of Ferguson's defeat, he started retreating into South Carolina; finally, the tide seemed to be turning for the South. At the battle, about 700 Loyalists were captured and as news spread, the Loyalists felt unsafe. Thus in 1780 the Dark Days seemed to be ending with hopeful prospects for a revolution very much alive.

The Treaty of Peace of Paris in 1783 officially ended the war. This was two years after Cornwallis surrendered. When a British officer, blindfolded, was led to Washington, he asked for a full day's armistice but was given only two hours. He came back with Cornwallis's surrender terms containing the proviso that his army be paroled in Britain. But Washington was stubborn to the bitter end and demanded that Cornwallis's army surrender as prisoners of war. Washington got his way.

POWS AND REPATRIATION

The Paris Peace Treaty specifically provided for POWs on both sides to be set free, but another important feature was an agreement that POWs did not have to be repatriated. Many German Hessians made this choice because they wanted to remain in the United States, which had more opportunities than their former country could offer them. The option of a POW not to be repatriated was fully respected by the United States in the treaty.

In 1976 the bicentennial of the American Revolution was celebrated. The memorial for the Revolutionary War soldiers who died in British prison ships was built in 1908. A *New York Times* article entitled "Resurrecting Patriots and Their Park" described this shrine to American prisoner of war patriots at Fort Greene Park in Brooklyn.

The crypt, inside the Prison Ship Martyrs Monument, was opened to inspect for damage and determine what work was needed to restore the monument and then make it more accessible to the public.

The parks commissioner of New York City, Henry Sterns, reflected on the monument and regretted that it was a lost chapter in American history about which people knew very little. The monument was personally dedicated by William Howard Taft in 1908. Inside the crypt were twenty heavy slate boxes that contained thousands of bone fragments of men who died on the prison ships in New York harbor. The article, which was written by Douglas Martin, included a picture of the prison ship *Jersey,* which held up to 1,200 prisoners at a time.

Martin reported further that according to research, black slaves were in the ship to fulfill their masters' military obligations. People today seem to be aware of the memorials to veterans of both Korea and Vietnam, but not many are aware of this great tribute to Revolutionary War prisoners of war who fought the battle for independence.

In *Newsday,* August 25, 1996, ex-POWs of our country honored their predecessors on the prison ships of the American Revolution "to raise awareness of the lesser known part of our history." They had not been recognized and seemed to have been forgotten.[22]

NOTES

1. Larry G. Bowman, *Captive Americans: Prisoners during the American Revolution* (Athens: Ohio University Press, 1976), 4.

2. Bowman, *Captive Americans,* 6.

3. Bowman, *Captive Americans,* 10.

4. Bowman, *Captive Americans,* 11.

5. David Sterling, ed., "American Prisoners of War in New York: A Report by Elias Boudinot," *William and Mary Quarterly*, 3rd series, 13, July 1956.

6. Charles Metzger, *The Prisoners of the American Revolution* (Chicago: Loyola University Press, 1971).

7. G. W. Allen, *A Naval History of the American Revolution* (Williamstown, Mass.: Corner House, 1970), 628–29.

8. Bowman, *Captive Americans,* 27.

9. Charles Paullin, *The Navy of the American Revolution* (New York: Haskell, 1971), 245.

10. Paullin, *Navy of the American Revolution,* 272.

11. C. Brian Kelly, "The Morning That Charles Lee Dallied Too Long in a New Jersey Tavern," *Military History*, February 1996, 90.

12. Edward J. Lowell, *The Hessians and the Other German Auxiliaries of Great Britain in the Revolutionary War* (New York: Harper, 1884), 64.

13. Lowell, *Hessians and Other German Auxiliaries,* 291.

14. Geoffrey Perret, *A Country Made by War* (New York: Random House, 1989), 35.

15. John Chester Miller, *Triumph of Freedom, 1775–1783* (Boston: Little, Brown, 1948), 169.

16. Paullin, *Navy of the American Revolution,* 267.

17. Walter Hart Blumenthal, *Women Camp Followers of the American Revolution* (New York: Arno, 1974).

18. William Ordway Partridge, *Nathan Hale: The Ideal Patriot* (New York: Funk & Wagnalls, 1902), 47.

19. Miller, *Triumph of Freedom,* 537.

20. George F. Scheir and Hugh F. Rankin, *Rebels and Raincoats* (Cleveland: World, 1957), 189.

21. Henry Steele Commager and Richard Morris, eds., *The Spirit of '76,* 2 vols. (Indianapolis: Bobbs-Merrill, 1958), 476.

22. *Newsday,* August 25, 1996, A26, A48.

3

The Quasi-Undeclared Naval War with France

The period from 1783 to 1825 can be called a "mixed bag" for the new nation, as it was involved with France, the Barbary Nations, and the War of 1812 with Britain. With the defeat and capture of Burgoyne's army came the support of France, and on February 6, 1778, two treaties were signed at Versailles—the treaty of amity and commerce and the treaty of alliance. Strictly fulfilling the obligations of these treaties, however, would have made the United States an ally of France against Britain. It was not prepared for this contingency from an economic point of view and consequently decided to maintain an attitude of strict neutrality. Another important fact was that it had no navy.

The so-called Quasi-War with France was the country's first limited undeclared war. It started as a result of a disagreement with France about the U.S. role in the West Indies and initiated two years of naval war along the Atlantic coast. The Quasi-War affected the creation of the U.S. Navy, which prepared the country for the "mixed bag" of problems it would experience in both the Tripolitan War and the War of 1812 with Britain. Difficulties with France, the Tripolitan nations, and Britain included not only a number of prisoners but also a new classification of prisoners, one acquired by the process of impressments.

From 1783 to 1865, there were nine treaties between the Barbary pirate nations and the United States (excluding the Treaty of Peace of Paris, which ended the Revolutionary War). The last one in 1825 merely ratified amended articles for the treaty of 1799. Also negotiated in this time period were the 1800 treaty (finally proclaimed in December of 1801), which ended hostilities with France, and the Treaty of Ghent signed on December 24, 1814, which ended the War of 1812.

The Genêt Affair in 1793 generated a series of problems in diplomatic relations with France that lasted until 1798 and ushered the United States into the period of undeclared naval warfare that is the major focus of this chapter. Edmond Genêt, a French ambassador, circulated letters authorizing Americans to attack British commercial vessels. This was viewed by George Washington as a violation of American neutrality.

Because of his actions in the United States, Genêt was declared persona non grata, but he did not respond to his ambassadorial recall because he was afraid to return to France in view of the French Revolution. He remained in the United States and married the daughter of New York's Governor Clinton.

BRITISH CONTROL OF THE SEAS

Since 1783 Britain had been smarting from the loss of its American colonies. The United States, following the treaty with Britain, had no way to protect its ships at sea, and the British had control of the sea. The lack of an adequate navy was something Thomas Jefferson, minister to France, complained about in 1785. In that year two American merchantmen were captured by Algerian pirates and twenty-one Americans were taken into custody. A ransom was demanded for the American prisoners in Algerian hands. In 1793 eleven more vessels were captured by Algerians and more than 100 prisoners were sent to Algerian harems and quarries. Jefferson's efforts to protect American commerce were not successful.

John Jay's treaty of 1794 with Britain was an attempt to erase the strain on the country. The British were impressing American seamen into their navy and ordering the seizure of American merchant ships headed for French ports. It was John Jay's job to settle the outstanding issues, but, unfortunately, the treaty with Britain was a poor one and caused internal conflict. The treaty did not make any guarantees against impressments, did not provide for the freedom of the seas, and did not gain any commitment from England to halt seizure of American ships or cease impressments of American sailors.

France heightened tensions with the United States as a result of the XYZ Affair of 1797. The man who created this problem, the French minister Talleyrand, claimed no knowledge of the affair. Secretary of State Timothy Pickering, in a 1797 report, maintained that spoliations and maltreatment of American ships at sea were being committed by French warships and privateers. He further charged nonpayment of French debts in the West Indies, seizure of cargoes, noncompliance of contracts for French supplies, and violations of the treaty of amity and commerce. In short, he read the riot act against France.

The French claimed that American seamen serving on enemy ships should be considered pirates even if the British had impressed them and that they could be hanged on a French ship if captured. The logic of this was brutally incomprehensible. Pickering's report contained three incidents that clearly violated the rights of American vessels and their men.

On December 25, 1796, the *Commerce* complied with an order from a French privateer to surrender and then four men were wounded by a burst of cannon. In February 1797 the French privateer *Hirondale* captured the schooner *Zelpha* and forced the captain and crew to leave the ship. Finally, there was the case of the *Cincinnatus*. A French armed brig captured it in March 1797 and tortured its captain when he refused to declare his cargo English property so it could be confiscated lawfully. The captain did not submit, despite the torture of thumbscrews. He and his ship were let go after provisions and property aboard his ship were illegally removed. If ever there was justification for all-out war with France, the years 1796 and 1797 demonstrated such a declaration. A direct result of French totalitarianism was the creation of the U.S. Navy on April 30, 1798.

Congressional acts followed authorizing the purchase and construction of more vessels, suspension of trade with France, and the establishment of another arm of the military, the U.S. Marine Corps. On
June 5, 1794, in preparation for the creation of the U.S. Navy, the
first officers had been selected, including six captains, two of whom
served in the American Revolutionary navy. One main restriction
was that all work on new ships would cease in case peace was concluded with Algiers. This condition was met by the treaty of September 5, 1795, with Algiers, the fifth article of which stated that no
person could be removed from an American ship nor could anyone
be molested. A supplementary congressional statute adopted allowed
for the completion of three of the ships.

The administration of John Adams was to be mainly concerned
with events of the Quasi-War. Adams was very disturbed to learn
that the French Directory had issued a decree that violated the commercial treaty of 1778. The decree eliminated the principle of free
ships and free goods and also stated that any American found serving under an enemy flag would be treated as a pirate. Adams hoped
that difficulties could be resolved in an honorable way, but this
would proved to be very difficult to achieve. The fact that the French
government authorized its privateers and private armed vessels to attack American shipping created a lucrative business for raiders in the
Caribbean. Alexander de Conde commented that the French ships at
times "were hardly distinguishable from pirates."[1]

French actions on the high seas served to improve relations between the Americans and the British, something the French did not
like. Nevertheless, the English navy persisted in stopping and
searching American ships at sea. The British policy of impressments
did not stop despite American protests.

Alexander Hamilton, a staunch Federalist, was working out plans
for a frontier war when he received a letter and manuscript from
Christopher Gore, a friend of his in London, a Federalist lawyer who
was serving on a commission provided for in the Jay treaty. Gore's
report seemed to justify full-scale war with France.

FRENCH RAIDS AT SEA

In 1797 the American government simply could not stop French raids without a navy. The French attacked American shipping within sight of Long Island Sound and also near the entrance to Delaware Bay.

In June 1798 the *Ganges* was patrolling coastal waters between Long Island and Virginia, but its captain did not catch any French ships, which it was authorized to do by Congress. American laws were really only half measures; consequently, says De Conde, "from the American point of view, our clash with France was a Quasi-War. It was a limited war that Americans fought only at sea under self-imposed restrictions."[2] Thus no prisoners of war were taken on American soil by either side.

With French privateers making handsome profits against American ships in the Caribbean, the secretary of the navy ordered the newly formed navy to demonstrate its presence in this area and capture French seamen.

Near Egg Harbor, New Jersey, in July 1798, the *Delaware*, under Captain Stephen Decatur, captured the *Croyable*, the first prize of the American navy. The fifty-three prisoners taken by Decatur were brought to Fort Mifflen. Decatur turned over the *Croyable* to his navy, which renamed it the *Retaliation*. John Barry was ordered to sail with the *Delaware*, the *Herald*, and the *Pickering*, and asked the governor of Puerto Rico to release American prisoners held there who had been captured by French cruisers.

About four months later, the *Retaliation* was recaptured by the French. Lieutenant Bainbridge, commanding the *Retaliation*, was following two ships he thought were English. He found out all too late that the ships were French frigates and was so close to the ships that he could not escape. He struck his colors and was ordered on board the *Volontaire* to surrender. The next day the *Volontaire* took the *Retaliation* and a prize brig to Basse Terre. American officers were kept on the French frigates while the crew of the *Retaliation* was sent ashore to prison to join many other American seamen. The men there were suffering from starvation and poor treatment. Bainbridge was given parole on shore and managed to get an order for better treatment of the prisoners from General Desfourneaux. Ultimately Bainbridge and the other American prisoners, nearly 250, were released and sent back to the United States. Members of the *Retaliation* crew who were not landed at Guadaloupe managed to recapture the vessel and escape with it.

On January 18, 1799, Lieutenant Bainbridge left Guadaloupe with an agent of Desfourneaux carrying a letter from the general to the president of the United States. They arrived on February 13 at Philadelphia. Desfourneaux was trying to get on the good side of President Adams by releasing the captain of the *Retaliation* and his seamen and by saying in the letter that he wanted to consider Americans as friends. The fact that the American navy was doing such an excellent job in the West Indies was fully recognized by Desfourneaux. On March 3, 1799, the sufferings of American prisoners and their impressments led to a congressional act allowing for retaliation in any way against captured French citizens.

Strong resentment against the French was seen well before the retaliatory act of March 3, 1799, when four laws were passed by the Federalists: the Naturalization Act signed by the president on June 18, 1798, the Alien Friends Act on June 25, 1798, the Alien Enemies Act on July 6, and the Sedition Act on July 14. Another act, often forgotten, was the Logan Act, signed on January 30, 1799. The Sedition Act, which even Alexander Hamilton did not approve of, seemed to be unconstitutional. The two alien acts were never used by John Adams. The Logan Act, however, became an issue during the Vietnam War.

The Logan Act provided for fine and imprisonment for any American who without proper governmental permission tried to deal with a foreign government in opposition to our foreign policy. It was not concerned with acts by private citizens that might lead to war but was directed at preventing people from meddling in foreign policy or sabotaging it.

French prisoners of war in the United States complained about their treatment, but the secretary of the navy responded that their rations were adequate; they were given clothing and blankets and officers were permitted to leave the United States on parole. Toward the end of March 1799 the *Retaliation* was sent back to Guadaloupe with French prisoners in exchange for Americans.

A store ship was sent out from Boston and was met by a French privateer. The American ship fired on the privateer and immediately sent its boats to the relief of the French sailors. Sixty men were saved from the *Amour de la Patrie*. About the same time, the *Tartuffe* was captured, and Commodore Barry took many prisoners. Under a flag of truce he went to Guadaloupe to exchange French prisoners for American seamen, but he was fired on and not allowed to land. The French governor assured Barry that there were no American prisoners on the island. Barry was very skeptical about this but allowed the French prisoners ashore.

One other major naval development, which became the first important battle of the so-called Quasi-War, pitted the warship the *Constellation* against the French *L'Insurgente* on February 9, 1799. The commanding officer of the *Constellation* was Thomas Truxton, a navy veteran from the Revolutionary War. The French captain had been ordered by Desfourneaux not to attack American ships, and when he was captured, wondered why he was fired on since he thought that France and the United States were not at war. Truxton simply replied that the French captain was his prisoner and refused to return the ship to Desfourneaux. Truxton was defiant of Desfourneaux, whom he considered to be insincere in his feelings of neutrality. When Congress passed the Retaliatory Act on March 3, Desfourneaux personally declared war against the United States. Desfourneaux, a minor French public servant, could not make such a decision for France as a nation.

President Adams wrote to his navy secretary on August 5 and directed that all French prisoners be sent to the United States, not

Guadaloupe. They would be allowed to work or fight on American ships. If they were to be returned, their written parole should be taken so that they would not serve in any war capacity until they were exchanged.

Many Americans wanted a full-scale war but Adams did not. Suspicious of those who did not agree with his foreign policy toward France, President Adams had signed the Logan Act. The president and the State Department, guided by the Senate Foreign Relations Committee, were the only agencies which could direct such policy.

The navy persisted in hunting for French ships in the West Indies, especially near Guadaloupe, and Captain Truxton, who previously had had trouble with Desfourneaux, became the commanding officer of the *Constitution* and the squadron situated at Guadaloupe.

Early in the morning on February 1, 1800, he spotted the French frigate *La Vengeance,* which was transporting military passengers and thirty-six American prisoners of war from Guadaloupe to France. Truxton didn't know about our POWs on board. He engaged the ship while the American POWs, who had been impressed, were permitted to remain below during the battle. After the action they were brought back to the deck where they operated the pumps. Truxton's men and the enemy had suffered damage to their ships and there were many casualties on both sides, but losses on the *Vengeance* were more numerous. Witnesses reported that the French ship struck its colors, but darkness prevented Truxton from seeing this. If Truxton had known the ship had American POWs on board, would he have engaged it? The answer to this question is not known. This was the last major battle of the Quasi-War. Although it was somewhat indecisive, Americans considered it a victory.

On August 3 the *Trumbull,* under Captain Jewett, captured the *Vengeance.* The ship, along with its prisoners (the French crew), was sent to New London. Previously, on June 27, there had been only fifteen American POWs at Guadaloupe who were about to be released through an exchange. At the same time on St. Christopher, north of Guadaloupe, there were about 180 French prisoners.

American ships were occasionally captured off the Brazilian coast and farther north and east, but at Cayenne on French Guiana, according to an account in the summer of 1800, the Americans were not considered prisoners. They were not given any allowance nor were they qualified for an exchange. The justification for keeping them on prison ships was to maintain good order and to protect their health, conditions quite different from British prison ships of the Revolutionary War. Gardner in his book *Our Naval War with France* reports in a footnote that this fact was stated in the *Massachusetts Mercury* (October 3, 1800).[3]

The *Enterprise* captured three French ships and recaptured some American ships. One of these ships had passengers who were army officers, including a general. At the same time two American sailors were being held for killing two Frenchmen in recapturing their ships. The two prisoners were not treated well and attempts to exchange them proved to be in vain. The French general and others were held as hostages. Retaliation on both sides didn't seem to be called for. The general was paroled to Guadaloupe, where he obtained the release of the Americans.

After cruising for ten days off Bermuda, the *Experiment*, under Lieutenant Charles Stewart on September 1, 1800, arrived at Guadaloupe and confronted the French privateer *Deux Amis,* which had seized many American merchantmen. The French ship quickly surrendered. Up to September 1800 and later, American ships were capturing French ships as prizes, and, of course, accumulating French prisoners.

An American brig destined for Barbados captured the French ship *Berceau* while it was being repaired and towed it to port. Captain Senes was paroled and placed on board the American ship. The prize ship was brought to Castle Island and left under guard while the officers were paroled. On January 15, 1801, the United States purchased the *Berceau*, but under a treaty with France the *Berceau* was given back to France, sailing on September 26, 1801. This treaty, called the Convention of Peace, Commerce, and Navigation, is also known as the Treaty of Mortefontaine. It was long, including twenty-seven articles, and was concluded on September 30, 1800, with ratification coming in Paris July 31, 1801. The Convention of 1800 did not solve existing issues, but it did serve to end the hostilities.

In 1800 the new American navy reached a high in seizing armed French ships. In a footnote De Conde states that "in less than three years of Quasi-War the Navy captured one French frigate, defeated another, captured three privateers, sank four, recaptured more than 70 merchant ships and reduced seizures drastically."[4] This, of course, meant fewer American seamen becoming prisoners of war.

As unscrupulous as Talleyrand had been previously, he contributed significantly to the peaceful resolution of the undeclared war. When John Adams sent the treaty of Mortefontaine to the Senate, he had lost the presidential election to Thomas Jefferson. The submitted ratification was defeated but was resubmitted by Adams, and the necessary two-thirds vote was acquired. It would be up to Jefferson, the next president, to persuade the French to consent to the Senate's reservations and to conduct the final negotiations on the Convention of Mortefontaine. The stage was almost set for the War of 1812 with England but was delayed by the Barbary pirates, whose war began with the advent of Jefferson's administration. Fortunately, the Quasi-War with France prepared the Americans for the Barbary pirates as well as the War of 1812 with England.

NOTES

1. Alexander De Conde, *The Quasi-War* (New York: Scribner's, 1966), 8.

2. De Conde, *Quasi-War,* 126.

3. W. Allen Gardner, *Our Naval War with France* (Boston: Houghton Mifflin, 1909), 196.

4. De Conde, *Quasi-War,* 418.

4

The Tripolitan War

The war with the Barbary pirate nations was the first against an Arab despot and represented an early challenge to U.S. foreign policy. Four nations along a thousand-mile stretch of the coastline of North Africa made up the Barbary States: Morocco, Algiers, Tunis, and Tripoli. These countries had already caused problems in the 1500s and 1600s for European nations. Morocco was a rich and developing monarchy while the others belonged to the Ottoman Empire and owed loyalty, in name only, to one supreme leader. Because the trade of all four consisted of piracy, they were called pirate nations. This piracy was nothing more than blackmail, bribery, or tribute.

To say that the Barbary pirate nations started their war after the United States' undeclared naval war with France is an erroneous statement. Although there was no official declaration of war for many years, an unofficial one had been going on for quite some time. The war had early precedents.

Miguel Cervantes had been held prisoner in Algeria for five years in the early 1600s. John Ward, an Englishman who once served in the navy, became a pirate and by 1609 had turned his back on his nation and raided English coastal towns. Even England's protective money had not spared American colonists trading in the Mediterranean. In 1622 England concluded a treaty with the bey of Tunis to free English slaves by paying tribute to guarantee no future trouble.

That agreement laid the foundation for other major European treaties with Algiers and Tripoli.

After the Revolutionary War, Americans no longer enjoyed the protection of the British navy against the Barbary pirates in the Mediterranean Sea. The United States tried to gain British cooperation in the Treaty of Paris but was refused it.

AMERICAN PRISONERS

Whipple tells us that in 1678 the Barbary pirates seized the merchantman *Pincke* from New York and held her captain, Jacob Leiser, his two sons, and eight crewmen for ransom.[1] Churchgoers in New York City collected money to pay off the ransom.

By July 1785 Algerian pirates captured two U.S. ships and seized as prisoners twenty-one Americans and a Spanish woman passenger. The ransom demanded was $2,800 per person. The American people as well as the media expressed strong sentiments against these actions. The Articles of Confederation Congress claimed poverty.

In 1784 the Boston brig *Betsey* was taken and three months later the American schooner *Maria* was seized off Cape St. Vincent; the next to be taken was the *Dauphin* near Cadiz, which was taken to Algiers.

In 1786 the United States made a treaty with Sidi Mohammed, sultan of Morocco. Article 6 of the treaty stated that American prisoners were not to be made slaves but would be considered as either ex-citizens or goods seized by a Moor and would be released. In the case of war, article 16 said that prisoners were not to be made slaves but were to be exchanged. These were the two main provisions (there were 25 in all) that concerned prisoners, and the policy was continued with some variations by the sultan's successor. None of the other states, however, agreed to such a policy.

In 1793 Portugal and Algiers signed a peace treaty, but this had bad effects for the United States because it opened up the Straits of

Gibraltar to the pirates, who then had easy access to the Atlantic to prey on unprotected U.S. ships. In the summer of 1793 the pirates, proving that international law meant little to them, captured eleven American merchant ships and made prisoners of war of more than 100 Americans who were placed in Algerian harems and quarries.

One particularly tragic event of 1793 involved the Boston brig *Polly* and her crew. A forecastle hand named John Foss wrote a book about his captivity and ordeal after he and others were ransomed.

The *Polly* was captured by the brig *Balazera* in the Atlantic. Of the 119 Americans held in Algiers, six died from the plague that swept through the dungeons in which they were held, twenty-one succumbed to the harsh life of the Algerian prison, and some were rendered incapable of earning a living because of the treatment received. Some fortunate POWs were given jobs in the harbor area cleaning and fixing ships and carrying supplies from different parts of the city.

From the very start, the prisoners were treated poorly. After plundering the ship, the pirates tore off the clothes from the backs of the prisoners. The dey had four of them wait on him personally and the rest were bound hand and foot with chains in the prison. Dupuy and Baumer vividly describe the conditions of the prisoners.[2] The same conditions are described in Whipple's book *To the Shores of Tripoli*.[3]

In 1792 a group of American prisoners sent a plea to Congress about their seven years of captivity. Their message was sent by Captain O'Brien of the *Dauphin* to ministers of New England and New York to plead their case before their legislatures. The number of prisoners was increasing with each ship captured.

PRISON TORTURES

Prisoners were starved and punished with an overseer's whip and a pointed instrument used to urge on a beast. Those who were stubborn and didn't respect the Muslim religion were beaten on the soles of their feet with a stick called a bastinado. Whipple's book *To the Shores of Tripoli* describes this torture quite well in a footnote. Other tortures included burning at the stake or stabbing with a sharp stake. Although reports of atrocities committed against POWs served to incite congressmen and administrative officials against the Barbary nations, England, France, and Spain still thought it convenient to pay tribute to avoid problems with the pirate countries.

TREATIES

In later years more treaties were consummated with some of these powers. The treaty of peace and amity with Algiers on September 5, 1795, specifically noted in article 3 that ship's crews of both nations should not be molested, and article 5 prevented the commanders of Algerian cruisers from removing anyone from an American ship. A treaty of peace and friendship with Tripoli on January 3, 1797, acknowledged that the pasha had received the money and demands he made and would receive no further tribute; also, citizens on a seized prize ship would be released. The same year, a treaty of peace and friendship with Tunis (in August) provided for the release of citizens found on an enemy ship and also the restoration of any slaves taking refuge on an American ship. The same provisions were made for any POWs escaping to Tunisian ships. The next major treaties were with Tripoli in 1805 and with Algiers in 1815 and 1816.

PAYMENTS AND PROBLEMS

In March 1794, Congress voted to build six frigates with the understanding that the program would be stopped if the prisoner issue was resolved. This would pacify the sentiment that prevailed against the pirates. When an agreement for the release of prisoners was reached with the bey of Algeria in 1795, ship construction was abandoned. Unfortunately, the prisoners were not released immediately and the final release did not occur until 1796.[4] Allegedly twelve of twenty-one men captured in 1795 were repatriated to the United States, seven died of the plague, one of consumption, and one in a madhouse.

The United States did not make ransom payments on time to keep the enemy happy nor fulfill a promised bonus of a brand-new frigate of thirty-six guns. That warship, to be called the *Crescent*, was ready for sailing on July 4, 1797, but Americans weren't enthusiastic about giving an enemy a formidable present that could be used against them.

The launching of the *Crescent* made Bashaw Yusul Karamandi of Tripoli very envious. Of the three leaders at that time in North Africa—the dey of Algeria, the bey of Tunis, and the bashaw of Tripoli—Karamandi of Tripoli was the greatest troublemaker and the greatest power, a fact that motivated him intensely. He had seized the throne quite illegally by killing one brother and exiling the other, who was the real heir.

Buying off trouble with the dey of Algeria led to an entanglement with another murderous ruler, the bashaw of Tripoli. Paying such tribute to Algiers simply made for more problems with the pirates in years to come.

The warship construction program had been stopped, and it then became the problem and responsibility of Secretary of War Henry Knox. Ironically, he found a pair of Quakers interested in warship design and subsequently three ships, the *Constitution*, the *President*, and the *United States*, were built. Now the United States was in a position to deal with not only the Barbary pirates but also the French, who were trying to get a bribe and an inexpensive loan just to talk. In 1798, however, Congress strengthened the U.S. position when it authorized the Navy Department to build twelve ships of war and create the U.S. Marine Corps.

Over the next three years one French frigate was sunk, another captured, 111 privateers captured, and four destroyed.[5] About seventy American merchant ships were recaptured and the Quasi-War with France was coming to an end. A squadron of three frigates and two sloops was now sent off to make a strong impression on the impatient bashaw.

On May 14, 1801, the bashaw of Tripoli had his men cut down the flagpole in front of the American consulate. He was relying on President Thomas Jefferson to be a pacifist and an appeaser. As early as 1786 Jefferson, then minister to France, had been one of a few who considered it wise to fight the pirates rather than pay them at the first hostage crisis. But as president and commander in chief, he faced the possibility of a war with Tripoli and had a change of heart about the problem of paying tribute.

The cost of piracy to the United States was not insignificant. In 1798 the United States paid Tunis jewels and small arms, as well as $107,000 in succeeding years. Tripoli demanded a yearly tribute of $100,000 from 1787 on, but it was never paid. In 1796 and 1799 over $80,000 was paid, and in 1802, $6,500 to ransom the crew of the *Franklin* from prison. As Dupuy and Baumer point out, the money paid in tribute to this nation, about $2,000,000, was "sufficient to have built an imposing fleet."[6]

On January 21, 1801, Captain William Bainbridge sailed into Algiers and unloaded his passengers. He gave the required tribute to Yusuf and demanded release of all the prisoners. This brought a threat against him. He took the French citizens back on his ship and on January 30 sailed out of the port. The navy officer expressed his feelings as follows: "I hope I may never again be sent to Algiers with a tribute, except it be from the mouth of a cannon."[7] In the near future this wish would be fulfilled.

The chopping down of the flagpole was like a declaration of war. Three squadrons under Commodore Edward Preble were dispatched in September 1803, and one of the ships in his squadron was the *Philadelphia.* Preble himself had been a POW on the infamous prison ship the *Jersey* during the Revolutionary War.

The *Philadelphia* was sailing in the Mediterranean on October 31, 1803, when Captain Bainbridge saw what he thought to be a merchant ship heading for the port of Tripoli. Preble detailed the *Philadelphia* and the *Vixen* to blockade the port. When the *Philadelphia* came under heavy fire from the enemy, Captain Bainbridge had to surrender because his ship, the largest in the navy, had run into a shoal and wasn't in a position to fire its guns against the approaching enemy. An attempt to scuttle the ship was a failure.

PRISONERS ONCE MORE

The crew of 309 officers and men became prisoners, much to the delight of the bashaw, and all men were held for ransom. Enlisted men and officers were kept separate and officers were treated better. This was the second time Captain Bainbridge had to endure prisoner of war status. For him and his men it meant an eighteen-month imprisonment. His sailors were divided into two groups. The skilled were assigned the task of fixing up the *Philadelphia* and those who were reluctant were under the threat of the whip. The unskilled had to construct their own prison in a warehouse that was filthy and unsuitable for habitation. Others were put to work building harbor defenses. Even if there had been a Geneva Convention then, it wouldn't have done any good. At least, according to Fowler, the prisoners were not subjected to torture. Five seamen died and five, much to the dismay of Bainbridge, converted to Islam and swore allegiance to the hated bashaw.[8] Preble learned about this from a British frigate's man on November 10 and was shocked. The safety of all the prisoners roused great concern on the international scene, and although there were mediation offers from several quarters in the European community, Preble preferred direct retaliation to diplomacy and engineered his own plan. His operation consisted of boarding the *Philadelphia* and burning it. On the night of February 16, 1804, the plan was enacted and within thirty minutes the men returned to the *Intrepid* from which they had come. This was one of the most daring (and fortunately very successful) raids ever attempted by the

U.S. Navy, and it included, according to Dupuy and Baumer, prominent personalities who would serve in the War of 1812.[9] The next main event of the Tripolitan Wars came under the leadership of William Eaton, consul to Tunis and former army officer. His expedition was romanticized in the motion picture *To the Shores of Tripoli* (1942), starring Maureen O'Hara, Howard da Silva, and John Payne. Payne played the role of Marine Lieutenant O'Bannon. Before O'Bannon left for his assignment, however, he took a bride back home, so the role played by Maureen O'Hara was fictional.

William Eaton seemed to be playing the part of a navy officer. He was determined to put down the pirates, but unfortunately Commodore Richard Valentine Morris would not allow him to execute his plans to get rid of the bashaw. Eaton returned to the United States and sought the approval of President Jefferson, who gave his permission.

Eaton's plan was to dethrone the bashaw and restore the rightful heir, who was somewhere in Egypt. Eaton had to find him and build an army of Arabs and Tripolitans who disagreed with the bashaw and ultimately conquer the bashaw's forces. Hamet Karamondi was found and was willing and eager to regain the throne from which he had been ousted. Lieutenant O'Bannon and his marines and other men, in conjunction with the forces under Eaton, were successful in their venture. The city of Derne surrendered and Eaton left the cleanup to Hamet Karamondi.

Captain Hugh Campbell, the commanding officer of the *Constitution*, did not bring any reinforcement or consolation but told Eaton that Tobias Lear, Consul General to Algiers, had negotiated a treaty with Yusuf. On February 23, 1805, there had been a convention in which Hamet Karamondi provided that American prisoners in Tripoli would be released without ransom. In case of war between the parties, captives would be treated as prisoners of war, not as slaves, and would be exchanged. Neither ransom nor tribute would be required as a condition of peace. A secret addenda said that Hamet would deliver the bashaw and Murad Reis, the bashaw's high admiral, to the U.S. commander in chief in the Mediterranean, to be held as hostages. In the Tripolitan Treaty negotiated between Yusuf Pasha and Consul General Tobias Lear on June 5, 1805, once again prisoners would be exchanged, but there was a secret provision. If Hamet's wife and children were returned to him, the pasha feared renewed hostilities with his brother; therefore the pasha would be permitted four years in which to deliver up his brother's family, who were under his control. The treaty was heavily criticized, but at least the war was over and no more tribute would be paid. Yusuf had received $60,000 cash ransom for the *Philadelphia* POWs. This left only Algiers and Tunis as potential blackmailers.

After Commodore Samuel Barron returned to the United States, his successor, John Rodgers, sailed five frigates and several brigs into the Tunis harbor on August 1, 1805, to make an impression on Hamouda, the bey. Consequently the United States was given "most favored nation" status. Hamet went into exile and was finally reunited with his wife and children, whom Yusuf had held in prison.

Achmet, the bey of Algiers, was not happy about delays in receiving his tribute and naval stores. The Algerians seized three merchantmen, but later one escaped. Consul General Lear was able to secure a temporary peace and a release of vessels and prisoners.

In 1810 the bey of Tunis was threatening war, and Hadji Ali, a new dey in Algiers, was in command when the War of 1812 started. The Treaty of Ghent signed, President James Madison, Jefferson's successor, wanted to make the Mediterranean safe for sailing and asked the Congress for a declaration of war against Algiers. He received it on March 3 and by early May two squadrons were steaming into the Mediterranean to make a fact of the president's wish. The two men leading them were veterans Stephen Decatur and William Bainbridge.

Omar of Algiers was stunned when Decatur's squadron sailed into his harbor on June 29, 1815. Not only had his maritime policies failed, but the Americans were holding 500 of his subjects as hostages, tribute was discontinued, American ships or citizens would no longer be subject to capture, and, finally, all American prisoners would have to be released. After Decatur refused a truce, Omar asked for three hours. Now the Americans were doing the demanding and readied to attack the remaining Algerian ships. The dey's barge came alongside Decatur's ship with ten prisoners and a white flag. These visits to Tunis and Tripoli put the finishing touches on the Barbary Wars as the U.S. Navy demonstrated its sea power. Further difficulties with the Barbary powers were petty, and the United States maintained its navy in the Mediterranean Sea for a long time. But already it was experiencing major problems with England, which led to the War of 1812.

NOTES

1. A. B. C. Whipple, *To the Shores of Tripoli* (New York: Morrow, 1991), 293.

2. Ernest Dupuy and William H. Baumer, *The Little Wars of the United States* (New York: Hawthorn, 1968), 27.

3. Whipple, *To the Shores of Tripoli.*

4. Robert Albion and Jennie Barnes Pope, *Sea Lanes in Wartime: The American Experience, 1775–1942* (New York: Norton, 1942).

5. Geoffrey Perrett, *A Country Made by War* (New York: Random House, 1989), 91.

6. Dupuy and Baumer, *Little Wars,* 29.

7. Dupuy and Baumer, *Little Wars,* 34.

8. William M. Fowler Jr., *Jack Tars and Commodores: The American Navy, 1783–1815* (Boston: Houghton Mifflin, 1984).

9. Dupuy and Baumer, *Little Wars.*

The War of 1812

According to Theodore Roosevelt, land operations in the War of 1812 "were hardly worth serious study."[1] Yet many prisoners of war were taken in land battles, and some of these cases proved to be very controversial. Roosevelt further states "the only real noteworthy feat of arms of the war took place at New Orleans and the only military genius that the struggle developed was Andrew Jackson." Naval engagements were more successful than army battles because of a lack of competent military men. On the other hand, many naval personnel had received excellent training and experience in the Tripolitan War.

The army generally was not prepared at the start of the war. The only army ready to wage the conflict was, according to Geoffrey Perret, "in the wrong place, in the west, gathering together at Dayton, Ohio."[2] The aged William Hull led the forces in Detroit, which was then inhabited by the Indians and French trappers. Heading the British was the governor-general Sir George Prevost, whose forces consisted of British regulars and the King's Indian allies.

IMPRESSMENT

Most historians would agree that the principal cause of the War of 1812 can be summed up in one word—impressment. This took place on the high seas and sometimes very close to U.S. shores. Another factor was interference with the American economy and trade by Great Britain, but the real issue was impressment, about which James Zimmerman wrote an entire book. Britain claimed it was only taking back its subjects. But when the British took natural-born U.S. citizens, the country became greatly aroused.

When or how impressment originated is controversial. Briefly defined, impressment is taking prisoners and forcing them to fight against their own nation or another nation friendly to their captors. Generally it happened on the high seas, but prisoners were also kidnapped from taverns or the streets at night by a group called the press-gang.

Taking prisoners who were naturalized Americans did not seem to antagonize Congress as much as taking American-born citizens. A parallel in the twentieth century occurred when mainland Chinese were taken by the Chinese Communists to fight against South Korean and U.N. forces in Korea.

British impressments started, according to Robert Leckie, when "the magnetic chain of events drawing our country into the War of 1812 began in 1801."[3] Americans found themselves in an economic cross fire between France and England. Having won their political independence from England, they were concerned about their economic independence, with England enforcing a blockade off U.S. shores by capturing American ships and impressing sailors and privateersmen.

Some military historians, such as Captain Dudley Knox, contend that the War of 1812 started as early as 1793. The United States was neutral and Americans were dealing with both England and France and were making great profits, although at considerable risk. They were starting to get involved in the "economic cross fire" mentioned previously, even before the undeclared naval war with France.

Impressments from private ships were not numerous during the colonial period, but there were some. One case resulted in three days of rioting in Boston. That incident involved the impressments of a group of sailors, ship carpenters, and laboring landsmen by a Commodore Knowles. The rioting in Boston forced the colonial governor to flee for his personal safety. Fortunately, the men impressed were granted their freedom after the riots.

In 1769 a court case arose when Michael Corbett was charged with killing a British frigate lieutenant with a harpoon. The British officer was trying to impress Corbert and his friends from their ship. The defense counsel was John Adams, who claimed the impressment was illegal. The verdict was justifiable homicide and the lieutenant was judged to have had no authority for his actions from the Lords of the Admiralty. Years later the same John Adams defended British soldiers in their court-martial after the Boston Massacre.

England resented losing the Revolutionary War and was, according to Bradford Perkins, hoping to "even the score."[4] The John Jay treaty (1795) did not even mention impressments and thus met with great opposition from the United States citizenry and the president. No one had any idea that the impressments issue would bring about a war that would be concluded by a treaty that did not even mention impressment.

In 1795–1796 there were impressments in the West Indies area. Both Frank Updyke in *Diplomacy of the War of 1812* and James Zimmerman in *Impressment of American Seamen* attest to vigorous impressments from April 1795 to April 1796 in the waters near England and the West Indies. There was also a great increase in impressments between 1797 and 1802. This was corroborated by the reports of American consuls and agents for seamen from 1803 to 1806.

According to Zimmerman, impressment "was said to be far worse than the bondage inflicted on the 300 seamen taken captive in Tripoli for whose rescue the government had sent out extra frigates. Impressment was worse than *Algerian bondage* because those impressed were required to commit murder in fighting battles with nations with whom the United States was at peace."[5]

The turning point, according to Captain Mahan in *The War of 1812*, was the Chesapeake Affair on June 22, 1807.[6] This brought war closer, although President Madison's war message to the nation did not come until five years later. Once the war was started, more prisoners would be taken as a result of naval sea actions, naval actions on the Great Lakes, and land engagements.

Theodore Roosevelt tells us that "for years before 1812 the number of impressed sailors was in reality greater than the entire number serving in the American navy," and "they never lost their devotion to the home of their birth, more than two thousand of them being imprisoned at the beginning of the war because they refused to serve against their country."[7] If there was any hatred, it was against England but not the British. There were no impressments into the American navy, in strong contrast to methods used by the Royal Navy. There were no picked crews on the American side, although it was not easy to get personnel for the navy. Neither James Madison nor Thomas Jefferson ever said that England did not have the right to take American seamen. Both presidents tolerated impressments but only when it happened in British ports and to British subjects, according to Bradford Perkins.[8] In the first year of the war the British admiralty conceded that almost 20,000 Englishmen were serving in the American merchant marine, and the last report in January 1812 by Secretary of State James Madison stated that since 1803 England had impressed 5,257 men. England claimed that the correct number was only about a thousand. At the end of the war about 1,800 impressed seamen were released and this number did not, of course, include men who had escaped, died, or been released during the war.

England's supposedly valid reason for persisting in impressments had at first been the need for men when fighting the French and then later when fighting American rebels. It had to use impressments to keep the navy adequately manned, and the United States was a convenient country from which England could pilfer merchantmen and seamen.

Perkins tells us that the Royal Navy from 1805 to 1809 was seizing American ships every two days, and an American living in England claimed that the actual rates were much higher. Perkins quoted John Quincy Adams, who referred to impressment as "kidnapping upon the ocean" and a Boston newspaper called it "barbarous thefts of American citizens."

THE *CHESAPEAKE* INCIDENT

With the *Chesapeake* incident in June 1807 the lid was almost blown off. The *Chesapeake* did not anticipate hostile action as it set sail from Chesapeake Bay for the Mediterranean. The decks were filled with supplies not yet stored below, which was a tragic blunder, since the ship was in no position to answer the challenge given by the British *Leopard*. Commodore James Barron was fired on when he refused to surrender. The attack on his ship resulted in eighteen wounded and three deaths. Four alleged British deserters were removed from the *Chesapeake*.

President Thomas Jefferson's pacifism was now considerably diminished. He ordered British warships to leave American waters and stay away. This was, however, unenforceable. The *Chesapeake* incident would have been perfect justification for an immediate declaration of war on Britain, but such a declaration did not come until five years later when responsibility passed from Jefferson to Madison.

Samuel Bemis writes that "impressment was the most corrosive issue ever existing between the United States and Britain,"[9] and Frank Updyke says it "was the most aggravating and the most persistent" of American grievances.[10] Donald Hickey says that the British government agreed to release impressed Americans whose citizenship could be proven, but the appeals through diplomatic channels could take years, given the slow communication of the time. Many British sailors were deserting and the Royal Navy wanted to stop them. An impressment bill was presented to Congress but was attacked by both parties. The bill eventually managed to get through Congress and was signed by President Madison, who was charged with the supervision of enemy aliens. General James Mason was made supervisor over British prisoners of war. He made matters worse for British POW officers and aliens because he demanded a parole of honor for both aliens and POW officers living beyond the tidewater. Officers were generally treated more kindly and paroled in large towns and even sent home with the usual stipulation that they not fight anymore until officially exchanged. Often militia soldiers were sent home because they were considered part-time soldiers; enlisted men were the poor souls at the bottom of the ladder who were confined until exchanged. They were usually placed in state prisons located not far from the northern frontier, especially in Kentucky and Massachusetts.

THE PRISONERS

American prisoners were often held in prison ships, and also in jails spread throughout the British Empire. The most infamous prison of all was Dartmoor in England. More will be said about conditions at Dartmoor at the end of this chapter.

Separating officers and noncommissioned personnel was customary on both sides in a conflict. While Americans released British seamen claiming to be deserters from the Royal Navy, the British, in marked contrast, did not; they demanded verification. When the Treaty of Ghent was signed in 1814, some were still being held in prison.

Americans treated British POWs much better than the British treated American POWs, although Hickey noted that Captain David Porter permitted his men to tar and feather a British subject. This was a real exception to the rule. Americans learned from the Revolutionary War how to cope with the POW problems that arose in the War of 1812. Thus a person was named to head a group called the commissary general of prisoners, whose duties were to "supervise and conduct prisoner of war activities in the United States." This person was the aforementioned General James Mason.

At the same time, provision was made in London to appoint a commission to arrange for an exchange cartel. Both countries maintained representatives to help nationals in enemy hands and to bring about exchanges.[11]

GENERAL HULL

The War of 1812 opened on land in the middle of the summer of 1812 with the campaign of General William Hull, a Revolutionary War hero, on the Michigan frontier. Unfortunately, the news of the declaration of war reached Canada before Hull had learned of it and this ruined any possibility of a surprise.

Fort Mackinaw was surrendered by its garrison of sixty Americans to British and Indian forces of almost 600. Reports of the victory of the Indians at Michilimackinac encouraged all the Indians to come together under Tecumseh. Near Brownstown, the American Colonel Van Horne, with some 200 men, was ambushed and routed by Tecumseh and his Indians.

Although Hull had proven he was no coward in the Revolutionary War, he had a great fear of the Indians, perhaps because his son, daughter, and two grandchildren were traveling with him. On August 16 Hull crossed back to Detroit with British General Isaac Brock, Tecumseh, and 1,000 Indians close after him. Brock threatened Hull with torture and massacre by the Indians and consequently Hull surrendered without a fight against Brock's Indian forces and British troops. Of this episode Geoffrey Perret writes, "It was the greatest capitulation between the Revolution and Bataan. Hull gave up 2,000 men . . . and a reputation for courage."[12] General Hull received a court-martial for this surrender.

Brock had never seen Indian warfare; Hull had experienced it. Brock refused to grant Hull the honors of war. American regulars were taken as POWs and the Ohio militia was paroled and told to find their way home.[13]

The court-martial panel for General Hull was stacked against him. It was headed by General Dearbon, and Hull was refused access to War Department records required for his defense. The verdict was innocent of treason but guilty of cowardice and neglect of duty. He was sentenced to be shot, but a recommendation for mercy was made to President Madison because of Hull's age and prior military service. The president approved the sentence but remitted the penalty.[14]

Hull and most of the regulars were put on ships for transport to Montreal to be held there until officially exchanged. A few of the married officers, accompanied by wives, were given paroles at Newark. At Detroit the British held on to prisoners considered to be deserters from their ranks, but eventually they were taken to Montreal. Ohio militiamen were given lake transport behind Indian lines and released on parole to make their way home overland.

In retrospect, Hull had had no prospect of reinforcements and the fear of the Indians certainly had not helped his situation. Brock's warning that he might not be able to restrain his Indians was another strong factor for Hull's surrender. Some believe there was ample justification for his action. Historian Alec Gilpin clearly blames the secretary of war and the administration.[15]

The next commander was William Henry Harrison of Tippecanoe fame. The Fort Dearbon garrison was commanded by Captain Nathan Heald. On August 15 Brock attacked Detroit. Out of Detroit marched regulars, militia, women, and children and Captain William Wells. They were met by 400 Indians. Heald ordered his regulars to storm the enemy position while the Miami guard of Indians stayed out of it. Heald surrendered after the Indian chief promised to spare the lives of the survivors, a promise that was not kept.

Meanwhile, the Niagara offensive was delegated to General Van Rensselaer, whose forces consisted of militia, regulars, and a fleet of eighty boats. His objective was to cross over and attack the enemy at Queenston Heights. The ensuing conflict was a success at the outset but became a failure because of a lack of reinforcements; 250 Americans were killed or wounded, and 900 were taken as prisoners of war.

IRISH AMERICANS IN THE BATTLE OF QUEENSTON

The battle of Queenston on the Niagra River on October 13, 1812, greatly roused the country. Twenty-three of the prisoners taken during the battle became controversial because of their status. The British government maintained that these soldiers were British subjects not eligible to be considered POWs; they would have to be returned to England to stand trial for treason. Once again the principle invoked was "Once an Englishman always an Englishman," which denied the validity of American naturalization.

This incident led to one of the most embittered controversies of the 1812 war and eventually put an end to the exchange of all prisoners. Before the cartel ship sailed, British officers came on deck and conversed with the prisoners and set aside twenty-three who, because of their Celtic brogue, had been identified as Irish.[16] One person who championed their cause, who himself was a prisoner seized at Queenston, was Winfield Scott, who eventually rose to the rank of general and played an important role in the Mexican War and Civil War.

Scott heard the commotion about the Irishmen from below and dashed up to the deck where he denounced what was happening and emphatically told the prisoners to shut up. The twenty-three were hurried off and manacled on board a British frigate, which then headed for England where they would be tried for treason on the theory that subjects of the prince regent could not expatriate themselves. Scott was given parole status by the British, who paid no attention to his arguments.

When Scott arrived in Washington he continued his tirade about the British action on the Quebec cartel ship and sought out the secretary of war. The Senate immediately passed a bill giving the president retaliatory powers and the House agreed. At the first possible opportunity a number of British prisoners were confined. The governor-general, Sir George Prevost, was notified of this retaliatory measure, and was informed that the British prisoners would be given the same treatment as the Irish American soldiers. This was only the beginning.

Prevost responded by placing forty-six American officers and noncommissioned personnel under confinement. He threatened to kill two Americans for every British officer executed and vowed to pursue the war much more aggressively if any harm should come to British POWs. The United States countered this by confining more POWs and not allowing any paroles. Men's lives seemed to be hanging in the balance, but there was no serious attempt or intent to execute POW officers on either side.

To make matters worse, some Federalists sided with the British. Donald Hickey tells us in *The War of 1812* that in one instance British POWs in a jail were given pistols, probably by Federalist sympathizers who had not been searched. The results were that nine escaped, five were recaptured, and those who remained escaped to Canada. In the final analysis, the U.S. and British governments realized that they were acting like children and should treat prisoners more humanely.[17] General Winder, another former paroled POW captured in the Battle of Stony Creek in June, was given a parole on January 14, 1814, for sixty days. He was delegated by the U.S. government to negotiate a POW exchange. Both sides got involved in talks, but did not resolve anything.

What was beyond negotiation, however, was the fate of the twenty-three Irish Americans. They would not be included in the exchange, but one objective was successfully accomplished: the Irishmen would ultimately be treated the same as other American prisoners held in England. Of the twenty-three, two would die of natural causes and the remaining would ultimately be returned to the United States. There were other cases of attempted trials for treason, but the fear of retaliation was the factor that really saved them.

MORE RETALIATIONS

After the battle of Queenston there was another controversial incident involving POWs. The battle of Beaver Dams in June 1813 resulted in the capture of fifty-nine men of the 14th Regiment. They were sent to England because they were British subjects. In retaliation, a similar number of British soldiers were confined as hostages by General Harrison in the battle of the Thames. Much correspondence was exchanged between General James Mason and Colonel Thomas Barclay in charge of POWs for both countries, respectively, concerning conditions and POW exchanges.

In the winter of 1814 came the first American break when General Winder held POWs near Quebec, men captured at the battle of Stony Creek on June 13. For a year, unsatisfactory efforts had been made to effect an exchange, but in June 1814 he was granted a parole because he had spoken of trying to end the problem of hostages as a retaliatory measure.

Sir George Prevost wanted the matter settled favorably, but Winder could not persuade President Madison to drop the retaliatory program. He then returned to Quebec as a hostage himself. Madison, however, decided to drop the program and gave Winder authority to deal with the program and negotiate an exchange for all or any of the officers held as hostages or in regular prisons. Winder himself had to agree not to reenter military service until exchanged British prisoners arrived in Canada. A convention resulted on April 16 that provided for a mutual exchange; the prisoners could return to the military and naval service after May 15. The twenty-three Irishmen remained in England until repatriation under the provisions of the Treaty of

Ghent. General Winder had greatly impressed both Madison and Monroe and was given a command (on paper) that included the defense of Washington, but he suffered defeat at Bladensburg.

Walter Lord relates a brief humorous incident in *The Dawn's Early Light* that took place on August 21, 1814. A Lieutenant Gleig learned that there was an American rifle company ahead of him and rushed there with a group of his own men. Unfortunately, he was too late, but he found two men armed with muskets and bayonets who claimed they were simple country folks out shooting squirrels. Gleig laughed it off and seized the two as prisoners of war for the British army.[18]

When General Winder proceeded to Bladensburg, he sent a patrol toward Marlboro and two prisoners were captured who revealed that the British would not be marching that day.

President Madison had the mistaken idea that he as commander in chief would be presiding over the troops at Bladensburg with General Winder under him, but this simply was not to be. This was the only time in history that an American president as commander in chief was on a field of battle. But when he realized that in the field everything was out of his hands, he told the cabinet members with him that military matters should be in the hands of the military. He said, "Come, General Armstrong, Colonel Monroe, let us go and leave it to the Commanding General."[19]

COMMODORE BARNEY

Another interesting sidelight told by Walter Lord concerned American Commodore Joshua Barney who said to the British Admiral Cockburn and General Ross upon his capture, "Well, Admiral, you have got hold of me at last." The admiral expressed regrets that he was seeing Barney in such a state. After a brief discussion between Cockburn and Ross, Cockburn advised Barney that he was paroled immediately, and when asked where he wished to be taken, Barney responded a tavern near Bladensburg. General Ross called a surgeon to take care of the commodore's wounds and ordered a party of soldiers as stretcher-bearers. Cockburn detached Captain Wainwright to accompany them and see that proper attention was given to the commodore. Walter Lord commented that "all these officers proved fully up to that infinite courtesy that so often marked exchanges between opposing commanders before the twentieth century."[20]

Of course, there were some bad instances during the War of 1812 on the part of high-ranking British officials. One such example was the negative attitude of Colonel Proctor on January 12, 1813. On that day the British and Indians counterattacked U.S. forces. General Winchester himself was captured and became a POW and the British commander, Colonel Proctor, did not restrain the Indians when they tortured and massacred Americans.

DR. WILLIAM BEANES

A well-respected American civilian was a temporary prisoner of war. Dr. William Beanes, an elderly physician from Upper Marlboro, was captured by the British for his role in jailing General Ross's stragglers.

Two people, John S. Skinner, American prisoner of war agent, and Francis Scott Key, a Georgetown lawyer, asked for presidential permission to visit the British fleet under a flag of truce and to negotiate the release of the doctor. Madison approved and sent them to General Mason to make the preliminary plans. Dr. Beanes was clearly a noncombatant who was forcibly taken out of his bed in his home.

Mason notified Colonel Thornton, senior officer of the British wounded in Washington, that a flag of truce would be going down the line and that any open letters British prisoners wished to send to the British army would be gathered together for transmittal—a generous gesture. All did not really go according to calculations, but the letters were delivered and ultimately the two Americans met the commander in chief on the flagship.

The doctor received harsh treatment, which was unusual for a prominent, wealthy civilian prisoner of war. Ross said he would release the doctor but not right away. He could not let the doctor go early because British plans and preparations had been discussed openly in his presence and that of the two agents.

VARIOUS NAVAL BATTLES

Naval battles on the ocean and the Great Lakes contributed more prisoners to each side. On May 16, 1811, before the War of 1812 was officially proclaimed, there was the *Guerriere-President* incident, which was preceded by an encounter with the British sloop of war *Little Belt*.

The British frigate *Guerriere* was cruising along the New Jersey and Long Island shores. Commodore Rodgers of the *President* was sailing from Annapolis to New York when he was told by the captain of a coasting vessel that a New Jersey youth had been impressed from an American brig near Sandy Hook and placed on a frigate thought to be the *Guerriere*. On May 16 Rodgers thought an approaching ship was the *Guerriere* and was determined to talk to the captain and persuade him to release the Jersey boy.

The British ship, when it saw the American ship, headed south with the *President* in pursuit. Rodgers demanded that the ship identify itself when 100 yards separated them, but the British response was a shot on Rodgers's ship. (Later there would be some controversy concerning who actually shot first.) There was a brief action between the two ships. A broadside from Rodgers's ship silenced the fire of the enemy ship, and Rodgers waited in case it was necessary to render assistance to the enemy ship.

At daylight the next day Rodgers sailed within talking distance of the enemy and sent out his first cutter under the command of Lieutenant Creighton to get the necessary information. Creighton returned with the information that no help was necessary and that the name of the British sloop was *Little Belt*. No prisoners were taken as a result of this action, but it was a possible impressment that triggered the problem. Once again the strength, determination, and importance of the U.S. navy was demonstrated. The British ship limped away to Halifax; there was no attempt to capture it because war had not been declared.

The next main naval action involved the *Constitution* under Captain Isaac Hull (a nephew of General Hull) and the *Guerriere* under Captain Dacres. These two ships confronted each other on August 19, 1812. Up to this time the British navy had not been tested in battle against the U.S. Navy. When the *Constitution* fired on the enemy ship, the destruction was terrible. Both sides tried to board each other, but the motion of the two ships prevented them, and ultimately Captain Dacres had to surrender. The *Guerriere*'s wounded counted sixty-two, which included the captain and several officers. Both wounded and nonwounded became prisoners of war. The next day the *Guerriere* was set on fire and blown up.

In the battle between the two ships, the *Guerriere*'s 267-man crew included ten Americans who did not want to fight against their own countrymen and were permitted by the British captain to remain below. Dacres received a court-martial for his failure in this matter.

About two months later, on October 18, 1812, the U.S.S. *Wasp* under Captain Jacob Jones and the British *Frolic* under Captain Whinates engaged each other. The *Wasp* had been sent to England with letters for American ministers to Britain, and war was officially declared while it was on the return voyage. The *Wasp* left Delaware on October 13; two days later a small storm occurred and on October 17, when good weather returned, the men on the *Wasp* noticed several ships to the east. A brig was leading six vessels. The brig ran up a Spanish flag, but this did not fool the Americans. In the ensuing conflict much damage was done to the *Frolic* and many of its crew were killed. The *Wasp* had some damage and some killed also.

An American seaman once impressed by the British became a hero in the battle. Captain Jones ordered his Lieutenant Biddle to sail the *Frolic* to a southern port, but the sight of a seventy-four-gun British ship dashed American hopes. Both the *Wasp* and the *Frolic* were retaken. Prize crews were put on board and the American sloop and its captives were sailed to Bermuda. There Captain Jones was exchanged and returned to the United States, where he was treated as a victorious captain. A sum of $25,000 was voted by Congress as prize money for distribution among the crew. The *Wasp* flew the British flag but was soon lost at sea, a fate that would also be endured in 1942 by the aircraft carrier of the same name.

Another October naval encounter, on October 25, was between Stephen Decatur of the frigate the *United States*, and the British frigate the *Macedonian* under Captain John Carden, who had to surrender his ship and men. Decatur, we should remember, had distinguished himself in the Tripolitan War. The confrontation between Decatur and Carden was disastrous for Carden, who made a fatal mistake. Carden thought Decatur's ship was the *Essex*, a ship less powerful than the *United States*, and consequently his own ship never really had a chance. The prize and its captor arrived at Newport harbor on December 4 and Decatur was acclaimed as a hero. The *Macedonian* officers and crew numbered 300. A total of thirty-six were killed and sixty-eight wounded; the wounded and non-wounded were simply added to the growing numbers of British prisoners.

The closing days of December 1812 saw the *Constitution* under Commodore Bainbridge and the *Java* under Captain Lambert in a naval battle. The *Constitution* was cruising off the Brazilian coast. Bainbridge himself had been a prisoner for some time because of negotiations with France. He was sent to the United States in his own vessel filled with freed American prisoners. With the defeat of the *Java*, Bainbridge ordered Lieutenant Parker of the *Constitution* to take over the frigate captured after the battle. Captain Lambert had been fatally wounded in the battle and his ship was burned. All its prisoners were taken to San Salvador and then paroled.

The beginning of the next year of the war, 1813, saw a confrontation involving the *Comet*, a privateer commanded by Captain Boyle, who was waiting in a Brazilian harbor for the chance to seize one of three ships getting ready to sail to Europe—one large armed ship and two armed brigs. A Portuguese man-of-war shot a broadside against the *Comet,* whose captain retaliated immediately, and the Portuguese ship was cut to ribbons. The ship the *Bowes* also surrendered and a prize crew was dispatched to board it, but a man-of-war arrived on the scene and fired at the rowboat, which was then forced to return to the *Comet.* The *Comet* and the *Bowes* managed to make it to the United States. On the way more important prize captures were made and all got safely to the wharf in Baltimore.

On January 17, 1813, in a brief action, the *Viper* under Lieutenant J. D. Henly was captured by the British frigate *Narcissus* under Captain Lumly. A few weeks later, on February 8, the schooner *Lottery* under Captain John Southcomb was on her way from Baltimore to Bombay. Nine boats commanded by Lieutenant Kelly Nazer were sent to attack the *Lottery.* The *Lottery* was boarded after a battle in which Southcomb was fatally wounded and some of his men were wounded or killed. Southcomb was taken aboard the *Belvidera* under Captain Richard Byron, the British squadron commander. He was well treated but unfortunately died. His body was taken ashore, and as Theodore Roosevelt states, "he was granted . . . every mark of the respect due to so brave an officer."[21]

On February 24, 1813, the American sloop *Hornet* under James Lawrence engaged and sank the British *Peacock* under Captain Peake. On February 4, Lawrence had captured the brig *Resolution* and set it on fire because he did not want to man it. Lieutenant Shubrick set out in one of the *Hornet*'s boats, and when he reached the captured ship, he found that all but a few of the slightly wounded had been removed. There remained one boatload more, but the ship sank so fast that thirteen crewmen and three American seamen went down with the ship. The boat from the *Peacock* broke away with four on board. Every effort had been made to save lives. Lawrence hoped that the escapees could make it to the shore but thought they were lost.

Lawrence's treatment of prisoners was always good. Mustering the next morning revealed that 277 people had made it on board. This included the crew of the American brig *Hunter* captured by the *Peacock* only a few days earlier. The officers of the *Peacock* were treated so well that they did not really think of themselves as prisoners. They had been given clothing by their captors, who had devoted themselves to removing the wounded and other prisoners. On arrival in New York the officers of the *Peacock* published a statement expressing in the warmest terms how much they appreciated how they were treated.

A subsequent action on March 16 resulted in the British Lieutenant James Polkinghorne's setting out to attack the private schooner *Dolphin* and three other ships, the *Arab*, the *Lynx* (both of which surrendered almost immediately), and the *Racer*, which gave up after a battle. The *Dolphin* was then attacked and boarded.

On April 4, 1813, in a brief action, the schooner *Norwich* captured the British privateer *Caledonia*. The privateer lost seven men in the encounter. On September 5 the brig *Enterprise* under William Burrows and the *Boxer* under Samuel Blyth met in a battle in which both captains were killed at almost the same time. Both ships arrived at Portland, where the two commanders were laid to rest.

The last major sea action of 1813 involved the British brig *Shannon* under Philip Broke and the U.S. frigate *Chesapeake*. Broke was waiting near Boston in the spring of 1813 to take on the *Chesapeake*. In May the *Chesapeake* got a new captain, James Lawrence, who was anxious to even the score with the British. He left the harbor on June 1 and the *Shannon* poured a devastating fire on the *Chesapeake* when it sailed within range. The resulting tragedy saw Lawrence, fatally wounded, reportedly issuing his famous command, "Don't give up the ship!" His crew was beaten in hand-to-hand combat and trapped below decks. The *Chesapeake* became one more captive ship of the British.

Thus the United States did not fare too well on the ocean in 1813. During 1814–1815, however, its fortunes improved. Three new vessels were built or purchased and a grand total of seventy-nine prizes were seized by ships of various sizes.

In 1813, on the Great Lakes, when Canadian militia and British regulars outnumbered Americans almost three to one, the British lost heavily. Americans lost almost 290 army and navy prisoners. Of ten British losses on the Great Lakes in 1813, one was seized at York, two burned, and nine captured by American forces. Theodore Roosevelt provides a chart of British losses with each ship's tonnage and guns. In marked contrast, there were only two American losses. The new U.S. Navy did much better than the U.S. Army.[22]

From the summer of 1813 on, the Royal Navy created a tight blockade off the American coast. This forced many frigates to stay in port, which produced a severe economic blow to the American people and in particular to residents of the island of Nantucket, which will be discussed later in the chapter.

In early 1814, the *Essex* under Captain David Porter entered the neutral civilian harbor of Valpariso, and three British men-of-war appeared on the scene. The *Phoebe* came alongside the American ship and although Porter made a run for the sea, unfortunately a small squall struck and disabled his ship. Two of the British ships initiated an attack on Porter's ship. Porter was realistic and practical about the situation and allowed his crew to jump overboard to try to swim three-quarters of a mile to freedom. He struck his colors but insisted that the British conduct was unethical, which of course was denied. Porter reported fifty-eight killed, sixty-six wounded, and thirty-one missing. British Captain Hilyer decided to parole Porter and his crew and sent them to the United States, despite the protest of Admiral Cochrane in command of the coast of North America.

Lieutenant McKnight, Captain Adams, Midshipman Lyman, and eleven seamen were exchanged on the spot for some of the British prisoners on board the *Essex*. McKnight and Lyman took the *Phoebe* to Rio de Janeiro and then left on a Swedish vessel. They were taken off the vessel by the *Wasp* under Captain Blakely and were lost with the rest of the crew of the ship. The others arrived safely in New York in the summer.

Another brief engagement came on April 29, 1814, between the *Peacock* under Captain Warrington and the British sloop *L' Epervier*. The British commander soon realized it was useless to fight and his ship was boarded. As soon as some of the shot holes beneath the wharves were fixed, attention was given to caring for the wounded and prisoners. Discovered aboard were three impressed American seamen, one of whom had been killed. Captain Warrington was determined to save the prize if possible, and he put it in charge of Lieutenant J. B. Nicholson and ordered him to sail to Savannah. When two large enemy frigates approached from the north, Nicholson yelled to Warrington to remove the crew from *L'Epervier* and leave him and sixteen men to handle the ship. Warrington agreed and tried to draw off the approaching ships. Nicholson stayed on course and on May 1 brought the brig safely into Savannah. Three days later the *Peacock* arrived.

Throughout 1814 the sloop *Wasp* had a profitable cruise in European waters. The commander, Captain Johnston Blakeley, during a four-month cruise, captured thirteen British merchantmen and fought two of the best brigs of the Royal Navy.

One ship destroyed was the *Reindeer,* from which prisoners were removed. Anxious to get rid of these men, Blakeley put them on a Portuguese brig he overhauled and sent them to England. Unfortunately Blakeley and his ship were lost at sea.

The battle of Lake Champlain was fought September 11, 1814. Under the leadership of Lieutenant Thomas Macdonough Jr., the American squadron was as successful as Perry had been. His ships were fewer than those of his enemy, but he was so successful, Barnes says, that "as soon as Sir George Prevost saw the results of the action out in the water, he gave up all ideas of conquest, and began the retreat that left New York free to breathe again."[23]

In early January 1815, however, Stephen Decatur lost his frigate the *President*. It grounded heavily on a sandbar and could not escape. His undoing was accomplished by the *Endymion*, although the enemy ship was rendered useless for combat. Two enemy frigates, *Pomone* and *Tenedos*, came up against Decatur, who had to surrender. The British did everything in their power to make the wounded comfortable and treated enemy officers courteously and kindly. Decatur himself was a cabin prisoner on board the *Endymion* and was given, along with his officers, freedom on the island of Bermuda. On his return to the United States he was treated as a hero. He was vindicated for his failure by a military court of inquiry.

On February 20, 1815, the *Constitution* under Charles Atewart took the *Cyane* in a moonlight battle and then the *Levant* under Captain George Douglass. Captain Gordon Falcon of the *Cyane* and his officers were sent as prisoners to the *Constitution* and added later would be the captain and officers of the *Levant*. Both enemy captains were treated as honored guests at a dinner aboard the *Constitution*. The capture of these two enemy ships, the Battle of New Orleans, and the later sinking of the *Penguin* could not have taken place if all the parties involved had known of the president's ratification of the Treaty of Ghent. Barnes writes that "the *Cornwallis* fired the last gunshot of the War of 1812."[24]

ROBERT FULTON

Many histories do not mention the battle of Stonington or Robert Fulton, since the battle had little significance. Any student of American history should remember Robert Fulton for his steamboat, but his other projects were significant for the War of 1812. They represented a new type of warfare that would be related to events leading up to the battle of Stonington, led by the British ship *Ramillies,* and would be relevant to prisoners of war. These events are described by James De Kay in *The Battle of Stonington*. The subtitle of the book, *Torpedoes, Submarines, and Rockets in the War of 1812*, is more descriptive of what the book is really about.

Robert Fulton invented a "turtle boat" that could be submerged and used to attach torpedoes to the bottoms of ships. A near victim of this device was the *Ramillies* under Captain Thomas Hardy. In this war the world saw "the world's first generalized application of underwater warfare."[25]

Jeremiah Holmes was very involved in the events preceding the *Ramillies* incident. He was the master of the sloop *Hero* and lived in Mystic, Connecticut. He sailed for New York and avoided the British blockade and joined the pilot boat, the American schooner *Ulysses*. He was at greater risk running the blockade because if he were captured, it meant hanging. Because Holmes had deserted the Royal Navy, De Kay tells us,[26] he would never have been exchanged as a POW. Holmes was impressed into the British service by the *Trident,* shouting all the while that he was an American lieutenant. He endured three years of forced service, as pleas were made everywhere to no avail. Later he was transferred to the *Saturn,* which sailed off to the Mediterranean. On board he became an expert on cannons. The admiralty therefore refused to give him up and never allowed him on shore for fear that he would flee. He made two escape attempts near Gibraltar and Africa.

Holmes knew that the *Nimble* and *Revenue,* two Mystic River schooners captured off Cape Hatteras, would have their crew sent off to prison in Bermuda, so he managed an escape in Portsmouth one winter day to an American ship. He arrived home in March 1807 and took over the *Hero*. He finally decided, however, to sell his share in the ship and pursue another job.

In April 1813, the *Hero* hunted down and captured a British brig under one of Captain Hardy's lieutenants and took the brig as a prize, holding the crew for ransom. Hardy sent a letter of negotiation to the Connecticut governor and an exchange of prisoners was effected in New London waters at the end of May. Hardy had threatened the destruction of New London, an important factor in achieving the exchange. Prisoners were returned to the *Ramillies,* which flew a flag of truce.

In March 1813, a congressional act was passed that encouraged destruction of enemy ships and the use of "torpedoes, submarine instruments, or any other destructive machines whatever."[27] In essence, therefore, a whole new type of warfare was being encouraged by Congress.

On June 15, 1813, John Scudder placed on the *Eagle*, a rebuilt and refurbished schooner, ten 40-pound kegs of gunpowder with a quantity of sulphur mixed in it deep below the deck. There were two firing mechanisms fixed to the top of this ship, which was really a self-propelled floating bomb. Scudder's objective was to sink the *Ramillies*. Scudder left the boat, which the British seized, and the resulting explosion showered pitch and tar on the deck of the *Ramillies* almost a mile away. If it had been any nearer, it would have been disastrous for the *Ramillies*. A remarkable fact about this attempt was that it had been engineered by civilians and not the military.

Captain Hardy sailed his ship to Gardiner's Bay and quite often he and his officers were hosted by the island's owner. This information was brought to the attention of Decatur by Joshua Penny, a local pilot and spy from Long Island. Thus arose the possibility of kidnapping Hardy on shore. In late 1813 the plan concocted involved Joshua Penny's guiding four small boats from the American squadron at night from New London to the Island. To protect Penny in case of capture, Decatur signed him on as a seaman. In actuality, all Penny's previous activities had consisted of espionage and dirty tricks. Five men were captured and five left on the beach. All five were given paroles, since they were not important and the whole operation had been aborted. If it had been successful, it would have been a real psychological coup for the Americans.

Aboard Hardy's ship was a John Carpenter, an American seaman from Norwich who had been impressed five years earlier. Carpenter was able to notify his father, who wrote to Hardy and begged for his son's release. This played well into Hardy's strategic plans and the father was permitted to come aboard the *Ramillies* and speak to his

son. Upon confirmation of his nationality the young sailor was released. This diplomacy was viewed as a stroke of ingenuity in local
eyes. Unfortunately, other men who had asked for release on the
same grounds were not as lucky as John Carpenter. Hardy then proceeded in a determined way to eliminate all enemy ships, and he
took possession of all islands in the area.

Jeremiah Holmes, living on the eastern bank of the Mystic
River, was still under the sentence of death as a British deserter. He
armed a small ship with which he aided the grounded *Victory* off
Fisher's Island, thus preventing the British from taking the *Victory*
as a prize.

THE FIRST SUBMARINE TORPEDOES

Two weeks after the explosion of the *Eagle*, a Norwich man introduced submarines to the War of 1812. On July 10, 1813, the *New
York Herald* ran a story of three attempts to use a diving boat under
the *Ramillies* to blow a hole in its bottom. The first two times were
not successful and although the third involved placing some type of
"time bomb" under the ship, this also proved to be a failure. The
name of the person, probably from Saybrook, remains a mystery, but
he had designed and built a working sub during the American Revolution. Hardy wasn't taking any chances and had his ships constantly moving around and his ship's bottom checked carefully every
two hours both day and night. Meanwhile, in the Chesapeake Bay
area, Fulton's contribution was a "torpedo" that was similar to what
today is known as a mine.

Hardy sent letters to the Connecticut governor to the effect that in
the future his ship would carry on board fifty to one hundred POWs
who would share the same fate if his ship were attacked.

The subject of torpedoes was discussed between Decatur and a
man named Weldon or Welling (his first name is still under dispute).
He tied Decatur to the emergence of torpedo warfare in Long Island

Sound. This person also met Joshua Penny, who had unsuccessfully attempted to kidnap Captain Hardy.

When Hardy was informed about the presence of Penny, he sent his first lieutenant into Sag Harbor during the day to learn where Penny lived. The lieutenant returned with the information and that night, with a squad of marines, he dragged Penny out of his bed to the docks. On ship Penny was put in irons and placed on bread and water rations while he constantly proclaimed his innocence.

The local militia commander, Major Benjamin Case, directed a formal demand for Penny's release. The letter explained that Penny was a native-born citizen of East Hampton and a noncombatant who could not be legally held as a POW. Hardy's intelligence, from both sides of the sound, was excellent. Hardy wanted to take Penny to Halifax, and he was well on his way to Nova Scotia when it was learned that President Madison had retaliated by ordering two British POWs to be held as hostages for Penny's return. The British in Halifax felt Penny would be seen as a martyr and were concerned about their own two POWs being held as hostages.

By this time U.S. military prisons were overflowing and the government would have to secure additional areas for such prisoners. At Ipswich a jail held sixteen sailors, and eighty British officers captured at the battle of Thames were held in Newport, Kentucky. At Chillicothe there was a detention camp with British officers and sailors guarded by the U.S. marshal of Ohio. They had been seized by Commodore Perry on Lake Erie. Fort Sewall in Massachusetts and the Kentucky State Penitentiary at Frankfurt also held POWs.[28] Tucker tells us that American prisoners in Canada were poorly treated; because of the great need for more accommodations for POWs the British were considering transport to England.

Prevost had many U.S. officers in the Beaufort jail near Quebec. Both General Winder and Chandler had been captured in the battle at Stony Creek. Eager to get rid of his prisoners, Prevost gave Winder a sixty-day parole to go to Washington. Winder went to Baltimore. He reached Plattsburg from Quebec on May 20, 1814, and then started for the capitol again. President Madison needed an officer to defend the capitol and his choice was Winder.

The battle of Stonington, as already noted, was insignificant. It was a lop-sided American victory, according to De Kay. On the fourth day of the battle the British simply withdrew. Why the British attacked remains a mystery. Perhaps Hardy wanted to destroy civilian property. When he was questioned afterward, his reply was that he thought torpedoes were being manufactured in the village, but there was no sound basis for this claim.

NANTUCKET

The blockade of the U.S. coast had a special effect on the island of Nantucket. This island had fared well under the protection of the British king and under the influence of the Quakers in the early years of the American Revolution. According to Whipple, the island's economy had been based on whaling since the early 1700s.[29] People there wanted to remain neutral in the War of 1812 in order to pursue economic growth and development.

The Quakers continued their dominance in 1812 and saw no point in getting involved in the new war; thus, a policy of neutrality would again be the rule. A year before the threat of war, economic difficulties began to emerge for the people of Nantucket: both Jefferson's economic warfare and the British coastal blockade from Chesapeake Bay to New London, Connecticut, were disastrous to the whaling industry of the island.

Rear Admiral Henry Hotham, who commanded the British ships from Nantucket to the Delaware, was instructed to investigate the situation on Nantucket. If the residents there were as disturbed as they said they were, they would be granted permission to import supplies. In return for such consideration they would have to declare themselves absolutely neutral in the war. A number of discussions followed, and a committee elected at a town meeting signed such a declaration. The town meeting also voted not to pay taxes to the United States during the war. The agreement was honored by the British government, which then ordered the release of Nantucket men among the prisoners of war in Dartmoor prison. Unfortunately, there is no evidence reported by historians (including Horsman, who wrote extensively on Dartmoor's prisoners) that this was actually done. Prisoners were still being held at Dartmoor even after the signing of the Treaty of Ghent.

DARTMOOR

At the end of the war horror stories started emerging about prisoners in Dartmoor. Donald Hickey addressed the conditions of Dartmoor in *The War of 1812* (1990), as did Horsman in his book. A very early account was also contained in Basil Thomson, *The Story of Dartmoor Prison.*

Basil Thomson was a prisoner for seven years at Dartmoor. The Department of the Admiralty felt that Dartmoor was "a most eligible and healthy situation for housing sick and wounded seamen and prisoners of war."[30] Thus was laid the foundation for the place in which thousands of American men would be incarcerated as a result of the War of 1812. Those imprisoned there earlier were Frenchmen and other nationalities who had fought against British policy. Once the War of 1812 started, the garrison forces had to be gradually increased to maintain captured American naval, army, and merchant service officers.

From the spring of 1813 to the early summer of 1815, American prisoners were at Dartmoor. Reginald Horsman described Dartmoor as "a prison of remarkable contrasts: on the one hand smallpox, pneumonia, and floggings; on the other music, dancing, fencing, and theatre."[31] Americans created their own courts to punish thefts and maintain internal law; the British prison governors—members of the Royal Navy—did not interfere. Some flogging punishments were just as cruel as those imposed by order of seamen's courts, which consisted of American officers on naval ships.

By April 1813 there were so many American POWs (Thomson tells us there were about 1,700, of which 700 were on ships)[32] that fear of revolt spurred the movement to Dartmoor prison. Thomson further relates that fifty-nine Americans enlisted in the British navy to escape Dartmoor.[33]

In the beginning of August 1814, American officers started moving to Section Number 6, and plans for digging an escape route started. Everyone swore on a Bible not to divulge the plan. They went down 20 feet and then tunneled 250 feet outside of the prison walls. By the end of August three tunnels were under way. Unfortunately, one tunnel was discovered, which prompted queries about who might have betrayed the tunneling prisoners. A secret court was convened and some were arraigned. There was strong evidence, but the men were removed to the guardhouse for protection until ready for a cartel. They were threatened by other Americans, and one escaped to the country where he worked as a blacksmith until he was discovered and returned to Dartmoor on April 1, 1815, a month after ratification of the Treaty of Ghent.

Other prisoners escaped and made their way to Tarbay. They seized fishing boats and sailed to the French coast. We know that none were taken alive but not how many really escaped. The initial difficulty for an escaping prisoner was that he had to cope with the surrounding moors, which in winter were cold and icy.

Horsman's article tells us that "of the Americans sent to Dartmoor about one out of seven was black."[34] At that time the American navy recruited black seamen and it was a good opportunity for free Negroes. Until late spring 1815 the black barracks at Dartmoor were in Section Number 4. A problem arose at the end of the war when many blacks refused repatriation if their ship's destination was a Southern port.

The American agent Beasley did not show any haste in securing ships to take prisoners home, for which he was criticized by prisoners.

Unfortunately, there soon followed a tragedy in which British troops fired on unarmed prisoners, killing four and wounding thirty-one.

THE TREATY OF GHENT

When negotiations were begun at Ghent to end the war, U.S. envoys were still demanding a cessation of impressments. The men selected by the president were competent and well known and were willing to act on their own if necessary. They were much more competent than their English counterparts. In June 1814, President Madison decided to drop the issue of impressment, a rather ironic twist, for that issue had precipitated the war. The U.S. envoys were then able to deal with other issues and come to a final agreement. Samuel Bemis in *A Diplomatic History of the United States* asserts that the issue was never really settled, although "Great Britain has ceased the practice since 1813."[35] On Christmas Eve 1814 the document that ended the war was signed.

While the Treaty of Ghent was being signed, there were over 5,000 American sailors in Dartmoor. Article 3 of the treaty said that all prisoners of war taken by either side on land or sea should be returned as soon as practicable after treaty ratification and upon the prisoners' paying debts they might have incurred during their captivity. An interesting point of article 10 was that both England and the United States desired to abolish slavery, which was considered to be irreconcilable with the principles of humanity and justice. This point, of course, was finally settled in the United States by an internal conflict, the Civil War.

One other battle of the War of 1812 was the Battle of New Orleans, whose victor, Andrew Jackson, was seen as a brilliant tactician. This battle took place after the Treaty of Ghent; with modern means of communication there simply would not have been any such battle. Even after the battle some sporadic naval warfare continued until news could reach distant vessels.

NOTES

1. Theodore Roosevelt, *The Naval War of 1812,* 3d ed. (New York: Putnam, 1882), ix.

2. Geoffrey Perret, *A Country Made by War* (New York: Random House, 1989), 107.

3. Robert Leckie, *The Wars of America,* rev. ed. (New York: Harper & Row, 1968, 1981), 229.

4. Bradford Perkins, *Prologue to War: England and the United States, 1805–1812* (Berkeley: University of California Press, 1961), 6.

5. James F. Zimmerman, *Impressment of American Seamen* (New York: Columbia University, 1925), 112.

6. Perkins, *Prologue to War,* 168.

7. Roosevelt, *Naval War of 1812,* 32–33.

8. Perkins, *Prologue to War,* 88–89.

9. Samuel Bemis, *A Diplomatic History of the United States*, rev. ed. (New York: Holt, 1942), 144.

10. Frank Updyke, *The Diplomacy of the War of 1812* (Baltimore: Johns Hopkins University Press, 1915).

11. George Lewis and John Mehwa, "History of Prisoners of War Utilization by the United States Army, 1776–1943," Pamphlet 20-213 (Washington, D.C.: Department of the Army, 1955), 22.

12. Geoffrey Perret, *Country Made by War*, 109.

13. John R. Elting, *Amateurs to Arms! A Military History of the War of 1812* (Chapel Hill, NC: Algonquin Books of Chapel Hill, 1991), 34.

14. Elting, *Amateurs to Arms,* 34.

15. Alec R. Gilpin, *The War of 1812 in the Old West* (Michigan: Michigan State University Press, 1958), 124.

16. Glenn Tucker, *Poltroons and Patriots*, vols. 1–2 (Indianapolis: Bobbs-Merrill, 1954), 192.

17. Donald Hickey, *The War of 1812: A Forgotten Conflict* (Urbana: University of Illinois Press, 1989), 157.

18. Walter Lord, *The Dawn's Early Light* (New York: Norton, 1972), 66.

19. Lord, *Dawn's Early Light,* 124.

20. Lord, *Dawn's Early Light,* 138.

21. Roosevelt, *Naval War of 1812,* 173.

22. Roosevelt, *Naval War of 1812,* 283.

23. James Barnes, *Naval Actions of the War of 1812* (New York: Harper, 1896), 215.

24. Barnes, *Naval Actions of the War of 1812*, 263.

25. James Tertius De Kay, *The Battle of Stonington: Torpedoes, Submarines, and Rockets in the War of 1812* (Annapolis, Md.: Naval Institute Press, 1990), 5.

26. De Kay, *Battle of Stonington*, 16.

27. De Kay, *Battle of Stonington*, 29.

28. Glenn Tucker, *Poltroons and Patriots*, vols. 1–2 (Indianapolis: Bobbs-Merrill, 1954), 493.

29. A. B. C. Whipple, *Vintage Nantucket* (New York: Dodd, Mead, 1978), 181.

30. Basil Thomson, *The Story of Dartmoor Prison* (London: William Heinemann, 1907), 3.

31. Reginald Horsman, "The Paradox of Dartmoor Prison," *American Heritage Magazine*, February 26, 1975, 13–17, 85.

32. Thomson, *Story of Dartmoor Prison*, 97.

33. Thomson, *Story of Dartmoor Prison*, 106.

34. Horsman, "Paradox of Dartmoor Prison," 14.

35. Bemis, *Diplomatic History of the United States*, 145.

6

The Mexican War

The first confrontation between Mexico and the United States resulted in American soldiers being taken as prisoners of war in April 1846. War was declared on May 13 by President James Polk, but in essence, the Mexican government considered that a state of war already existed because of a train of events that included the Texan proclamation of independence on March 2, 1836, the annexation of Texas to the United States on March 3, 1837, Texas statehood in 1845, and finally the movements of General Zachary Taylor in 1846.

Texas was a thorn in the side of Mexico. When its first president, Sam Houston, sent a representative to Washington to seek recognition of Texas, Andrew Jackson, on his last day in office, recognized it. But his two successors, Martin Van Buren and William Henry Harrison, did not do anything more about the situation. John Tyler succeeded Harrison and on Tyler's last day in office he informed Houston that Texas had been admitted into the Union by a joint congressional resolution. Thus the wheels were set in motion for the incoming expansionist president, James Polk, to lay the foundation for the incident that would precipitate the first imperialistic war for the United States.

Like the War of 1812, this one was fought on land and water: the Gulf of Mexico and the Pacific coastal area. Whereas the American army was inferior to the navy in the War of 1812, the army in the Mexican War proved to be the superior force. The navy, however, played an important role in transporting army troops and blockading coastal areas.

TEXAS BECOMES A STATE

On July 4, 1845, Texas became a state and General Zachary Taylor's troops disembarked from a navy ship at New Orleans. This infantry regiment was to protect the newly admitted state, if necessary, from a foreign invasion. Taylor was simply preparing for any contingency.

The United States claimed the Rio Grande as its boundary and thus the ownership of the land between the Rio Grande and Nueces Rivers was disputed. The president's attempt to have U.S. envoy John Slidell negotiate the boundary with Mexico was a failure. Consequently, General Taylor was ordered to the mouth of the Rio Grande from Corpus Christi, something the general himself had recommended as early as October 4, 1845.

The United States was not really prepared for war, but this didn't faze General Taylor. As Robert Selph Henry puts it, "Into that war in the spring of 1846, the two nations drifted through a fog of misunderstanding and a welter of war talk."[1]

WAR BEGINS

The U.S. forces started their advance at 10:00 A.M. on March 8, 1846, led by Colonel David Twigg's regiment of dragoons and Major Ringgold's artillery battery. The American army sent guarantees to Mexican officials and residents that civil and religious rights would not be violated. Then Taylor sent out a scouting party under Captain Seth Thornton and sixty-three dragoons. On April 25, General Torrejon, with all of General Mariano Arista's cavalry and some infantry, came upon the American dragoons whom, after a brief battle, they surrounded and captured. The results were eleven American casualties, some wounded, and some captured; thus the first American prisoners of war of the new conflict had been taken.

CAPTIVES

Among the captives was Captain Thornton. His Mexican guide informed the base camp about the ambush. General Torrejon sent a courteous note to General Taylor that he had no hospital facilities for the wounded but that the other officers and men were being held as prisoners.

The next major step for General Taylor was to send a note on April 25 to Washington. He said he had received a communication from General Arista that hostilities had commenced and "I regret to report that a party of dragoons sent out by me on the 24th to watch the course of the river above on this bank became engaged with a very large force of the enemy, and after a short affair, in which some sixteen were killed or wounded, appear to have been surrounded and compelled to surrender. Not one of the party has returned, except a wounded man sent in this morning by the Mexican commander, so that I cannot report with confidence the particulars of the engagement or other fates of the officers, except that Captain Hardee was known to be a prisoner and unhurt. Captain Thornton and Lieutenants Mason and Kane were the other officers. The party was 63 strong. Hostilities may now be considered as commenced."[2]

Fortunately Captain Thornton was a survivor. He would later report that as a prisoner he had been treated kindly and that one dragoon who treated him rudely was punished by General Arista.[3]

In a letter written by Captain Hardee on April 26 he described the circumstances of his capture. He also mentioned his concern for his men's treatment and arranged with a Mexican officer to deliver himself and his men as POWs to be treated "with all the consideration to which such unfortunates are entitled by the rules of civilized warfare."[4]

General Taylor exchanged enough prisoners to recover the command of Captain Thornton. Wounded prisoners were sent to Matamoros and wounded officers were granted paroles. General de la Vega and a few other officers declined paroles and were then sent to Major General Gaines.[5] The exchange of prisoners took place on May 11. La Vega had been captured in the battle of Resaca de Palma on May 9. Thus the first major exchange of the war was conducted in a civilized manner.

After the very first confrontation of the war the public cry taken up by the newspapers was "American blood shed on American soil." But this was a form of propaganda comparable to that used in the so-called Boston Massacre by colonial newspapers of the American Revolution. That colonial event had not been a massacre, and there was a critical question whether the American soldiers killed by the Mexicans were really killed on American soil. The Mexicans maintained that all Texan territory to the Louisiana line belonged to them and any movement into Texas would constitute an invasion of Mexico.

COLONEL TRUEMAN CROSS

Several events had prompted Taylor to create the scouting mission for Thornton. On April 10 Colonel Trueman Cross, Taylor's quartermaster, left the fort alone for a horseback ride up the river and never returned. Taylor ordered cannon fire to guide the colonel back, but he did not return. Riding with a group of officers up the river one day, Lieutenant French came across a blue coat that he thought belonged to Cross. Subsequently, another search patrol was ordered. It was led by Lieutenant Porter, the brother of a future navy admiral. Eleven days after Cross disappeared, his body was found. His death was attributed to a heavy blow to the skull. The rumor back in the camp was that he was killed after being taken prisoner by a guerrilla band. Colonel Cross was buried with full military honors on April 24.

More and larger patrols were sent out to investigate. The killing of Cross would not have been a sufficient cause for war, but the Thornton confrontation with regular Mexican soldiers, on American or Mexican soil, was a precipitating factor.

When General Ampudia ordered Taylor to take his men to the other side of the Nueces, Taylor replied in the negative. He also asked the naval commander of the Rio Grande to prevent the Mexicans from using the river. The navy had transported Taylor's men to New Orleans and now was being asked to perform its other major function of the war—forming a blockade. In the Pacific area Commodore John Sloat's responsibility was to seize San Francisco and blockade other California ports.

THE BATTLES OF PALO ALTO AND RESACA DE LA PALMA

When Commodore David Conner thought it likely that Taylor would be attacked, he landed 500 bluejackets and marines under Captain Gregory of the frigate *Raritan* to garrison the base. According to Conner, this was done on May 8. In 1846, two important battles resulted in U.S. victories—the battle of Palo Alto on May 8 and Resaca de La Palma on May 9. When news came of Taylor's victory at Palo Alto, there seemed to be no need for the navy relief columns. However, the sailors and marines stayed until May 13 because of the possibility of a raid. Taylor thought the Palo Alto victory would chiefly be accomplished by bayonet, but it actually became an artillery duel.

A prairie fire brought a temporary halt to the fighting. As dusk approached, both sides continued to fire on one another. Arista retreated, hoping to find a better position the next day. Taylor's scouts saw that Arista was trying to hide his troops in the brush on the banks of the Rio Grande at a place called Resaca de la Palma. Troops on both sides were exhausted. On the morning of May 9, the Mexicans seemed to have disappeared.

After returning to terrain more appropriate for an advance, Lieutenant Sam Grant, given his first battle command, ordered a charge, but there was no resistance. He captured several Mexicans, including

a wounded colonel. Grant assigned a guard to escort the prisoners to
the rear. Dragoons under Captain Charles May suffered heavy losses
and tried to speed back. When May galloped back to American lines,
he brought with him a prisoner of war, Major General Romolo Diaz
de la Vega, who had been the acting commander in the field of all
Mexican troops.

The battle between the Mexicans and Americans degenerated
into a rout. Taylor's forces pursued the fleeing enemy to the Rio
Grande. The battle was a clear-cut victory, although it was rather indecisive. Taylor sent his wounded and all Mexican prisoners back
to Point Isabel. The capture of de la Vega and about a hundred others constituted a great moral victory. Arista's right wing, supposedly the strength of his army, "crumbled like a sand fort struck by a
wave."[6]

CATHOLIC PRIESTS ACCOMPANY THE ARMY

John Edwards Weems asserts that President Polk, probably inspired
by a suggestion from Secretary of State Buchanan, had invited the
Catholic bishop of New York to the executive mansion and asked
him to help recruit Spanish-speaking priests to serve with the U.S.
Army in Mexico. The main purpose of this was to assure the Mexicans that we would not rob churches. Bishop Hughes agreed and
later priests accompanied the army to fulfill this objective.[7] From the
very beginning, Mexican soldiers and their commanders tried to entice many Catholic American soldiers to change sides and join the
ranks of a Catholic nation.

A source known as the *Woodstock Letters* supplies a detailed account of chaplains in the Mexican War. The military does not have
records of chaplains for this war. In May 1846, there was no legisla-
tion that allowed for the appointment of chaplains, but by executive
discretionary power, or perhaps similar to what today would be
called executive privilege, such provision was made by President

Polk. Thus two Jesuits became the first officially commissioned U.S. Army chaplains.

Secretary of War Marcy wrote a letter to Father McElroy, S.J., saying that present laws did not allow the president to appoint and commission chaplains, but that the president could have people perform duties appropriate for chaplains. A similar letter was sent to Father Rey, S.J. Information was given to both concerning pay and travel.

The two Jesuit priests joined Taylor's army of occupation in the Rio Grande, and Taylor was so notified by the War Department. The two priests were given cabin passages to Point Isabel from which they received safe conduct to General Taylor's headquarters. Marcy's letter was classified as confidential.

Father McElroy served in Matamoros, where General Taylor was located before marching against Monterrey. Father Rey went with the troops. Unfortunately he was murdered by Mexican bandits at the end of the campaign against Monterrey. Father McElroy ministered mainly to the wounded and dying at the hospital, both Americans and Mexicans.

A *Woodstock Letter* dated 1841 describes the first navy chaplain. He boarded the ship the *North Carolina* off Norfolk in early December 1824 and was buried at sea on September 20, 1825. Father Adam Marshall, S.J., was hired as official schoolmaster to the midshipmen but also acted as chaplain to Catholic sailors.

GENERAL AMPUDIA'S SURRENDER

In the late summer of 1846 the war was progressing in favor of the United States, which had won almost all of northeastern Mexico by the end of 1846. When an emissary from a Mexican commander arrived at Taylor's headquarters offering to surrender the city of Monterrey but not the garrison, Taylor demanded complete surrender and General Ampudia finally conceded. Taylor took Monterrey and all public property but allowed Ampudia's soldiers to keep their horses, small arms, and a number of large guns as long as they returned beyond a line of about forty miles. Monterrey was then Taylor's. Unfortunately Polk did not approve of Taylor's allowing prisoners such paroles. The terms seemed very generous, and Polk considered recalling Taylor, but that would make him a martyr. The release on parole actually was a fait accompli. Polk had the right to make such a recall if he desired, as Truman recalled MacArthur during the Korean conflict.

THE DEFEAT OF THE *TRUXTUN*

On August 12, 1846, came the first loss of a navy ship. The twelve-gun brig *Truxtun* went aground off a reef at the mouth of the Tuxpan River about 120 miles north of Vera Cruz as Captain Carpender came too close and his brig settled on the reef. This left his ship in a precarious, unprotected position, with a full gale in progress. Carpender initially refused to surrender to General Antonio Rosas, but ultimately he had no choice and capitulated. Before he surrendered, however, he sent a party under Lieutenants Bushrod Hunter and Otway Berryman for help. The two lieutenants escaped in one of the brig's cutters and sailed successfully to Anton Lizardo in a Mexican coastal vessel that they had captured.

During the first week of September 1846, Commodore Conner reported receipt of a Mexican offer to exchange Commander Carpender and his *Truxtun* crew for General de la Vega and his officers captured at the battle of Resaca de la Palma. While Conner was waiting for a formal acceptance of the exchange from Washington, he secured a parole for his crew, and on September 22, four of the officers and thirty-eight of the men were sent to him. A revenue cutter was dispatched to Tuxpan to pick up the other three officers and thirteen men. On October 27, Conner informed the Mexican government that Washington had approved the deal.

TABASCO AND TAMPICO

Commodore Matthew Perry was anxious to seize Tabasco, and Conner agreed with this measure. Perry was tasked to accomplish the mission with seven ships and a landing force of 253 men under Captain Forrest.[8] On the evening of October 16, the navy ships left their anchorage. The small commercial town of Frontera, located at the mouth of the Tabasco River, fell easily, and for seventy-two miles upriver the weakly defended Tabasco was easy prey for the navy squadron. The successful action at Tabasco did much to raise the morale of the navy squadron. The port of Tampico later proved to play an important part in General Winfield Scott's success against Vera Cruz.

In the early hours of November 15, Commodore Conner's squadron at Tampico had to endure difficult weather. One of his brigs, the *Somers*, was capable of performing blockade duty even in bad weather. On November 26, the ship, under Lieutenant Raphael Semmes, was enforcing a blockade of Vera Cruz. He sailed close to the shore and put a boat over the side. The boat contained Lieutenant James Parker, Midshipmen John Hynson, R. Clay Rogers, and five men. Daringly and audaciously they boarded a Mexican ship whose crew they overwhelmed, but with some noise. A guard on *San Juan de Ulboa* yelled and demanded to know what was happening. In excellent Spanish, Lieutenant Parker responded that his men were drunk and that he was putting them in irons.

There wasn't enough wind to take the ship back as a prize to the *Somers* so the navy contingent of eight men burned the ship and returned to the *Somers* with seven prisoners.

ROGERS TAKEN PRISONER

A few days later Midshipman Rogers participated in another daring adventure near Vera Cruz. He and surgeon John Wright volunteered for shore mission to search out a route to a certain building near the beach. The building had a powder magazine. If this could be located, a landing party might be able to take it out. The search was fruitless on the nights of December 3–5. They tried again, but the next attempt proved to be Rogers's undoing as the two men were seized by a Mexican patrol. Wright successfully escaped but not Rogers. Although he was in full uniform, there was fear that he would be treated as a spy. This was not the case, but the Mexicans refused to grant him a parole.

Four months later, when General Winfield Scott went to Mexico City, Lieutenant Semmes joined him for the sole purpose of securing the release of Rogers. Rogers's case generated much military correspondence within the American military and naval structure as well as between the U.S. and Mexican governments. Much of this correspondence is contained in Executive Document no. 56, some details of which follow.

The official dispatch of Semmes to his mission was a letter from Perry on his flagship, fully authorized by Secretary of the Navy John Mason, with, of course, presidential approval. The order was dated April 29, 1847. Semmes's reply to a previous verbal order tells of his interview with Colonel Wilson, governor of the city, and afterward with General de la Vega. Semmes was promised cooperation to effect the exchange, which was in the hands of the Mexican federal government. He told de la Vega that the U.S. government was determined to obtain the release and that if it were not given, the United States would consider retaliation on Mexican prisoners.

General Scott's aide-de-camp informed Semmes of a change of plan that would prevent Semmes from dealing directly with the Mexican government. Semmes wanted this change of plan put in writing. Scott himself replied in writing that Rogers was being held as an honorable prisoner of war and not as a spy and was on parole in Mexico City. Semmes wrote that Scott had unofficial talks about Rogers's imprisonment. There was direct talk with a

Mexican government official about his exchange as well as that of the Encarnacion prisoners captured during the previous February (see below). These men would be released after the battle in the valley of Mexico in the following August and September. It remained a mystery why 5,000 POWs were released on parole at Vera Cruz and 4,000 at Cerro Gordo without anything being said about an official exchange of Mexican POWs. The fact that Rogers was on parole in Mexico City was not known to the U.S. government when Commodore Perry sent Semmes on his mission of mercy.

Had it been known, Semmes probably would not have been sent and would not have written his remarkable book about his experiences. A scholarly written account, it is a primary source of information about much of Mexico and the war itself. Semmes was very lucky that he was not on the *Somers* during this time, since it was caught in a storm while it was pursuing a blockade runner. The ship sank, drowning thirty-two of the crew of seventy-six, and twelve men were captured by the Mexicans. Those remaining were picked up by boats from the British, French, and Spanish men-of-war stationed at Sacrificios.

ENCARNACION

General Scott was informed personally by President Polk that he would lead the expedition to take Vera Cruz and Mexico City, but well before these battles the Encarnacion prisoners were taken. A scouting expedition precipitated the war, and although scouting is always a recommended procedure, it led to the capture of the Encarnacion prisoners.

On January 19, 1847, General Butler assigned Major Gaines of the 1st Kentucky Calvary to a scouting detail. He was accompanied by Captain Cassius Clay and about thirty to forty men. They made a circuitous journey and two days later arrived at the hacienda of La

Encarnacion, about fifty-three miles from San Luis Potosi to San-
tillo road. At the hacienda he was met by forty or fifty members of
Major Borland's Arkansas cavalry. Borland's orders from General
John Wool were to go to the hacienda and then report back immediately.

When it was learned that a small force of Mexicans was at El Sal-
ado, about thirty-five miles farther on, Borland decided to seize it
and sent back for reinforcements. Gaines's forces joined Borland's.
Soon it became apparent that the distance was probably sixty miles
and there was doubt that such a force existed. When rain started to
fall, the Americans decided to return to La Encarnacion for the night
for a good rest. A good rest it was! In the morning they were surrounded by Minon's cavalry brigade, which took them very easily.
As Henry says, Minon "at once relieved their embarrassment by taking them under his full—indeed close—protection."[9]

Two days later Captain Heady of the Kentucky Cavalry, with
eighteen men, was sent by Brigadier General Lane to find out what
had happened to the detachment. They arrived at a ranch where there
was liquor and got drunk. The officers were extremely careless and
two sentries fell asleep. The stage was set on the morning of January
23 for the Americans to be surrounded and taken by the enemy without a shot being fired. One man escaped while he was a prisoner on
the march south, and he brought back news of the captured Americans to Saltillo; in all, there were six officers and sixty-six privates.
A few days later another scouting party consisting of two officers
and seventeen men was added to the total number of captives. All
these prisoners were marched to Mexico City and were not released
until the following autumn.

DESERTIONS AND LOSSES

On Wednesday, January 27, 1847, the first of Antonio López de
Santa Ana's infantry began their 240-mile march from San Luis to

Saltillo. A part of his group was the infamous company of Irish volunteers, deserters from the American army, called the San Patrício Battalion.

American losses were bad in the fighting at Buena Vista, but Mexican losses were worse. Taylor defeated Santa Ana on February 22–23 and the next major engagement was at Vera Cruz. On March 19, General Scott landed at Vera Cruz and on March 29 the Vera Cruz garrison surrendered. It was joint thinking and planning by army and navy, with boats especially made for more than 1,000 men to be put on shore, which led to the eventual victory. The attack on Vera Cruz involved a supply job by Commodore Conner's squadron as well. The night of March 27 saw the final capitulation, and, under the terms granted, the Mexican garrison was allowed to march out with the honors of war and put down their weapons. Then the officers and men were given paroles with the usual stipulation that they would not fight again until an official exchange was effected.

Before the war, when General Taylor's men were at the Nueces, the army had been suffering from expiring enlistments and sickness. Desertion also became a problem. Mexican authorities offered men land to get them to desert, and the Mexicans played on the religious side of the aforementioned Irish Catholics. Two captured dragoons received royal treatment, and these two men returned with glowing stories of attractive Mexican women and congenial people. The desertion rate increased, especially in the first few days.

John Eisenhower writes that after fourteen men swam the river one night, General Taylor ordered guards to shoot. After two men were killed and some drowned trying to swim across the river, desertions began to diminish.[10] A contingent of about thirty men successfully crossed enemy lines, and thus, says Robert Selph Henry, it was "to form the nucleus of what was to become the San Patrício Battalion of United States deserters in the Mexican Army."

The War of 1812 had a group of loyal U.S. Army soldiers, who as prisoners of war held by the English were considered traitors. But that was because England had not recognized their naturalization as

U.S. citizens. The San Patrício battalion members were deserters, who, if captured, would have been POWs due for military court-martial and possible execution.

THE SAN PATRÍCIO BATTALION

Typical of the deserters was Sergeant John Riley. He was an Irish-man who had deserted from the British army in Canada, served briefly as a West Point drillmaster, and later became a sergeant with the 5th Infantry. One Sunday morning, April 12, 1846, he swam across the river to Mexico and did not return. Later he claimed that he had been "seized with the desire to go to church." It is quite pos-sible that another motivating factor was the offer of thirty-two acres of good Mexican land by the Mexican government, an offer that at-tracted many other soldiers. The likelihood that the love of God prompted him to desert, in view of his record, was not realistic. Whatever the motivation, he had much company during the later pe-riod at Matamoros when over 200 men saw fit to desert, many of whom, like Riley, were foreign-born soldiers and had not readily adapted to American culture.[11]

Robert Miller describes the circumstances of Riley's desertion. Riley had received a pass to attend the Mass that a Matamoros priest was saying on the Texas side of the river. But Riley "went south" and when he did not return, he was classified as a deserter. Riley claimed two and a half years later that he was an American prisoner of war and had not deserted of his own free will. Accord-ing to his account, after several days of interrogation he was given a choice of enlisting in the Mexican army or being shot. His choice was the Mexican army as a first lieutenant. He rose to higher rank and fought against his former comrades. Not all American desert-ers joined the Mexican army, but by the middle of April those who did join represented the main framework of the San Patrício bat-talion and eventually engaged in four major battles against their former country. The commanding officer of this legion into which the San Patrício were merged was Colonel Francisco Marino. His two company commanders were Captain John Riley with a brevet rank of major, who led the first company, and Captain Santiago O'Leary, also a brevet major, in charge of the second company. In the summer of 1847 Riley attempted to recruit captive Yankee soldiers while Colonel Marino used physical force to enlist others.

At the end of summer 1846, General Taylor led his force into Mexico to take Monterrey, which was well defended by expert gunners, and also some of the San Patrícios led by Riley. The battle of Monterrey extended from September 19 to September 24, 1846. By the morning of September 23, both sides were exhausted and reached a compromise surrender of the Mexicans by early morning. But the war dragged on. Taylor took Monterrey and all public property but permitted General Ampudia's soldiers to keep their horses, small arms, and a battery of six guns, provided the Mexicans retired beyond a line about forty miles south of the city.

On February 20, 1847, Lieutenant Chamberlain, with a platoon, reached a hilltop overlooking a plain that contained Rancho Hediona. After hearing shots, he turned to his second in command, Lieutenant Sturges, to seize the hacienda. Lieutenant Sturges did not return, but the Mexicans were taken as prisoners of war. In a footnote, John Eisenhower tells us that Sturges was a Mexican prisoner for eight days. During the Civil War he became a brigadier general.

Mexican prisoners were ordered to prepare the breastworks for a coming attack. Colonel May could not determine the number of approaching Mexican soldiers, whom he considered to be a part of General Santa Ana's main body. So he ordered the excess animals to be released and the prisoners to be shot. Eisenhower says that the orders were "fortunately obeyed."[12]

Eisenhower states further that Santa Ana's quick exit from Encarnacion probably prevented Santa Ana's noticing a "strange presence lurking in the Mexican camp." This strange presence was Ben

McCulloch boldly observing everything he could, after which he made his way back to report to General Taylor on February 21.

THE LAST BATTLES OF THE MEXICAN WAR

On the morning of February 22, 1847, Santa Ana issued a warning to General Taylor to surrender or have his forces cut to ribbons. A very polite answer was given by Taylor's chief of staff. As author Robert Selph Henry says, "Major Bliss reduced Taylor's explosive oral answer to a polite note begging leave to say that I decline acceding to your request," which Henry says is "an 1847 equivalent of a later American General's 'Nuts.'"[13] This reference involved General McAllister's answer in World War II to a German demand of surrender.

The battle of Buena Vista was really a succession of separate fights and not just one encounter. Losses on both sides were heavy, but the Mexicans suffered more. For the Americans, this victory meant that the war in the north was over. A part of the enemy's force had consisted of members of the San Patrício Battalion. In this battle Santa Ana lost 1,800 killed or wounded and 300 captured.

The siege of Vera Cruz was accomplished by General Winfield Scott, starting in November 1846 and lasting until March 1847. Ships brought most of Scott's army to a meeting place on the island of Lobos. Lieutenant Sam Grant was on one vessel and Scott's staff was on another. Scott had designed a type of craft for landing troops on the Mexican coast, but not all of his forces had arrived yet. He wanted all his men in and out of Vera Cruz before the yellow fever season began. This Sam Grant was Ulysses S. Grant, who led the North to a military victory in the Civil War and later became president of the United States.

On March 9, 1847, Scott decided to move to Vera Cruz. This date, according to John Edward Weems, was the first D-day landing in U.S. military history. On March 26, the firing ceased under a truce and two days later the terms of capitulation were signed. The terms provided for the parole of Mexican soldiers, with their promises not to fight again unless they were officially exchanged. Freedom of worship was another guarantee for the Mexicans.

Colonel E. A. Hitchcock witnessed part of the surrender ceremony. It was his responsibility to oversee the paroling of the Mexican soldiers after they marched out and stacked their arms. Hitchcock thought the Mexicans were rank crazy, since officer prisoners included 5 generals, 18 colonels, 37 lieutenant colonels, 90 captains, 180 lieutenants, but only 5 majors.[14] This was the case because many high-ranking personnel were political appointments. The surrender of Vera Cruz was complete.

On April 17, 1847, the two-day battle of Cerro Gordo began, which resulted in another American victory and 3,000 prisoners, creating an embarrassment for the Mexicans. Scott was probably relieved when more than a thousand managed to escape. General Santa Ana fled the scene early and on May 22 went to Mexico City and reclaimed the Mexican presidency.

After the battles of Buena Vista and Cerro Gordo, the Mexicans no longer had an army, but Santa Ana was not one to give up easily. He was already organizing for further resistance as Scott was getting ready for his next objective, Mexico City.

On August 20, 1847, retreating and advancing forces converged at Churubusco, where one of the bloodiest battles of the war was fought. It marked the zenith of the San Patrícios and their last battle in the war as a unit. Combined American offensives against a bridgehead and a fortified convent at Churubusco began before noon and almost 200 Mexican prisoners were captured. Miller tells us that the American victory yielded 1,259 prisoners, including 104 officers, one of whom (Anaya) was a former president, and another, Colonel Gorostiza, a cabinet member and former minister to the United States. The majority of seized San Patrícios either surrendered or were taken to the convent while the rest fled to a bridgehead where they were captured.[15]

On August 20, 1847, eight of Santa Ana's generals became prisoners and the next day, after a meeting of officials on both sides, a short armistice was arranged. But the Mexicans were still maintaining that the Nueces River was the proper border and they also discussed the imprisonment of the San Patrícios, whom they wanted released.[16] This last demand, however, was denied completely. Thus the fate of these men would be decided by military courts-martial.

There was no love lost between General Santa Ana and General Gabriel Valencia, commander of the Mexican army of the North. But in an army in which so many politicians received their rank, Santa Ana could not get rid of Valencia. Valencia ignored Santa Ana's orders and moved ahead to Padiermas. The battles of Contreras and Churubusco were fought within a few hours of each other on August 20, 1847. An American attack broke up Valencia's men and Santa Ana stood by brazenly and offered no help. Scott had not expected a victory, and after the battle he maintained he killed 7,000 and captured 813 prisoners, including 4 generals.

A negotiated truce failed, and even the Mexican people expressed indignation against Santa Ana. Hostilities were renewed, but this merely paved the way for the real end of the war.

The castle of Chapultepec, Molino del Rey, and Casa de la Mata were the last main fortifications outside the city. Molino del Rey lasted only two hours and many Americans were killed. American troops used ladders to go up the steep grades and by nightfall had control of Mexico City. They took about 1,000 prisoners, along with many weapons and ammunition.

THE CAPTURE OF THE SAN PATRÍCIOS

Captured at the Convent of Churubusco, the San Patrícios recognized some of their former officers leading the attacking American soldiers. Riley wouldn't let his Mexican comrades surrender or retreat, and the final results were disastrous. Among the attackers was a company of spies consisting of renegade Mexicans. This situation was very appropriately described by Fairfax Downey as follows: "So in the last clash on the Convent, traitors fought traitors."[17] Then, of course, came decision time for the San Patrícios.

All Catholic priests in American lines urged Riley's liberation by exchange or ransom.[18] Subjecting him to severe punishment might effect more resistance against the U.S. Army's attempt to seize Mexico City. General Scott listened very carefully to all appeals and decided that Riley had not deserted in time of declared war. He deserted during or immediately after the battle of Palo Alto, which happened before the official declaration of war by Congress. (In 1999, *One Man's Hero*, a film that presented Riley as a martyr and starred Tom Berenger, was released.) The twenty-six who had deserted once war was declared were definitely within the jurisdiction of the Articles of War. On September 10, the death sentence was imposed on those so condemned; fourteen were stripped, branded, and drummed out of the camp; and sixteen were executed on a gallows, with five Catholic priests attending. One prisoner who had been a loyal and faithful soldier for many years received a pardon. Apparently he had fallen under the influence of Riley. In the same company his oldest son had refused to desert.

Even after the mass executions of San Patrício soldiers, desertion continued after Churubusco. According to statistics, the total number of deserters during the war was 9,207: 5,331 regulars and 3,876 volunteers out of a total of 39,197 casualties from all causes.

Many would say that the sentence of death would have been just, even though the war was not officially declared, because these men returned to fight against the United States. The chapter on Korea discusses the case of twenty-one turncoat American servicemen who did not take up arms against their former comrades. When the fighting was over, they were prisoners of the Communists who decided against repatriation to the United States.

Much of the military was angered by the fact that Riley was not hanged. Naval officer Ralph Semmes highly approved of the executions.[19]

Many articles have appeared in magazines and periodicals about the San Patrícios, and in 1989, Robert Ryal Miller published his *Shamrock and Sword: The St. Patrick's Battalion in the United States and Mexican War*. This is an extremely thorough and generally excellent account of this particular group.

Not all of the San Patrícios were of Irish origin. Some had immigrated from other European nations and some were Native Americans. All had been promised money and land grants, and the Mexicans made a special appeal to Roman Catholics to join them.

Sergeant Riley was well schooled in artillery and he trained the Mexicans in its use. The San Patrícios were ready to fight to the death since capture meant execution as traitors and deserters.

The San Patrícios were involved in the battle of Buena Vista and earned the respect of General Taylor. They took part in the battles of Cerro Gordo and Churubusco. At Churubusco, Riley did not allow his Mexican comrades to surrender or retreat, but they were defeated and taken as prisoners. What helped bring about this victory was a spy company of renegade Mexicans who joined the Americans. They acted as scouts to the Americans and thus were fighting against traitors, and the San Patrícios fell by the scores.

Those captured were placed under heavy guard as they awaited their courts-martial and were sentenced to be hanged for desertion. Riley was lashed and branded with a D for deserter and would labor as a convict as long as the U.S. Army was in Mexico. He was drummed out of the camp and he and other deserters had to dig the graves of those to be hanged.

On November 11, 1847, General Anaya, who had been captured at Churubusco, was elected interim president for the remainder of Santa Ana's term. In early February 1848, a peace treaty was signed by U.S. envoy Nicholas P. Trist and the plenipotentiaries of Mexico. The Treaty of Guadalupe-Hidalgo officially ended the war.

Article 4, paragraph 4 of the treaty required that all prisoners seized on land or sea be restored as soon as possible after exchange of ratification of the treaty. Article 8 addressed itself to the property rights of Mexicans residing within territorial limits of the United States.

The next major action for many army and naval officers would occur in the Civil War as Northern and Southern soldiers were pitted against each other; thus the Mexican War turned out to be the training school for Northern and Southern officers of the Civil War.

NOTES

1. Robert Selph Henry, *The Story of the Mexican War* (New York: De Capo, 1961), 37.

2. Henry, *Story of the Mexican War*, 17.

3. Henry, *Story of the Mexican War*, 17.

4. Henry, *Story of the Mexican War*, 21.

5. Henry, *Story of the Mexican War*, 25.

6. Justin Smith, *The War with Mexico*, vol. 1 (Gloucester, Mass.: Peter Smith, 1963), 174.

7. John Edward Weems, *To Conquer a Peace* (Garden City, N.Y.: Doubleday, 1974), 162.

8. Syng Physick, *The Home Squadron under Commodore Conner in the War with Mexico* (Philadelphia, 1896), 40.

9. Henry, *Story of the Mexican War*, 371.

10. John Eisenhower, *So Far from God: The U.S. War with Mexico* (New York: Random House, 1989), 61–62.

11. Eisenhower, *So Far from God*, 62.

12. Eisenhower, *So Far from God*, 179.

13. Henry, *Story of the Mexican War*, 248.

14. Weems, *To Conquer a Peace*, 340.

15. Robert Ryal Miller, *Shamrock and Sword: The Saint Patrick's Battalion in the U.S.-Mexican War* (Norman: University of Oklahoma Press, 1989).

16. Raphael Semmes, *Memoirs of Service Afloat and Ashore during the Mexican War* (Cincinnati: Moore, 1851), 428.

17. Fairfax Downey, *Texas and the War with Mexico* (New York: Harper & Row, 1961), 130.

18. George Smith, *The Chronicles of the Gringos* (Albuquerque: University of New Mexico Press, 1968), 435.

19. Semmes, *Afloat and Ashore during the Mexican War,* 428.

7

The Civil War

Abraham Lincoln assumed the presidency of the United States on March 4, 1861, and inherited a problem from his predecessor, James Buchanan—the mess that became the bloody Civil War. The tragedy of this conflict was not only that Americans were fighting Americans but that prisoners of war were taken by both sides. Americans were mistreating and in some cases actually torturing and murdering fellow Americans.

The principles of POW exchanges were accepted practice in the American Revolution and the War of 1812. At the beginning of the Civil War neither side was well prepared to meet the crisis of housing and caring for POWs. In the early days of the Civil War, historian William Hesseltine says in his preface to *Civil War Prisons: A Study in War Psychology,*[1] "POWs were treated well by both sides. But when the procedures of cartel exchanges were stopped, prisons in the South became overcrowded and the Confederates themselves suffered much poverty. Even prisons in the North would experience difficulties for those confined in the prison." A contributing factor is that the war was fought mainly in the South, not the North, and lasted for four years. At the outset of the Civil War both sides thought the war would be of short duration. A notable exception was Robert E. Lee who early expressed the idea that the war might very well be as long as four years.

CIVIL WAR PRISONS

Andersonville emerged as the most infamous prison because of poor conditions and countless atrocities. Yet other prisons in the South and even some in the North were also bad, including Elmira in New York State and Fort Delaware in Delaware, which Ann Brown called "the most dreaded northern prison" in her article in the *Civil War Quarterly.*

There are huge numbers of primary sources (letters, diaries, reports, books) and secondary sources about life in Civil War prisons. The best accounts are those written by survivors, but it is unclear what role vengeance may have played in the mind of the authors.

A leading classic is Hesseltine, *Civil War Prisons: A Study in War Psychology* (1930). A more thorough, recent source is Lonnie Speer, *Portals to Hell.*[2] Both books contain excellent bibliographies with primary and secondary source materials that provide copious information on the topic of POWs.

What caused the atrocities and poor treatment on both sides? There were many factors, but Speer in his introduction says "neither side was more at fault than the other."[3]

At the beginning of the war, captives were often released on parole in the field. This seemingly sensible approach eliminated the necessity of housing, feeding, and caring for prisoners and would (hopefully) prevent soldiers from rejoining their ranks to fight once again. One reason offered in 1863 for terminating parole was the fear that soldiers would violate the conditions. Thus parole became a thorny issue, and stubbornness on the part of Abraham Lincoln and Jefferson Davis regarding POWs may have caused the war to drag on longer than necessary. Unfortunately, many Union prisoners thought their government had forgotten them.

Both the Mexican War and the Civil War had their origins in Texas and had prisoners taken before the actual declaration of war. Accepting the thesis that "American troops were killed on American soil," denied of course by the Mexican government, we can say that war began in Texas, as did the Civil War.

GENERAL TWIGG

General Twigg wanted to get his men out of Texas because he knew that problems would arise soon. He was a brevet major general who happened to be a Union Southerner. His men were spread out along the Rio Grande from San Antonio to the borders of New Mexico. The state of Texas decided on secession along with the other southern states, and this set everything in motion. Twigg had the choice of removing or surrendering his men as prisoners to Texas. A committee appointed Colonel Ben McCulloch to try to persuade (although some may argue that "threaten" might have been a more appropriate term) Twigg to yield without resistance, but Twigg declined. He would not surrender and he preferred to wait until March 2. He insisted on removing all his forces from Texas, but he did agree to give up public property with the stipulation that his men be allowed to leave with their weapons. The commissioners agreed with this, but unfortunately Twigg was removed and replaced by a Colonel Waite, who feared that there would be hostilities among his own men and that some would become POWs.

On January 28, 1861, Twigg was removed, dismissed for treachery, and court-martialed.

Colonel Earl Van Doren was ordered by the Richmond government to go to Texas and assume command there, which he did on April 11. His task was to prevent forces he considered POWs from leaving. The Confederate government authorized the capture of troops in San Antonio as POWs, claiming that since General Twigg was no longer in command, the Confederate government was not bound by previous promises. Thus, from April 23 to almost the middle of the next month, many Union contingents headed for the coast were confronted and taken prisoner.

Author Robert Denney in his *Civil War Prisons and Escapes*[4] describes the lack of ethics on both sides of the conflict. During the war in New Orleans, General Butler, not well-liked among Southerners and even some of his own men, learned about POWs who had violated their parole and subsequently had them convicted and sentenced to death in early June. Butler was a very harsh person and some argue that such a punishment was not justified and that they should have received lighter sentences. Some feel that their cases could not be compared to those of the San Patrícios in the Mexican War.

The seizure of the Union forces in Texas was offset to some extent by the seizure of a Missouri state militia unit. This group was meeting for an annual drill at Camp Jackson in St. Louis, Missouri, much as a weekend reserve unit would meet in modern times, but Captain Nathaniel Lyon considered many in the group secessionists and therefore surrounded the brigade with his own men and demanded that Brigadier General Daniel Frost surrender his men. Reluctantly he surrendered 669 men as prisoners. Later they were released on parole for the rest of the conflict. These incidents in Texas and Missouri took place before the real fighting started between the North and the South.[5]

Both sides needed to establish a POW policy. The Southern prison system resulted in haphazard policies as time passed and countless prisoners were taken. Only in the last months of the war did the Confederate government appoint a commissary general of prisoners, while on the other side more definite plans were formulated and experienced soldiers were put in charge.[6]

PRIVATEERS

A special circumstance at the start of the war concerned a life-or-death situation for certain POWs, if those involved could really be classified as POWs. In the spring of 1861, Jefferson Davis authorized the use of privateers. Privateers were also used in the Revolutionary War, the Quasi-War with France, and the War of 1812.

Lincoln retaliated with the threat that captured privateersmen would be charged with piracy and executed if found guilty. The Confederate government defied Lincoln by launching the privateer ship *Jefferson*

Davis on June 28, 1861. This schooner, based in Charleston, seized nine ships during the summer.

The first prize of the *Jefferson Davis* was the merchant schooner *Enchantress*. Sixteen days later the United States *Albatross* recaptured the *Enchantress* off the North Carolina coast and removed Walter Smith and five other crewmen. They were taken to Philadelphia and put on trial for piracy: the first test case for Lincoln's policy. The trial started on October 22 and Smith and his crewmen were found guilty and sentenced to death.

The next move was by Jefferson Davis. He told his secretary of war to give an order to the provost marshal Brigadier General John Winder that fourteen federal officers in Richmond were to be held as prisoner of war hostages for the safety of Smith and his men, and each time a sailor was executed, a hostage would be hanged. The names of six colonels were placed in a box to determine the order of execution.

New York Congressman Alfred Ely, a political prisoner, conducted the lottery. The first name drawn was that of Colonel Michael Corcoran, Irish-born leader of the 69th. He and eighteen of his men had been captured at Bull Run and were held hostage for Walter Smith and his men. This problem continued for months. Ultimately, Corcoran was released after a year as a hostage, the Confederate privateersmen were granted official POW status, and no one was executed. There were many incidents concerning hostages; throughout the course of the war at least 1,000 Americans became hostages.[7]

RETALIATION

On June 3, the *Savannah*, a small schooner, was seized as a prize by the U.S. brig *Perry*. The crew was placed in irons and sent to New York harbor. Jefferson Davis ordered Charleston officials to conduct the exchange of privateersmen and communicated to Lincoln to follow the same treatment of POWs and principles of humanity for those on the *Savannah*—a chance for retaliation if anyone on the *Savannah* was executed.

The threatened retaliation by Jefferson Davis was not a surprise. A colonel and two captains were being held in Richmond and it was expected that their paroles would be recalled. Thus retaliation became a way of life in the Civil War, more so than in the War of 1812.

In July 1861, there was a case of retaliation that involved a civilian. Dr. William P. Rucker of Greenbriar, Virginia, was arrested by the Confederacy as a spy. Consequently, the Federal army took three prominent area citizens as hostages. In October, however, an agreement was reached to release all of them.

Also in July 1861, Richard Thomas, a leader of Confederate irregulars, put himself in the spotlight by dressing up as a woman. When he was arrested, Virginia retaliated by picking hostages for him: a captain, three lieutenants, and three privates. This time, however, it took two years to effect an exchange for all.

In August 1862, the Confederate government in Richmond had seven Union officers. Federal Judge L. C. Turner ordered L. C. Baker, a State Department detective and spy, to arrest fourteen citizens of Fredericksburg and hold them as hostages for the safety of prisoners of war. Major General John Pope seized six citizens of the same town as hostages for the release of Union soldiers taken by the Confederates.

CIVILIAN HOSTAGES

In 1862 Major General Lowell Rousseau occupied Huntsville, Alabama. Lawless bands of Confederate sympathizers started shooting at Union railroad trains, which resulted in many deaths. On August 6, to stop this killing, Rousseau gathered together a number of influential citizens of the community and placed them on the trains as hostages. Using civilians in this way was an effective, though unethical, measure to make the trains safe.

Andrew Johnson, the military governor of Tennessee, also contributed to the violation of civil liberties. He had soldiers hold twelve Rutherford County citizens as hostages. His justification was that such a measure would guarantee the safety of Murfreesboro and prevent unlawful acts. Although this might have been the case, it still represented a violation of civil rights, even though this was not a great issue at that time.

Andrew Johnson came down hard on civilian secessionists. When he learned that seventy civilians from east Tennessee were imprisoned at Mobile because of their sympathies for the Union, he moved to arrest seventy secessionists. When he asked Lincoln if this action met with presidential approval, Lincoln approved.

The Confederate government in Richmond was aware that many strong advocates of secession were incarcerated in Northern prisons; consequently, on November 13, 1862, the Confederate government said it was holding about ninety POWs at Salisbury, North Carolina, as hostages for its citizens. A week later Union Major General T. C. Hindman said that a number of Southern citizens were held by Major General James Blunt for sick Federal prisoners in North Carolina.

JOHN KLEM

The year 1863 saw its share of retaliatory measures. Johnny Klem had tried to join the Union army in the spring of 1861 when he was only ten years old. Not discouraged when he was rejected, he enlisted in May 1863 in the 22d Massachusetts. On September 20 he was captured in the battle of Chickamauga but managed to escape. Promoted to lance corporal, he changed his name to John Lincoln Clem. In October 1863, he was captured again by the Confederate cavalry but was exchanged shortly afterward. The Confederates tried to use him as an example to show up the Union. Assigned to the staff of General Thomas, he was discharged on September 19, 1864. The last part of his life turned out to be quite a story.

He was appointed to West Point by General Grant but could not pass the entrance examination. Grant made him a second lieutenant in 1871 and Clem retired in 1915 as a brigadier general, quite a feat for a one-time private and prisoner of war.

MILITARY HOSTAGES

The highest-ranking hostage and POW of the Civil War was Confederate Major General William Henry Fitzhugh "Rooney" Lee. He was wounded and became a POW at Brandy Station, Virginia, on July 15, 1862. When he questioned his close confinement, he was told that the Confederates had two Federal hostages. A fellow prisoner of Lee was Captain John Winder, the son of the man in charge of all the Confederate prisons. These were two prize captives whose lives would be in serious danger if Union POWs in Richmond were executed. This posed a great problem for both sides and was not solved until February 1864, when all involved were exchanged.

In 1864 General Butler's forces used forty-two Texans as hostages under fire. His men were trying to dig a canal at Dutch Gap about seven miles before Richmond. Confederate mortars fired on his soldiers working on the canal, and Butler countered this by placing newly captured POWs in tents close to the canal. The enemy discontinued its fire for twenty-four hours but then resumed. This forced Butler to change his tactics and he sent the POWs to City Point, Virginia.

During the bombardment of Charleston in 1864 by Federal warships, a Confederate officer decided to copy Butler. Forty-eight Union prisoners were held in the city within range of their own artillery unit. This tactic was terminated by Brigadier General John Foster, who transferred from Johnson's Island a number of high-ranking Confederate officers whom he exposed to fire from the defenders of Charleston. The group included five Confederate generals, fifteen colonels, and fifteen majors.

General Sherman also resorted to retaliation on his march to the sea in 1864. He was furious when a land mine blew off the foot of one of his men and put groups of Confederate POWs at the head of columns to test the ground areas where such mines were suspected to be. We do not know if anybody was killed because of this tactic. The examples mentioned here are only some of the incidents in which hostages were employed in retaliatory measures.

Some historians, according to Speer on the very first page of his book, maintain that the firing on Fort Sumter was the first open act of hostilities, and that the first POWs of the war were part of a work detail at Castle Pinckney in South Carolina's Charleston harbor.

The commanding officer of all federal forts in that harbor was Major Robert Anderson. He had moved his men from Fort Moultrie to Fort Sumter, which was more suitable for defensive purposes. South Carolina's governor retaliated by ordering Castle Pinckney to be captured, and thus, on December 27, 1860, Colonel James Pettigre approached the castle with about 150 men. Seeing their approach, Lieutenant Meade and his group of workers closed the gates of the sides of the fort to challenge the enemy whose leader demanded surrender.

Lieutenant Meade turned down the offer of paroles and bitterly protested. Assured of fair treatment, Meade and his men were permitted to leave Fort Sumter. Fort Johnson in the harbor was captured six days later without casualties because it was not an active fort, and the next day Fort Pulaski on the Savannah River was similarly taken; also Fort Massachusetts on Ship Island on January 20.

The day after Lincoln assumed the presidency, March 5, 1861, he received a communication from Major Anderson that there was little food left for his men and he was desperate for supplies. Three days later, President Lincoln informed the governor of South Carolina that supplies would be sent to the fort. But General Beauregard was ordered by the Confederate government to demand the evacuation of the fort, and if such order was refused, to force the evacuation.

On April 11, the ultimatum was given to Major Anderson, who simply answered that he and his men would be starved out in a few days anyway if Beauregard did not destroy the fort. Beauregard promised not to do anything if Anderson would announce an evacuation date. Anderson replied that he would leave by April 15 if no supplies arrived. He was simply playing for time, but Beauregard would not take the bait and said that in one hour he would start firing. On April 12, 1861, at 4:30 A.M., this promise was kept. The bombardment officially opened the war.

WAR PRISONS

POW camps and prisons were well spread out throughout the Civil War. Both North and South had to use temporary facilities at the outset. Some temporary areas became permanent and some disappeared from the scene. Both Hesseltine and Speer mention areas in which such prisons were located, but Speer gives a more comprehensive list as well as a description of the types of sites that developed. Another listing of principal confederate prisons and their locations is given by Robert Kellogg in his *Life and Death in Rebel Prisons*.[8] Kellogg himself had been a POW but managed to escape. Given a furlough of thirty days, he wrote his experiences into a first-person narrative. His unit fought bitterly and surrendered with reluctance.

Speer assigned prisons to seven categories: (1) those that started as jails or prisons of small or medium size (Tombs prison in New York, which still exists today); (2) coastal fortifications (Fort McHenry and several others in Baltimore; Castle Pinckney in Charleston harbor); (3) old buildings such as warehouses and factories converted into prisons, used mainly in the South; (4) barracks surrounded by high fences, used chiefly in the North; (5) groups of tents surrounded by high fences; (6) barren stockades that had no shelter, the cheapest and worst type, such as Andersonville; (7) tracts of land on which prisoners were grouped and guarded by patrolling sentries. This final type was often used after major battles.[9] The North was better organized with Lieutenant Colonel William Hoffman as commissary general of prisoners. Within two weeks of construction, the new prison on Johnson's Island, intended to contain about a thousand POWs, had to admit almost 15,000 POWs the Union captured at Fort Donelson, Tennessee. The ideal location was an island because escape would be very difficult.

In June 1862, Colonel Hoffman became subject to the War Department rather than the quartermaster general, and the headquarters of his bureau, which dealt with POWs, was shifted to the capital. By the end of October 1862, he was responsible for all Union POWs released on limited parole in the North and supervised POW maintenance in all Northern POW camps.[10]

THE DIX-HILL CARTEL

While these developments were taking place, negotiations for the exchange of POWs were started and on June 22, 1862, Major General Benjamin Huger opened the proceedings between Major General John Dix of the United States and Major General D. H. Hill of the Confederacy. One month later, on July 22, the Dix-Hill Cartel was signed.

The cartel consisted of a short preamble, seven articles, and three supplementary articles. Article 1 had a detailed scale of equivalents for the basis of exchanges according to ranks of the men involved and also provided that privateersmen captured would receive the status of POWs and not pirates. The second half of that article seemed to be a major breakthrough. Articles 2–3 concerned civilian prisoners. The remaining articles dealt with procedures of parole and exchange. When the cartel was signed, the North and South were fighting the Peninsular Campaign, with large numbers of Union prisoners being captured by the Confederacy.

The signing of the cartel meant that POW numbers would begin to go down on both sides. But in 1863 the cartel agreements broke down. Naturally this meant increasing numbers of POWs on both sides.

What caused the breakdown? A number of factors were involved, such as the aforementioned privateersmen prisoners whom Lincoln wanted to consider pirates and the parole problem. There was also Jefferson Davis's attitude toward black prisoners, which will be discussed later in this chapter. Statistics given by Speer show that "by August 1864, the South had 67,500 POWs and that . . . more than 56,000 men had died as prisoners of war."[11]

United States military prisons could be found in the North, Midwest, and upper South. Charts at the end of Speer's book list about twenty-three states and Washington, D.C., with New York having the most with seventeen. There are 117 names of Southern military prisons, with Virginia having the most with forty. Among the Virginia prisons were about seventeen factories and warehouses converted to prisons. Needless to say, the economy of the South was greatly affected, a factor that contributed to its ultimate defeat.

Speer notes that "additional locations were used anywhere from several weeks to several months, while some were used throughout the war as depot prisons or gathering places before shipping POWs out to larger major facilities."[12]

The first battle of Bull Run took place the week before U.S. Quartermaster General Montgomery Meigs advised his government to prepare for the capture and care of POWs, but his words were offered in vain. The South was unprepared also. There was always the solution of parole. The Bull Run battle was on July 21, 1861. Almost 1,300 Federal prisoners were sent to Richmond, but this was the South's problem. In the early years of the war, the South did not have many prisons outside of Richmond. The number of POWs for both sides rose rapidly and then evened off for a while with the signing of the cartel in July 1862.

On May 10, 1861, prisoners at Camp Jackson were released on parole. This included the 669 men of the Missouri Brigade under

Brigadier General Daniel Frost, who had surrendered to Captain Nathaniel Lyon. The next month, on June 15, the twenty-man crew of the Confederate *Savannah* arrived in New York City after being captured on June 3. Major General George McClellan captured several hundred Confederate soldiers at Rich Mountain, Virginia, on July 11, 1861; all except two were granted paroles. The two excluded had once been in the Federal army. They had switched sides and were sent to Fort Lafayette prison in New York City.

The second year of the war continued this trend. While 1861 was chiefly a period of makeshift prisons to meet the crisis, 1862 saw a period of new prisons. Toward the end of 1861, Colonel Ebenezer Magoffin and about 1,300 Confederates were captured at Blackwater, Missouri, by General John Payne. This represented only a beginning for 1862, when the United States had 3,000 POWs and the Confederacy had 6,000. Magoffin became a disciplinary problem at Gratiot Street in St. Louis, Missouri, and was transferred to Alton, Illinois, after being sentenced to death.

The prison system on both sides in 1863 expanded tremendously. On January 17, Belle Island was reactivated for a short period of time, then emptied out, closed, and opened again. Midwestern and eastern prisons started emptying out because of the cartel agreement, but on January 31, about 1,665 prisoners were sent by train and 500 more added during the next two months. Conditions on both sides deteriorated. Overcrowding ended at Fort McHenry, Baltimore, Maryland, in August 1863, with the creation of a new Maryland prison. After the battle of Gettysburg in July 1863, the prison population increased considerably. Once the Confederates did not have enough men to maintain the line, their only choice was to surrender or retreat across a mile of open ground, which meant virtual suicide. Almost 4,000 Confederate soldiers were captured and this made General Robert E. Lee realize he was wrong in considering his own forces unbeatable.

By the end of 1863, both sides had to contend with numerous disasters and deaths, but the number of prisoners increased drastically as of May 25, 1863, when POW exchanges were terminated by General Halleck. He had no use for parole because he thought POWs simply returned to the war. Thus the system of parole was destroyed and was not used in subsequent wars.

THE LIEBER CODE OF WAR

In May 1863, Abraham Lincoln asked Dr. Francis Lieber to formulate a code of war that would set guidelines for how the Union army should handle POWs in the field and in captivity. Obviously Lincoln hoped for reciprocity from the enemy holding prisoners.

Lieber was the right man for the job. An outstanding academic figure in political science in the nineteenth century, he was educated in Germany and served as a soldier at Waterloo and in other famous European battles. He had been wounded in battle and later became disenchanted with the strict Prussian police as a civilian. After spending some time in their jails, he decided to emigrate, leaving Germany in 1826 for England and then moving to the United States.

In New York he distinguished himself as an American correspondent for German newspapers and edited a popular encyclopedia. His next position was chairman of history and political economy at South Carolina College, but since he detested slavery, he could not speak out as freely as he desired on that burning issue. In 1853 he published an essay on civil liberty and self-government, resigned his chairmanship, and went to chair the history and political science department at Columbia University in New York City.

At the request of President Lincoln in May 1863, he wrote *Instructions for the Government of Armies of the United States*. This represented the first comprehensive codification of international law issued by any government. Lieber's document was really meant for all countries. It was the first attempt to deal with prisoners of war and to consider them fellow human beings with lawful rights.

The document was intended to protect prisoners who were prisoners of a government and not the captors. The problem, of course, would be persuading all nations to accept its principles, and also enforce them. Nevertheless, the code was an important first step. Lieber had three sons fighting in the Civil War, the eldest for the South, who unfortunately was killed in the war.

There was no provision for traitors, guerrillas, or spies. Nathan A. Hale and Major André of the Revolutionary War and Gary Powers, the U-2 pilot shot down over Russia in 1960 (when there was no war), would not have been covered under the code, nor would Commander Bucher and his men on the *Pueblo* in 1968. Adolf Hitler's infamous commando order of autumn 1942—that enemies on commando missions should be slaughtered to the last man—was a clearcut violation of Lieber's code and all humanitarianism, and so also the actions attributed to Southern forces in the Civil War concerning members of the Black Phalanx.

As 1864 began, authorities on both sides were well aware of conditions prevailing in military prisons. By midyear General John Winder was given command of all prison facilities in Virginia, Alabama, and Georgia, and by November was named commissary general of all Confederate prisons. But Speer says "it was practically too late to exercise effective control."[13]

THE CONTINUING DISINTEGRATION
OF WAR PRISONS

Fort Delaware in Delaware Bay became a Union hellhole and the year of 1864 turned out to be the watershed period for military prisons on both sides.[14] The prisons were overflowing and the worst of conditions prevailed. With the establishment in the South of Andersonville and in the North of Elmira, it almost can be said that this was the era of concentration camps. At Elmira, almost 3,000 POWs died because of existing conditions while at Andersonville there were almost 13,000 deaths.

From the start, the Federal government tried to recruit prisoners, and escapes were always being attempted; some were successful and some were not. The first successful escape known involved Sergeants T. D. Parker, Franklin Cook, and R. E. Ellenwood of the 8th Infantry in August 1861 in Texas. The first documented escape of a Confederate from a Federal prison was First Lieutenant George Alexander at Fort McHenry. He had been charged with treason in committing piracy and for being a spy, but his wife secured for him a Federal uniform and on September 7 he made his successful escape. There were many other escapes between 1862 and 1865, tunneling being the favorite method.

Elmira Camp no. 3, in May 1864, was converted to house POWs and on July 6 the first POWs arrived—9,399 men transferred from Point Lookout in Maryland. One escaped on the way. On July 11 more arrived and on July 12, 502 more.[15]

On July 15 a fourth trainload of POWs was on the way to Elmira but collided head-on with a coal train outside Pennsylvania. Forty-eight POWs and seventeen guards were killed, ninety-three POWs and sixteen guards were injured, and five POWs escaped. They were the lucky ones.

On August 20, the so-called Immortal Six Hundred banded together. They represented POWs from fourteen states having regiments in the Confederate army. They were placed on the ship *Crescent City* and confined in the hold, somewhat reminiscent of POWs in the Revolutionary War. They remained in the hold for an eighteen-day trip to South Carolina.[16]

Major J. Ogden Murray, a member of the Immortal Six Hundred, wrote of cruelty to Confederate POWs in his *The Immortal Six Hundred*, the purpose of which was to let the world know what was being done to helpless POWs. He bitterly attacked Secretary of War Stanton and General Grant for refusing to exchange prisoners. Murray claimed that the cessation of exchanges was causing much of the suffering of Union POWs in the South. President Lincoln could have overruled that army order to relieve existing tensions in much the same way that Franklin Delano Roosevelt could have prevented by executive order Japanese internment after the bombing of Pearl Harbor.

Murray said that 22,576 Federal prisoners of war confined in the military prisons of the South died, while twelve out of one hundred of the Confederate prisoners of war confined in the Northern prisons died; the rate of death in Southern prisons was eight in each one hundred men.[17] Exchanges were promised but not accomplished. Murray was willing to admit that there were scalawags in his own group.

Cahaba was made a permanent prison facility in Alabama in January 1864. A second facility was built in 1864 in Georgia—Andersonville. The conditions in both Andersonville and Elmira will be discussed later in the chapter.

THE END OF THE WAR

The war officially ended April 9, 1865. Speer writes that the guards in Camp Ford in Texas, learning of the surrender, simply pulled out and left for their homes. The Federal government was not inclined to give an immediate release and moved as fast as possible to find Confederate prison commanding officers and other officers. Enlisted men were relatively safe from the clutches of the Union. The death of General John Winder left only one main scapegoat, Henry Wirz, who had been in charge of Andersonville.

After Appomattox the Federal government arranged for train and boat transportation for POWs from Southern prisons. The prisoners were required to take the oath of allegiance before their release. There was a fear of possible reprisals after the assassination of Lincoln on April 14, an event that shocked all in the North and many in the South.

Another tragedy was the explosion of the ship *Sultana* carrying 2,000 POWs, many of whom had been held at Cahaba. An estimated 1,500 to 1,700 died; the exact number is not known.

The surrender of General Robert E. Lee's forces to General Ulysses Grant on April 9, 1865, was an honorable and fair agreement. The person who established the policy was General Grant. The enemy officers had to give their paroles and not take up arms and had to wait for an official exchange to take place. Regimental commanders signed a similar parole for soldiers under them. Officers could keep sidearms, their private horses, and their baggage. They could return to their homes and as long as they obeyed their parole promises and obeyed laws where they lived, they would have no problems. The same courtesies were accorded Confederate soldiers in the West and South, and "altogether 174,223 Confederate prisoners of war were released on parole."[18] The rest of the prisoners would be released. Taking the oath was a prime requisite. The ordeal was over, but the prisons had taken their toll on everybody.

ANDERSONVILLE

Major Murray of the Immortal Six Hundred claimed that reports of cruelty by Southerners were as false as the tongues that spoke of them; Andersonville was a paradise in comparison with some Civil War prisons such as Elmira. Nobody, however, could call any prison, Union or Confederate, a paradise. Nothing good can be said about Andersonville. Its commandant, Captain Henry Wirz, never considered the possibility that he would be held accountable for what happened there, but he was tried by court-martial in Washington, D.C., and was convicted and executed.

The selection of Andersonville in such a remote location was designed to place persons far from the areas where the war was being fought. Ovid Futch relates that he was seven miles from the Point River, forty-two miles east of Chattahoochee, and 1,600 feet east of the depot at the Anderson station. Easy transportation between the railroad canal stop for prisoners and their place of confinement was an important factor. During the war there was much uncertainty about the transportation system of the Confederacy, since so much of the war was fought there. When the Union prisoners of war arrived at Andersonville on February 24, 1864, they had to enter a stockade not yet completed. Records show that even with an abundance of forest sites, good shelter was not provided for the prisoners. Robert Kellogg, who was a POW there, said that the increasing numbers of POWs made things worse.

Andersonville was chiefly for enlisted men, and, according to Futch, 329 persons escaped from this supposedly inescapable prison. Many of the escapees, however, were recaptured. The escapees primarily had been assigned to work details or were on parole.

In May 1864, a big escape was planned, but one of the leaders revealed details to Wirz. The POW was removed from the prison and rewarded for his treachery by Wirz. Ratting on his buddies would seriously endanger the life of an informer who remained in the prison camp. Kellogg relates how a Yankee traitor who was a shoemaker for the Jefferson Davis government came into camp and was "caught trying to entice others to work with him. . . . He was taken and half of his head shaved, and then left to make his way out, hooted and jeered by the whole crowd."[19]

One unfortunate feature of Andersonville was a group of several hundred POWs known as the Raiders. They enjoyed a lifestyle that was somewhat better than that of others because they stole from their fellow prisoners. They were organized into groups named for their leaders. The Raiders were always at work to stir up trouble. The camp finally became so incensed by them that its members tried some of them and sentenced some to run a gauntlet Indian style. Some of the Raiders were sentenced to the gallows. Captain Wirz entered the camp and turned over some Raiders to a vigilante committee to be hanged for murder and robbery. Solon Hyde says he thought all were foreigners but offers no evidence to back up his theory.[20] According to Hesseltine, many of the raiders were considered low life of New York City's slums. Wirz was not able to deal effectively with this problem.[21]

At Florence the prisoners were reminded of their previous experiences at Andersonville.[22] This officer's prison at Macon was another important Southern prison, but their rations were better than those given at Richmond, which contributed to Florence's better health conditions. Among the charges against Jefferson Davis and his cabinet was deliberately planning to murder POWs in Southern prisons; but at the end of the war the only Confederate who really suffered was Wirz.

The hospital conditions at Andersonville were very bad not merely because necessary supplies were unavailable but because its physicians did not sympathize with the sick under their care. Rations were meager, disease rampant, and sanitation poor. Almost 3,000 died in August and about 13,000 Northern soldiers were buried there. Many bodies were simply dumped into trenches instead of buried in coffins.

Andersonville did not have a permanent chaplain, which meant that prisoners had to conduct their own religious services. Major William John Hamilton, a Catholic priest from Macon, Georgia, found many Catholics when he visited Andersonville. He asked the bishop of Savannah to send some priests to help out, and in June Father Peter Whelan and Father Claverol arrived.

William Marvel tells us that Father Whelan was incorrectly identified as the only man of the cloth who entered the stockade. Many Protestants at that time did not trust Catholics because of prevailing anti-Catholic sentiments of the Know-Nothing party. Father Whelan's devotion and faith earned considerable respect for him. Captain Wirz was one of the people who "watched his tongue in front of him and granted him nearly everything he wanted."[23]

At Libby, Chaplain McCabe of the Protestant Episcopal Church endeared himself to the prisoners. He was captured at Winchester on June 16, before the first day's battle at Gettysburg. He aided the wounded and dying on the field of battle, which he refused to leave. He and the regimental surgeon were sent to Richmond to be placed later at Libby. Ambulances were placed at his disposal by General John Gordon.

Frank Bristol tells the story of how one day seventy-three captains sent for two chaplains, Chaplain McCabe and Father Brown, almost eighty years old.[24] These two chaplains selected two names from a hat—Captains Sawyer and Flynn—to be put into the dungeon and executed the next day. Because of some disagreement, however, the execution was delayed. A letter was written to Lincoln by one of the two POWs and McCabe saw a newly exchanged prisoner hide it in one of his boots. Ultimately the letter did get to the president in Washington. Coincident with these developments was the capture of Captains Lee and Winder, discussed earlier.

Chaplain McCabe was released from Libby and resigned his chaplaincy because of ill health on January 8, 1864. But in the fall he returned to army duty. His final residence would be in the Episcopal Office in Philadelphia.

POWs compared Elmira with Hades.[25] Its first POWs arrived on July 6, 1864, but it was soon filled far beyond its capacity. Its death rate was notorious and daily rations left much to be desired. Cold weather took its toll among the POWs, just as the heat did at Andersonville.

From Andersonville's POWs the Confederate army recruited 338 into its military service. In March 1865, near the end of the war, 138 joined the ranks of the Confederates. This defection did not surprise Kellogg in view of the conditions at Andersonville. Kellogg states in his book that at Florence he witnessed a prisoner being punished for an escape by being hanged by the thumbs.

Jefferson Davis reported that Dr. Joseph Jones, a physician and scientist, inspected Andersonville in August 1864 and said that existing poor conditions were the results of the soil, water, climatic conditions, and lack of vegetables and salt meats. In effect, Davis was saying that Wirz was not the monster he was supposed to be.[26]

Nothing was done to alleviate conditions at Andersonville. Wirz has been defended by some and certainly his trial did seem to lack mercy and fairness. The fact remains that Andersonville was no paradise, but neither was Elmira.

Clay Holmes in *The Elmira Prison Camp* draws on witnesses who knew or had been subjected to the difficulties there and presents facts. He refutes certain charges made about POW treatment. He admits that there was excessive suffering because of the climate and also admits to incidental cruelty but says that, on the whole, great consideration was given the prisoners. The North had cold weather and the South hot weather and nothing could really be done to alleviate these conditions. The POWs "were victims of conditions beyond the control of any human being."[27] Admittedly, not much could have been done for Southern prisons in an era when there was no air conditioning, but certainly better clothing and blankets could have been provided to Southern POWs in Northern prisons.

Futch calls Kellogg's narrative very acrimonious. Kellogg had been a prisoner himself but certainly could have exaggerated just as Holmes could have been prejudiced in his overview of Elmira. A footnote in Jefferson Davis, *Andersonville and Other Prisons,* points out that in Wirz's trial, certain prisoner witnesses in August 1864 swore that he killed prisoners at a time when he was on sick leave in Augusta, Georgia. S. W. Ashe in *The Trial and Death of Henry Wirz*[28] calls Wirz's death "a judicial murder." People who wanted to testify on his behalf were not allowed to do so. Jefferson Davis said, "The poor man was doomed before he was heard, and the permission to be heard according to law was denied him."[29] Wirz was executed on November 10, 1865.

Daniel Brown, author of *The Tragedy of Libby and Andersonville Prison Camps*, maintains that poor resources, poor planning, and mismanagement were to blame for what happened in Southern prison camps. Northern prison camps were affected to a lesser degree than Southern ones.

THE BLACK PHALANX

The general public knows little about black Union POWs, although there are books and studies on the subject. Black Union POWs constituted one of many issues that prolonged the war unnecessarily, since Jefferson Davis and Abraham Lincoln were at odds on the topic. Davis maintained that slaves were property under the U.S. Constitution and that of the Confederate States, and property recaptured from an enemy in war reverts to the original owner (if he can be found) or may be disposed of by his captor.

General Grant sided with the black POWs, but in so doing he prevented the exchange of white POWs. Exchanges could not be made officer for officer or man for man except in cases of the sick and wounded. Jefferson Davis made a final offer, which Lincoln refused. This wrangling prolonged the suffering and misery of prisoners on each side—all Americans.

The American Revolutionary War had blacks in the Continental Army, and the War of 1812 also had blacks serving. It should be remembered that Dartmoor prison in England held many black seamen and privateersmen as prisoners. By the time of the Mexican War a new army policy had emerged in which there was no room for blacks, and attempts to recruit them were opposed by both the civilian population and a number of military officials at the outset of the Civil War. Speer's book contains a short chapter about black soldiers and POWs. Joseph T. Wilson's book *The Black Phalanx*, sheds much more light on the subject. According to Speer, the first black regiment formed consisted of descendants of those who fought under Andrew Jackson in the War of 1812. General Benjamin Butler recruited free blacks (the 1st Louisiana Native Guard) to defend New Orleans, although they were not the first to fight against the enemy.

The real problem came when a Southern unit captured black Union soldiers. Five Union soldiers were captured, the three whites being exchanged and the two blacks being executed. Thus the Confederacy maintained different policies for white and black POWs.

Speer states that about 35 percent of black POWs captured by the Confederates died.[30]

When the Confederates met slaves in battle, they showed no mercy, and as far as the blacks were concerned, most were ready to fight to the death. Indeed, "though hundreds had been captured, none had been on parole, or among the exchanged prisoners."[31] This particular fact was brought to the attention of General Grant when captured black officers and men were hanged.

The author of *The Black Phalanx,* Joseph T. Wilson, was himself a member of the group and represents an excellent primary source of information. He was born in Norfolk, Virginia, in 1836 and later settled in New Bedford, Massachusetts, and became a seaman. When Wilson learned about the beginning of the Civil War, he set sail for New Orleans to find his father, who had been sold in that city. In New Orleans he enlisted and served in the 2d Regiment La Marine Guard, the 74th United States Colored Troops from which he was discharged September 10, 1862. He reenlisted December 18, 1863, in Company C of the 54th Massachusetts Colored Infantry. He was wounded in the battle of Oluster, Florida, February 20, 1864, and was discharged on May 8, 1864.

In 1862, blacks in New Orleans were being recruited into the Confederate Army, under Governor Moore's proclamation, into separate and distinct organizations from the whites. At the same time, blacks and Indians were enlisting in Union forces on the frontier, under the supervision of white officers. Wilson tells us that the Kansas Home Guard of two regiments of Indians included more than 400 blacks under the command of Custer, Blunt, and Herron. About 2,500 blacks served in Union forces from the Indian nations.[32]

The bill authorizing the arming of Negroes as part of the army was voted by both Houses of Congress and signed into law by Lincoln, July 17, 1862. Though this law allowed blacks to fight, the actual date of the first organization of troops of color is still disputed.[33] No further Negroes were recruited for the regiments created in 1862. What helped considerably was Lincoln's Emancipation Proclamation, which encouraged many officers to try to organize units of black troops.[34]

General Order no. 143 of the War Department established a bureau whose function was to record all details relating to organizing of units of colored troops. One main difficulty, however, which persisted for some time, was that these recruits did not receive the same pay and allowances given to white troops. Many generals opposed recruiting blacks into the army, even though their government had approved it. It took some time for many of these to change their minds. A series of subsequent battles proved the gallantry of African Americans and highlighted the atrocities committed against them as POWs.

THE BATTLE OF MILLIKEN'S BEND

The Battle of Milliken's Bend on June 7, 1863, was the first regular battle between blacks and whites in the valley of the Mississippi. The rebels took blacks as POWs and murdered them. This so enraged other blacks that they fought more aggressively in hand-to-hand combat. Confederate shouts not to give quarter to Negroes and their officers resulted in comparable feelings so that blacks also gave no quarter and fought to the death.

Prior to the battle on May 26–27, 1863, the siege of Port Hudson had taken place. General Banks was to make a final assault on it, but the garrison surrendered. One of the most efficient and brave officers was Captain André Callioux, a black man who demonstrated his ability and courage and was killed in the action. He was felled by a shell and died quickly. Not a single African American could be found alive after thirty-five were known to have been captured during the siege: all had been murdered.

The death of Callioux caused a sensation in New Orleans, and on July 11, 1863, he was given the full rites of the Catholic Church at his funeral, which was attended by Joseph Wilson.[35] Needless to say, the massacres at Port Hudson and Milliken's Bend were not forgotten by other black soldiers. At Milliken's Bend, although the Confederates were beaten, they provided the blacks with a firm determination to defeat the Southerners and to slaughter them. The blacks took 200 POWs, and the events of Port Hudson and Milliken's Bend became well known and spread throughout the army.

Morris Island had Fort Wagner, which became the prime target of the Union forces. Colonel Shaw of the 54th was among the first to arrive at the summit of Fort Wagner, where he was shot and killed. Emerging as a hero was Sergeant Carney, as only a few days earlier Captain Cailloux had at Port Hudson. The 54th suffered great losses and Carney became the first African American to receive the Congressional Medal of Honor. The Fort Wagner attack was an expensive one for the Union. The bodies of the dead, including Colonel Shaw, were thrown into common graves. In 1864 blacks fought in many battles throughout the year. That year at Fort Pillow, Confederates once again committed atrocities against black POWs.

ATROCITIES AGAINST BLACK POWS

General Nathan Bedford Forrest, a successful cavalry commander of the Confederate army, was responsible for atrocities against the Union's black soldiers. On March 24, about 1,500 Confederates stormed a garrison of 450 men at Union City. Surrender of the garrison was demanded but refused, and on the second attack Colonel Hawkins gave up against the wishes of his men, who preferred to fight it out. General Forrest pressed on, and on April 12, 1864, there was an extremely brutal battle at Fort Pillow, Tennessee, the next atrocity perpetrated against black soldiers. Under a flag of truce, Forrest demanded surrender and promised that the enemy would be considered prisoners of war. Major Bradford had assumed command of the Union force and refused the surrender, which met with immediate attack. The results were confusion and attempts to escape, and then the indiscriminate slaughter of soldiers, black and white, children, and women. Groups of soldiers were banded together and shot, including the sick and wounded. Many witnessed these atrocities, and their accounts were included in official reports. Forrest disclaimed knowledge of these events. Major Bradford was put on parole to attend the funeral of his brother. He did not return and was arrested later as a deserter but was shot and killed as he attempted to escape. There was much controversy over the events at Fort Pillow.

Black POWs were used to work on fortifications for the Confederate army and were accorded the status of POWs. The work they did would not have been allowed under the Geneva Convention rules if they had existed. Black POWs suffered incredibly. Ransom's Brigade in Suffolk, Virginia, in March 1864, was just as barbarous as their leader. His brigade was known not to take any Negro prisoners.

During the Atlanta campaign, the 44th United States Colored Infantry surrendered to Lieutenant General John Bell Hood at Dalton, Georgia. According to Confederate policy, the whites were paroled while the blacks were returned to slave status. Some blacks were turned over to state governments for trial and then returned to states for possible death sentences. It was not until February 1865 that POW status was recognized for blacks by the Confederacy. Jefferson Davis had finally seen the light.[36] Even Robert E. Lee believed that slaves could make effective soldiers; thus Davis signed the Negro Soldier Law passed by the Confederate Congress. Lincoln had always thought that it was the government's responsibility to protect all its citizens, especially soldiers, and that no distinction should be made concerning color in the treatment of POWs.

Wilson considers their treatment "the saddest and blackest chapter of the history of the war."[37] He comes down very hard on Jefferson Davis. Wilson had been a POW and an eyewitness to atrocities committed against his fellow blacks as a POW. At a congressional investigation hearing he testified seeing black sergeants being nailed to logs that were set on fire.[38]

NAVAL EXPLOITS

The Federal navy's role did not compare with that of the army. At certain battle sites near rivers, it aided the men fighting on land but was not heavily involved on the ocean. The Confederate navy's chief mission was to relieve the blockade. If any prisoners on either side were taken, there is not much written on the topic. On the same day, May 4, that General Taylor surrendered Confederate forces in Alabama, the Confederate navy surrendered.

William Brown relates an incident about William Tillman in June 1861. The privateer *Jefferson Davis* captured the *S.J. Waring* from New York and put on it a prize crew. Three of the original crew were retained, one of whom was Tillman, a steward and cook of the schooner, who was told he was then the property of the Confederate States and would be sold as a slave upon arrival in Charlestown. Armed with a club, Tillman went to the captain's cabin, struck him a fatal blow and then went to the deck and hit the mate. The crew was thrown into a panic, and Tillman, with a revolver, assumed command of the vessel. The enemy crew was put into irons and Tillman had become master of the ship. Thus his status as a POW had quickly changed to that of a free man and a hero. The *S.J. Waring* arrived in New York where its newly acquired master received prize money for the schooner.[39]

The Civil War was a very complex war from the standpoint of prisoners of war. It was a long, bitter struggle that ended in a victory not merely for the Union but for the black population of the entire country.

NOTES

1. William Best Hesseltine, *Civil War Prisons: A Study in War Psychology* (New York: Frederick Ungar, 1930).

2. Lonnie R. Speer, *Portals to Hell: Military Prisons of the Civil War* (Mechanicsburg, Pa.: Stackpole, 1997).

3. Speer, *Portal to Hell,* xiv.

4. Robert E. Denney, *Civil War Prisons and Escapes, A Day-by-Day Chronicle* (New York: Sterling, 1993).

5. Hesseltine, *Civil War Prisons*, 6.

6. Hesseltine, *Civil War Prisons,* ix.

7. Webb Garrison, *Military History,* June 1995.

8. Robert H. Kellogg, *Life and Death in Rebel Prisons* (Freeport, N.Y.: Books for Libraries Press, 1971), 19. First published in 1865.

9. Speer, *Portal to Hell,* 9–10.

10. George Lewis and John Mehwa, *History of Prisoner of War Utilization by the U.S. Army, 1776–1945,* Pamphlet no. 20-213 (Washington, D.C.: Department of the Army, 1955), 29.

11. Speer, *Portal to Hell,* 14, 16.

12. Speer, *Portal to Hell,* 331.

13. Speer, *Portal to Hell,* 174.

14. Speer, *Portal to Hell,* 278.

15. Speer, *Portal to Hell,* 243.

16. Speer, *Portal to Hell,* 248.

17. Speer, *Portal to Hell,* 22–23.

18. Lewis and Mewha, *History of Prisoner of War Utilization,* 41.

19. Kellogg, *Life and Death in Rebel Prisons,* 141.

20. Solon Hyde, *A Captive of War* (Shippensburg, Pa.: Burd Street Press, 1996).

21. Hyde, *Captive of War,* 145.

22. Hesseltine, *Civil War Prisons,* 25, 155.

23. William Marvel, *Andersonville: The Last Depot* (Chapel Hill: University of North Carolina Press, 1994), 141.

24. Frank Milton Bristol, *The Life of Chaplain McCabe,* 2d ed. (New York: Fleming H. Revell, 1908), 137.

25. Bristol, *Life of Chaplain McCabe,* 241.

26. Jefferson Davis, *Andersonville and Other War Prisons* (New York: Belford, 1890), 11.

27. Clay W. Holmes, *The Elmira Prison Camp: History of the Military Prison at Elmira, NY July 6, 1864 to July 10, 1865* (New York: Putman's Sons, 1912), 7.

28. S. W. Ashe, *The Trial and Death of Henry Wirz* (Raleigh, N.C.: E. E. Uzell, 1908).

29. Jefferson Davis, *The Rise and Fall of the Confederate Government,* 2 vols. (New York: 1881), 458.

30. Speer, *Portal to Hell,* 108.

31. Joseph T. Wilson, *The Black Phalanx: A History of the Negro Soldiers of the United States in the Wars of 1775, 1812, 1861–1865* (Hartford, Conn.: American Publishing, 1890), 315.

32. Wilson, *Black Phalanx,* 111.

33. Wilson, *Black Phalanx,* 112.

34. Wilson, *Black Phalanx,* 125.

35. Wilson, *Black Phalanx,* 187.

36. Benjamin Quarles, *The Negroes in the Civil War* (Boston: Little, Brown, 1953).

37. Wilson, *Black Phalanx,* 320.

38. Wilson, *Black Phalanx,* 332.

39. William Wells Brown, *The Negro in the American Revolution* (Miami: Mnemosyne, 1969).

8

The Spanish-American War

On April 26, 1898, Congress passed an act that declared war on Spain but said that war had actually existed since April 21. The treaty terminating the war was approved by the Senate on February 6, 1899, and was signed by the president the same day. Thus, to that date, the war represented the shortest in U.S. history. There was fighting on land and water in two main theaters of operations, the Pacific and Atlantic Oceans, more specifically the Bay of Manila in the Philippines and the Caribbean Sea.

The war presented a sharp contrast to the Civil War concerning prisoners of war. In the Civil War both sides were unprepared in regard to naval matters, but in the Spanish-American War the navy was much better prepared than the army.

The navy was organized into two fleets, the Atlantic under Captain William Sampson, acting rear admiral, and the Pacific, under Admiral George Dewey, located at Hong Kong. Sampson's chief of staff was Captain Chadwick; General William Shafter, a brigadier of the general army, was appointed as a major general of volunteers. The Spanish officer in charge of the Atlantic fleet was Admiral Pascal Cervera. Dewey received word on April 24 from the Navy Department in Washington that war had started between the United States and Spain.[1] The Pacific part of the war was completed in a few hours on May 1, 1898, with Admiral Dewey's victory in Manila Bay.

One difference between this war and previous wars is a lack of information on POWs. Very few Americans were taken as POWs, the chief ones being Hobson's naval crew and more than a thousand Spanish, chiefly naval, personnel. There were no real issues concerning poor treatment, since humanitarian principles guided both sides.

LIEUTENANT RICHARD PEARSON HOBSON

The most famous incident concerning POWs was the capture of Lieutenant Richard Pearson Hobson, a naval engineer, and his crew of seven. Admiral Sampson's objective was to keep Admiral Cervera's ships inside Santiago Harbor, and a special mission was conceived to accomplish this under the supervision of Lieutenant Hobson.

Hobson was born in 1870 in Alabama. His father was a Confederate army veteran who was wounded three times and then captured at Spotsylvania, where he spent the rest of the war as a POW. Young Hobson wanted a military career and chose Annapolis. He graduated in 1889, first in his class. He was an excellent athlete, particularly a good swimmer, which served him well in his attempt to be a hero during the Spanish-American War. He served in the Navy Department in Washington, D.C., with the Bureau of Construction and Repair for eighteen months, and was on the flagship of Admiral Sampson when war was declared.

Sampson's squadron left the day after war was declared to establish the blockade of Havana and lesser ports east and west of the capital.[2] Most authors writing about this war discuss the dangerous venture of Hobson and his men, but the best and most complete account of the mission and its aftermath of prison internment is Hobson's own book.

The operation called for the sinking of the *Merrimac,* a collier in the harbor, and thus the channel would be blocked to prevent Cervera's ships from escaping. Six men were required, two to be kept below, one person in the engine room, one in the boiler room, one to help with the torpedoes, and one at the wheel. Other necessities included a lifeboat in tow at the stern and a life preserver, a rifle, and revolver belts with boxes of cartridges. Being heavily armed made them ready for stiff resistance should they be captured.[3] Another important requirement was the ability to swim, if necessary, to a designated cove under the Morro Castle. If anything happened to Hobson, the senior petty officer would assume command.

There was no problem obtaining volunteers for the mission. Good light was also essential for the success of the difficult task, but as so often happens, the best-laid plans would prove futile. At the last moment the steering gear was disabled. All torpedoes were to be fired, but this proved useless. The men were being fired on by machine gun batteries on the slope. Two torpedoes exploded and the men had to make the best of the situation, which was far from good. They were swept over the side and their lifeboat had been torn away. Troops lined the shore and small Spanish boats were looking for survivors. In the cold water, Hobson and his men saw a boat coming toward them. Hobson called out to them to learn if there was an officer in the boat to whom he could surrender himself and his men. Thus the mission failed, and he and his men became prisoners of war.

At this time Hobson did not know that Admiral Cervera himself helped him into the boat. Hobson and his men, when brought to Cervera's main ship, were courteously treated and cared for. They were provided with dry clothes and facilities for washing, and Hobson was brought to the executive officer's wardroom for breakfast. At Morro Castle, their prison, the courteous treatment continued.

Hobson wrote a letter about his failure to Admiral Sampson, and when the American POWs left the ship, Hobson's men asked him to thank the Spanish crew for their kind treatment. Cervera also notified Sampson that his seven prisoners were all safe in his custody. The Spanish officers also were quite surprised at the excellent conduct of Hobson's men and remarked to Hobson what remarkable men he had.[4]

The confinement conditions at Morro Castle were not bad, but General Linares ordered the prisoners transferred to Santiago on Tuesday, June 7. They had been in prison for only four days and had never been treated disrespectfully by Spanish soldiers. Visits to Hobson by the British consul were a high point of Hobson's confinement.

On the journey all the POWs were blindfolded for about half a mile and then allowed to take off the blindfolds. They arrived at a famous location, the Ceibar tree, where there were two American officers with Spanish prisoners, three officers and a group of privates. An official prisoner of war exchange was to take place. The Spanish officer was to pick one of the officers in American custody.

This exchange is briefly discussed by several historians and by Hobson himself, but the best description of the exchange and events preceding it was rendered by Stephen Crane, author of many short stories and *The Red Badge of Courage*. Crane was one of many famous war correspondents assigned to cover the Spanish-American War.

In his book *Wounds in the Rain: War Stories*, Crane vividly describes the army's reaction when Hobson and his men approached the American lines. The nearby army "was majestically minding its own business in the long lines of trenches when its eye caught sight of the little procession." Then the men of the regular army arose en masse and "slowly lifted every weather-beaten hat and dropped it until it touched the knee. Then there was a magnificent silence, broken only by the measured hoofbeats of the little company's horses as they rode through the gap. It was solemn, funereal, this splendid silent welcome of a brave man by men who stood on a hill which they had earned out of blood and death."[5]

This certainly was a memorable exchange. Crane was famous for his description of the actual event. General Shafter stated, a few years after the war, that none of his men had ever become prisoners; he was, of course, talking of army men under his command and not naval personnel.

SPANISH PRISONERS OF WAR

This was not the case for the Spanish in the field and naval battles. Admiral Cervera and many of his navy men became POWs. Cervera, who had captured Hobson, was treated as humanely as he had treated Hobson and his men.

Cervera and the officers of his sunken destroyer were taken to the *Iowa* and then transferred to the *Harvard* and *St. Louis* for passage to Annapolis for officers and to Seaver's Island, Portsmouth, New Hampshire, for enlisted men, where they would be interned as POWs. On July 4 Cervera's fleet was destroyed.

According to Lewis and Mehwa, the war was so short that it was hardly classified as a war, with hostilities lasting about three months. These authors also assert that the war is significant because it represents the first time that a POW program was formulated in advance of the capture of prisoners.[6] It was thought that many prisoners would be taken after the proposed Santiago de Cuba campaign and the subsequent campaign against Puerto Rico. The large number of naval prisoners was not included in expectations.

The prisoners taken during the first attack on Santiago in early July were surprised at the humane treatment they received. Some of them were utilized as kitchen workers and some were used in the Hobson exchange described above.

The twin battles of El Caney and San Juan Hill on July 1, 1898, determined whether American forces in Cuba would succeed or fail. It was a close decision, according to Freidel.[7] El Caney was a small village of strategic importance because of its geographical position. The seizure of this village would cut off the possibility of reinforcements from Guantanamo, so this was important for General Shafter's purposes. The battle lasted nine hours and many were killed and wounded. El Caney surrendered. The Spanish commander was wounded in the leg by a bullet and then killed by a shot in the head. The total casualties of the Spanish numbered 235 killed and wounded and 120 taken prisoner.

The battle on the Siboney–Santiago road began two hours later than at El Caney. On the morning of July 3, General Shafter demanded Santiago's surrender with the warning that it would be heavily bombarded if it did not do so. Under a flag of truce, negotiations were carried on for a period of ten days.

On July 3, Spanish prisoners suffered casualties in the explosion of the *Vizcaya*: 323 were killed and 151 wounded out of 2,221 men; 1,813 were lost as prisoners.[8]

Approximately 24,000 Spanish surrendered on July 17, but they did so on the conditions of a parole and a promise that the U.S. government would grant them an early return to Spain at its expense. The troops who surrendered were disarmed, but their officers were not permitted to retain their firearms. The next objective was Puerto Rico, which would be given the same conditions. They agreed to a surrender after they heard of the signing of a peace protocol.

At the outset of operations in the Caribbean, General Shafter decided to land at Daiquiri without informing the army and the next day Daiquiri and Siboney "were handed over as bloodless gifts to the United States forces."[9] The Santiago campaign extended from June 22 to July 17, 1898. The Spanish General Linares did not desire to take a stand at La Guarimos after giving up the beaches without opposition. Once it was surrendered, the Americans would see no opposition on their march to El Pozo, which was halfway to the city.

Thus General Shafter had been very fortunate. He had been given much help in landing his troops by the navy and expressed his thanks to Admiral Sampson and the Navy Department. A total of about 6,000 men, according to Alger Russell's *The Spanish-American War,*[10] had been put on Cuban soil. According to Trask, "Some authorities attribute to Shafter no sense of coordinated warfare on joint operations, no understanding of the ways in which land and sea forces could operate in conjunction." But "others charge that Shafter did not wish to share the honors at

Santiago de Cuba with the Navy—that he aspired to capture the city and Cervera by himself."[11]

THE DEFEAT OF ADMIRAL CERVERA

The American victories at El Caney and San Juan Heights exposed Admiral Cervera's squadron to great danger. Consequently Captain Paredes decided that he would rather surrender his men to the *Oregon* than see them killed. On July 3 he lowered his colors and beached his ship. The result was that 1,720 officers and men became prisoners. Spanish ships started emerging from the channel a good distance from each other, but none really had much chance of success. The American naval victory on July 3 at Santiago de Cuba didn't remove the Spanish garrison there. This had to be accomplished by Shafter's army, but the naval victory was significant in that it guaranteed American command of the sea. Cervera emerged on July 3, but the Spanish squadron was devastated.

American seamen performed extraordinary service in rescuing Spanish crews from burning ships. Those saved who were not seriously wounded were placed on two ships to be taken to the United States. Seriously wounded were put on a special ship. Unfortunately, on one ship considerable trouble developed. A line was marked on the deck beyond which prisoners couldn't go. Crossing the line could be interpreted as perhaps an attempt to escape. The language barrier did not help the situation. A sentry fired his weapon, and the sound of it brought some prisoners to their feet. The volley of fire into a group of about 600 prisoners resulted in six Spanish killed, thirteen wounded. Order was restored over what was a tragic accident.

Cervera and his officers were confined at the U.S. Naval Academy at Annapolis; the enlisted men were sent to Portsmouth, New Hampshire, on Seaver's Island. Forty-eight men were disabled and placed on a hospital ship, the *Solace*, and later treated at Norfolk, Virginia.[12]

At Seaver's Island 20 officers, 3 surgeons, 2 chaplains, and 1,661 men were interned.

Admiral Cervera subsequently wrote a letter to Rear Admiral Sampson and expressed his thanks and praise to American sailors for the treatment they gave enemy prisoners. Thus relations were very cordial, something not seen in subsequent wars.

In an official letter to the commanding general of Santiago's forces, July 4, 1898, Major General Shafter informed him that Admiral Cervera was on board the USS *Gloucester* and was unharmed. He regretted, however, to announce the death of General Vara de Rey at El Caney, along with his two sons, on July 1. His body was buried with full military honors. Also, Lieutenant Colonel Vara del Rey was wounded and a prisoner with four others who were seriously wounded but would probably survive.

Shafter had considerable correspondence with General Juan Toral between July 3 and July 5. Shafter firmly believed that paroled prisoners returning to Santiago would relate their good treatment, thus creating a favorable atmosphere for the Americans in Santiago as well as for the contemplated exchange of prisoners for Hobson's crew.

On the completion of the exchange, Lieutenant Miley, representing Shafter, told the Spanish that hostilities would resume in an hour. Shafter made another demand for surrender. He did not want to see more Spanish or his own men killed. Three days later Toral consulted his home government and agreed to terms.

The surrender of Santiago took place on Sunday, July 17. After the Spanish stacked their weapons, Lieutenant Miley witnessed prisoners cooking horses brought out of the city, a good indication of the shortage of food among them. But the next day, supply ships arrived with food for all.

The transportation of all POWs was to be taken care of through British negotiators and this would include costs of passage, rations, and medical supplies that the U.S. government would provide. Thus, from August 10 through August 18, ten ships arrived carrying a total of 22,864 people. This included families of officers, priests, and hospital nuns.[13]

In Manila, where the Spanish fleet was defeated, the capital city fell on August 13, and about 1,300 were taken into custody. They were kept in a walled portion of the city, for the most part in churches and convents. The people who wanted repatriation were accommodated.

By September 17, all prisoners from Cuba were evacuated, the only exceptions being yellow fever victims and some soldiers who decided to remain. By October 1898 all troops from Puerto Rico had left. However, because of native insurrections, the process of evacuation lasted until 1900.

THE PHILIPPINE INSURRECTION

POWs were taken during the Philippine insurrection and were treated kindly and humanely. An amnesty act on April 1, 1900, released many, but those who were considered active insurrection agents, civilian officials, and other agitators were deported to the island of Guam. Two years later, on July 4, President Theodore Roosevelt, who himself had fought in the Spanish-American War, officially ended organized native resistance in the Philippines.

The Philippine insurrection started on February 4, 1901, and its leader had been Emilio Aquinaldo. Dewey had not captured all of the Philippine Islands. He had no land forces but established a rigid naval blockade of Manila. Aquinaldo, the insurgent leader, was a great concern. He had declared himself president on July 1 and consequently would have to be brought under control. He was determined to continue the fight and strike against Manila, and his forces took many American army troops as prisoners, some of whom were tortured. Some Americans even tortured the enemy in order to secure military information. A traitor was responsible for the capture of Aquinaldo on March 23, 1901, but guerrilla activities continued

until April 1902. The last important insurgent leader, Malvar, surrendered along with 8,000 to 10,000 troops. Finally, on July 4, 1902,
Theodore Roosevelt's proclamation closed out the problems and
amnesty was granted for all "except those convicted of murder,
rape, arson and other serious crimes."[14] The U.S. Navy really decided the outcome. As Leckie says, "A War for an island by con-
tending offshore powers has to become a naval war, or at least be
decided by sea power.[15] This was to be accomplished on two different oceans—the Atlantic and the Pacific. Perhaps General Shafter
had been correct when he did not want to share honors with the navy
for fear that the navy would receive more credit, but he certainly
recognized the importance of the navy, which would again prove its
importance in wars to come.

Shafter was not known for his diplomacy. Excluding reporters
from Santiago disturbed the media and many people, including Secretary Alger. But Shafter refused to change his mind because he
thought that the presence of many POWs and the media in the city
could cause trouble. Charles Brown in *The Correspondents' War*
says some historians theorize that if President McKinley had been
more forceful, war would have been avoided.[16] This line of thought
is developed by Walter Millis in his book on the war, *The Martial
Spirit: The Hawks of That Day*.[17] Although the media with its yellow
journalism may have led the way, even without them, many think
that war was inevitable.

NOTES

1. Richard H. Titherington, *A History of the Spanish-American War*
(Freeport, N.Y.: Books for Libraries Press, 1971), 144. First published in 1900.

2. Richard Pearson Hobson, *The Sinking of the Merrimac* (Annapolis,
Md.: Naval Institute Press, 1987), xiii. Originally published in 1899.

3. Frank Freidel, *The Splendid Little War* (Boston: Little, Brown,
1958), 53.

4. Hobson, *Sinking of the Merrimac*, 91.

5. Stephen Crane, *Wounds in the Rain* (Freeport, N.Y: Books for Libraries Press, 1972). First published in 1900.

6. George Lewis and John Mewha, *History of Prisoner of War Utilization by the United States Army, 1776–1945,* Pamphlet no. 20-213 (Washington, D.C.: Department of the Army, 1955), 43.

7. Freidel, *Splendid Little War,* 119.

8. Freidel, *Splendid Little War,* 231.

9. Ivan Musicant, *Empire by Default: The Spanish-American War and the Dawn of the American Century* (New York: Holt, 1998), 367.

10. R. A. Alger, *The Spanish-American War.* (Freeport, N.Y.: Books for Libraries Press, 1971)*,* 96–98.

11. David E. Trask, *The War with Spain in 1898* (New York: Macmillan, 1981).

12. Trask, *War with Spain*, 568 n. 4–5.

13. Musicant, *Empire by Default,* 507.

14. Lewis and Mehwa, *Prisoner of War Utilization,* 46.

15. Robert Leckie, *The Wars of America,* rev. ed. (New York: Harper & Row, 1981), 23.

16. Charles H. Brown, *The Correspondents' War* (New York: Scribner's, 1967), 442.

17. Walter Millis, *The Martial Spirit: A Study of the War with Spain* (Chicago: Ivan R. Dee, 1989).

9

World War I

The United States was involved in World War I for only a short time, but its operations were much more massive and complex than those of the Spanish-American War, even though the Spanish-American War had been fought in both the Atlantic and the Pacific. Also, the prisoner of war situation was quite different on both sides.

Quite a number of books have been written about World War I. John Keegan's recent book is excellent but concentrates on how the war happened and how it affected many things, not focusing on America's role in the war or on prisoners of war. Many other historians do not focus on either of these points. James G. Harbard, a general who represents an excellent primary source, gave very little consideration to POWs; neither did General Pershing in his memoirs.

American prisoners are considered in Fook's book *Prisoners of War*[1] and Dennett's *Prisoners of the Great War.*[2] A comprehensive account of the American role is contained in the volumes of the *United States Army in the World War, 1917–1919* (1990), but this is not in narrative form. This multivolume work contains military correspondence orders and summaries in their original form, and volumes 4–9 involve the military operations of the AEF (American Expeditionary Forces).

The "war to end all wars" did not accomplish that objective. Keegan says, "The Second World War, five times more destructive of human life and incalculably more costly in material terms, was the

145

direct outcome of the First."[3] Further, "no large European city was destroyed or even seriously devastated during its course as all German cities were by aerial bombardment during the Second World War."[4] World War II started in 1939 and "was unquestionably the outcome of the First and in large measure its continuation."[5]

THE UNITED STATES BECOMES INVOLVED IN WORLD WAR I

Early in 1917 President Woodrow Wilson broke off diplomatic relations with Germany. He was elected as a president who would keep the United States out of war, but conditions changed radically. The sinking of the *Lusitania* certainly helped effect a change in U.S. policy, but there were prior incidents that also provoked such change.

Two events contributed largely to changing the U.S. attitude toward Germany and influencing its involvement in the conflict. According to Daniel Smith, the first was the very clumsy German attempt to involve the United States with Mexico. Germany proposed an alliance with that nation by promising to return the states of Texas, Arizona, and New Mexico in what was called the Zimmerman telegram, which incensed both the government and the people. The second factor was the German decision to resume unrestricted submarine warfare.

On April 4 the U.S. Senate voted for war 82 to 6, and two days later the House voted for war 373 to 50; thus on April 6, the United States declared war on Germany. General John Pershing was designated as the general who would head the American Expeditionary Force (AEF). It was unfortunate that "the Army, however, was only a skeleton and to put flesh upon it was going to be a long task which would show no results at all for some time."[6] Pershing would have his hands full. Fortunately, the U.S. Navy was in much better shape, having proven itself in the Spanish-American War. The first American troops arrived in France on June 28 at the port of Saint-Nazaire.

Thousands and thousands of German POWs were taken by the Allied forces and Allied POWs by the Germans before the United States joined the fray, but once the Americans were fully committed, it was then their turn. But U.S. involvement had little effect on the field of battle for at least a year.

GERMAN SUBMARINE WARFARE

Two days after the U.S. declaration of war, April 8, the German submarine U-55 sank the British steamer *Torrington* off the coast of Sicily. The sub destroyed one of its lifeboats with fourteen people in it and quickly submerged to abandon twenty passengers hanging on to the hull of the sub, drowning everyone.

American convoys carrying troops to France from May 1917 to November 1918 were subjected to the dangers of German submarine warfare. Martin Gilbert writes that of 1 million American troops crossing the Atlantic, only 637 drowned because of German submarine warfare.[7] When the U.S. troopship *Tuscania* was sunk in February 1918, the convoy it was part of saved 2,187 of 2,397 aboard.

In November 1915, Admiral Dewey had written, "The submarine is not an instrument filled to dominate naval warfare . . . the battleship is still the principal reliance of navies, as it has been in the past." Brilliant as he was in the Spanish-American War, he was a poor prophet. In the war at sea unrestricted submarine warfare was to be a primary problem for the Allies.[8]

Most of the POWs taken in World War I were army and marine personnel on both sides, but the navies participated substantially. On November 17, 1917, the German submarine U-58 was destroyed. An alert coxswain on an American destroyer saw a finger telescope of the sub, and his ship headed for the area and dropped a depth bomb that destroyed the sub's motors. It then dropped a second depth bomb, and the badly damaged sub had to surface.

A shot struck the German commander, Captain Gustave Amberger, when he emerged from the sub. The destroyer attached lines to the sub to salvage it, but its crew managed to thwart the effort and scuttle it. As the sub went down into the water, the crew dove off it. Only one German submariner died, after efforts to resuscitate him failed. Thus Amberger, three officers, and thirty-five crewmen became American POWs. They were given food, warm clothing, and much better treatment than they expected. When placed on boats to be taken ashore, they cheered their captors.[9]

On May 31, 1918, the *President Lincoln* was 500 miles from land when it was sunk by the U-90 with the loss of three officers and twenty-three enlisted men. The sub surfaced and picked up Lieutenant Edouard Victor Isaacs as a prisoner but left his fellow survivors floating on rafts and lifeboats as they sang popular songs to keep up their spirits. At 11:00 A.M. two destroyers rescued them and brought them to Brest. On the way the U-90 was seen and twenty-two depth charges were dropped exploding near it. The sub, of course, was carrying the POW Isaacs. He was well treated on board and brought to Wilhelmhaven and later taken to Villingen.

Isaacs tried escaping several times, once by jumping from a speeding train, for which he was punished with two weeks of solitary confinement. In October he effected a successful escape and after many trials and terrors he finally swam across the Rhine to Switzerland. A few days later Isaacs was giving details of what he had learned about German submarines to intelligence officers when the armistice was signed. Four weeks after his escape he was in Washington, where Secretary Daniels personally congratulated him on all his efforts.

GERMAN POWS

The first German army POW captured by the Americans was Leonard Hoffman, a twenty-one-year-old male orderly, on October 27, 1917. He was shot and stumbled into an area of the 16th Infantry.

He was a POW for only a short period of time because a day after an operation he died in the hospital.[10] Within six hours of the arrival of the 16th Infantry, the Germans lay down a barrage and the raid resulted in three killed, five wounded, and eleven prisoners, the first of 4,434 to be taken as prisoners. Thus the AEF had its introduction to World War I.[11]

Prisoners were seized by combat patrols and as a result of air reconnaissance, which were the main sources of intelligence for both sides.[12] Alabama soldiers of the 167th Infantry gained a wealth of information and Croix de Guerres were given to all members of a patrol that captured two soldiers of the 7th Bavarian Infantry.

CARL DENNETT

Since so many POWs were taken before the United States entered the war, there was a well-established system of procedures and designations of camps for POWs. Dennett's book *Prisoners of the Great War* includes a table that lists seventy prison camps in alphabetical order and gives for each one the number of enemy officers, army NCOs and privates, navy officers, navy sailors, and finally, civilians. The totals given were 290 army officers, 3,156 army NCOs and privates, 2 naval officers, 10 navy sailors, and 144 civilians. Naval personnel numbered few, most of the POWs having been taken in small engagements and some in large battles. These totals were considered differently from enemy POWs taken.

Dennett's table of POW camps[13] lists those with the largest numbers as of November 13, 1918, being at Rastaff, Glessen, Limberg, and Villingen.[14] The author includes for each POW name, rank, regiment, prison number, and size of different clothing (e.g. coat, trousers, collar, gloves) and other pertinent information. Instructions on the form stated that each form had to be filled out and mailed at once and Dennett's name appeared at the bottom as deputy commissioner for the Department of Prisoners of War.

Carl Dennett was the Red Cross deputy commissioner to Switzerland in charge of taking care of the needs of American prisoners in German prison camps. He was the right man for the job because he had excellent knowledge of the camps and the prison rules, and he was familiar with such terms as working commando, reprisal camps, and what a "colis" brought to a starving man; thus he was aware of camp language and real troubles and problems in the camps. As he was writing about all nationalities of prisoners, French, English, and Belgians, and had spoken to the first group of American prisoners to emerge from Germany since the signing of the armistice.

Working commandos consisted of work parties sent out from the main camps; they could consist of a number of men or perhaps a single person sent to work on a large farm, factory, coal, salt or other mine, stone quarry, or highways or railways. These commandos could be situated far from their camp of residence and consequently would have guards watching over them where they worked. In the case of a group of working commandos, the overseer was a German noncommissioned officer called a *Feldivebel*, and he could be cruel or nice. Some single personnel were assigned to work without a guard, usually in an area where escape would be extremely difficult. Often the treatment accorded a POW depended entirely on the attitude of the overseer; farmers were more likely to give better treatment. This was understandable because bad treatment would result in poor work. Often a neutral delegate would be assigned to a camp having 3,000 POWs but was able to see only about 500 because so many working commandos were absent.

In September 1917, there were about 600,000 POWs whose address was given as Limberg camp. An annual inspection revealed the presence of only about 2,400 men. These were not necessarily American POWs. Dennett's table for this camp lists a total of 104

Americans, 4 officers, and 100 NCOs as POWs as of November 15, 1918.

The reprisal camps held POWs who had committed alleged offenses, usually where terrible conditions existed, and for which German military authorities sanctioned the administration of severe punishments.

The Kommandantur was the German government officer in charge of a prison camp. He was usually a high-ranking army officer and had supreme power in the camp. Dennett says that many of them would undoubtedly suffer the same fate as that given to the commanding officer at Andersonville prison after the U.S. Civil War: hanged for brutality.

Dennett states, "Never before in the history of mankind have such conditions existed with reference to prisoners as in the great world war."[15] In World War I, Germany did not provide adequately for POWs and did not give serious humanitarian considerations to its POWs "as human beings nor did it try to make . . . efforts to preserve their lives."[16]

AMERICAN POWS

When U.S. troops were sent to France in 1917, the American Red Cross acted promptly to help possible American POWs. The American Red Cross asked Ellis Loring Dresel, who had visited prison camps before the United States entered the war, and who was associated with the U.S. ambassador to Germany, to do whatever he could for the needs of Americans who might become POWs. In April 1918, the American Red Cross asked Carl Dennett to go to Switzerland to take responsibility for American POWs. A committee, consisting of the author from Boston and representatives from Scranton, Pennsylvania, Waltham, Massachusetts, Brookline, Massachusetts, and San Francisco, was sent to Switzerland. Due to the efforts of Randolph Stewart of Brookline, the repatriation of American POWs was well supervised and these men were promptly and comfortably returned to France.

When the commission arrived in Berne, not many American POWs (only 211 in Germany of whom 113 were civilians, 11 naval and 87 military personnel) were there.[17] In July 1918, the author was informed that more than a million American soldiers were in France and another million were to arrive. Thus steps had to be taken to provide food for an anticipated 50,000 POWs. The chief quartermaster of the American Expeditionary Forces (AEF) in France, General Rogers, had to pave the way to provide for the needs of American POWs—he had to rent places to store food and blankets and, of course, procure these materials as well.

The principal sources of information about American POWs in Germany were prison lists sent by the Germans, the minister of war to the Berlin Red Cross, and finally to the American Red Cross at Berne. During this process Germans demonstrated considerable inefficiency.

The AEF had no German POWs on June 1, 1918, since they had rather unwisely turned over all POWs to the French military forces. This resulted in a distinct disadvantage in trying to secure information on a reciprocal basis: the AEF had no real bargaining power. Dennett made this point rather clear—Americans had no POWs. If German POWs could be retained instead of being turned over to French forces, the situation would be much better.

Within a few weeks American military forces had more than 2,000 POWs and within four months more than 37,000 German POWs were in their possession. They arranged with general headquarters of the AEF in France to supply lists of all German POWs to the American Red Cross at Berlin, which then put them in a better position to demand reciprocity from the Germans for all information given on their POWs.

The federal government made arrangements with the Frankfurt Red Cross in Germany to send rosters to the American Red Cross at Berne of POWs taken by Germany. The procedure was to send postcards to all prison camps in Germany on which POWs would provide information about themselves. At the extreme left bottom of the cards were the words well, sick, and wounded. These cards were to be sent to Washington, but many were never mailed. Camp help committees were organized to assist the situation and were told to report without delay. This turned out to be an effective, faster method of communication than official prison lists. The time factor for locating POWs in Germany was cut in half.

When Germans captured POWs, they searched them for papers that might provide information and maps and then questioned them thoroughly. The methods varied; some used physical violence, and some POWs were killed. Dennett was strongly convinced that the United States never utilized such tactics.

The Germans tried threats and trickery and even placed spies among U.S. forces. Some spies could speak excellent English and wore American uniforms. Often prisoners were used as workers behind American lines and under the fire of American guns, as both North and South had done in the Civil War. Germany used many of these measures with American POWs in World War II.

German POW camps were usually surrounded by ten-foot-high barbed wire fences. The bed bunks were made of wood with two tiers, and mattresses had all types of materials that often harbored vermin. Cooking facilities varied. Some had excellent kitchens, some very poor ones. At times there wasn't enough fuel for the stoves. Recreational facilities and athletic activities were available and some camps had education classes, libraries, and newspapers.

ESCAPES FROM GERMAN CAMPS

Escapes were expected, especially if a camp wasn't far from the Swiss border. Notes were pinned under tables at supper that warned that there might be dictaphones planted in the lamps. This was, of course, a device not experienced in previous wars. The first

American POW to escape to Switzerland from a German POW camp was aviator Everett Buckley of Chicago, who will be discussed later in the chapter.

Some POWs who managed to break through fences and reach the frontier were recaptured and sent back to a farm in Donaueschingen. They then escaped from a field and ran five kilometers to the Danube, where they were caught again and sent back to Heuberg. Sentenced to thirty-one days but refusing to yield, they cut the bars out of a window and with seven other POWs fled to Bolhlege, where they were caught again and then sent to Varingengladt. They were placed on another farm where they received poor care. They missed an opportunity to see a doctor and in July 1918 were put on a working commando in a hayfield. They escaped again with the help of a map and compass and reached the Swiss border. They avoided three sentries and successfully got to Berne, where they were given money and clothing by the American Red Cross and sent to France. This case was truly an adventure for these POWs and exemplified their determination and ingenuity.

When the armistice was signed, about 75 percent of American POWs were situated in camps near the Rhine and close to the zone that would be occupied by the Allied armies.

There were a few individual events involving the taking of German prisoners that should be mentioned. On October 7 Sergeant Alvin York started for the hill at Chatel Chehery with his men. The Germans were putting their machine guns to full use and these guns were the objective of the seventeen American AEF soldiers. York's men ran after the Germans, who threw their hands up and yelled "Comrade." The one in charge pleaded to the Americans not to shoot and they would surrender. There was a hard battle from the Germans and a German major. Ultimately York captured 132 POWs and brought them back.[18]

Fooks, who had commanded the 3d Battalion, 14th Infantry and had been wounded, also states that two men of the 3d Battalion were captured in advanced posts. No enemies were captured, and he gives further statistics: 12 officers, 316 enlisted men, and 38 wounded American POWs.

AN ACCOUNT BY CLIFFORD MARKLE

Clifford Markle wrote an interesting personal commentary of the actual confinement of an American POW in Germany. Unfortunately there are not many accounts like this for World War I, in contrast to the many Civil War, World War II, Korean War, and Vietnam War narratives. The brief introductory paragraph to this primary source is given by William H. Taft, who says that the author was employed in his office in New Haven for a considerable period. When the war started, he joined the Medical Corps, was sent to France, and was ordered to the front. He was captured in April 1918.

The battle of Seichepray (which the author calls the Lexington of World War I) occurred on April 20, 1918. As a first aid man assigned to the infantry, Markle and other medical personnel were captured and taken to Germany. All men who wore rubber boots were deprived of them and forced to walk in their stocking feet across no man's land. This injured their feet and caused many infections. He and the other Americans had to carry a wounded soldier to the soldier's battalion and station. Chances of escape at this point were very slight. Depriving American soldiers of their boots was a common practice reported by Dennett to the American Red Cross.

Markle was sent to different locations to work—to make shoes, to milk cows, and even to work in a restaurant. It was easy to escape, but he held off for a while so he could gather sufficient food. When he decided to escape, however, he was thwarted. As he himself said, "Man proposes but God disposes." That same afternoon a guard came from Cologne to take him to a wire factory where he met ten Americans who greeted him from their bunks in the barracks to which he was assigned. All these Americans had been captured at the battle of Seicheprey and had been sent from Limberg prison camp to Cologne. In addition to the American POWs, there were 400 Russians, 80 Italians, and 6 Rumanians. The majority of the Russians had been working in Cologne for three years. (The United States, it should be remembered, had not been in the war as long as other nations.)

Facilities there were not bad. The men had running water for bathing in all barracks and once a week had shower baths at different sections where they worked in the factory. Thus they fared much better than soldiers at the front, but they were still POWs who would have preferred to be back in the trenches. Air raids took place two or three times a week, but nobody was injured, and the raids did not discourage the POWs, whose morale was good.

On November 9 a revolution started among the guards, who tore off their shoulder straps. This signified that they were no longer soldiers, and they even defied their officers. When the armistice was signed, they "passed by us very quietly, for although we expected the war to end inside of a month, we never dreamed that it actually had ended at that time."[19] The men hiked back to the camp and met nine other Americans; they left together on November 15. They boarded a train with English, French, and Italians and began their trip to France. On December 1 they rejoined their regiment and sailed for America four months later.

There are two other interesting POW accounts. Lieutenant E. H. Jones, in *The Road to Endor,* tells of two POWs at Yozgard, Turkey, who made their way to freedom. The second is Major M. C. C. Harrison and Captain H. A. Cartwright's book, *Within Four Walls.* Another book is *The Escaping Club* by A. Evans. These books were written by British officers and were published in England; they were British POWs whose reports make for interesting reading.

Although the United States was only briefly involved in World War I, the records of the adjutant general's office show that Americans captured about 48,976 Germans and about 4,120 Americans were captured from various combat missions.[20] Only a few American soldier POWs during World War I were charged as traitors. Privates Halas and Harry Nicholoff gave useful information to the enemy.[21]

LEGION OF THE LAFAYETTE

The Legion of the Lafayette represented the air battles in World War I for the American side. Three aviators in this group—Harold Willis, James Hall, and Christopher Ford—were forced to endure the indignity of being POWs.[22] Many of these aviators gave as much trouble to the enemy as prisoners of war as they had as active pilots, by trying to escape and keeping their jailers always on the alert. They did not believe that their prison confinement meant the war was over for them. They didn't have any previous knowledge of what POW camps were like nor did they know how to plan an escape or how to endure duress in a prison camp. At the very beginning of their flying missions they were well aware of the odds of being taken prisoner. Things were stacked against them if they had to crash-land in enemy territory. The enemy were arrogant, merciless, and as POWs, demanded their rights under the Hague Convention. But when the shoe was on the other foot and they were the captors, they paid little or no attention to the Hague Convention. Those who escaped from German POW camps often gave lectures on their escapes, offering advice and instruction on escape measures. In a way, this paved the way for formal pamphlets, books, and courses on the subject of escape, evasion, and survival in subsequent wars.

James Hall terminated his career in a POW camp. He was a POW in various German hospitals and POW camps until the armistice.[23]

Everett Buckley of Illinois was not injured in his plane crash. He was surrounded and roughed up by a crowd, but amazingly a German military officer came to his defense and rescue by riding into the crowd with his sabre slashing away, and that officer actually injured some Germans. Never before had anything like this ever happened.

Buckley was put on bread and water for eighteen days. He was subjected to extended questioning at the "Karbrriche Hotel" by German intelligence officers. Buckley refused to answer questions and was sent to a prison camp at Heuberg, Germany. In a month he planned a successful escape. He reached the Swiss frontier where he was recaptured. His whereabouts were never released by the Germans nor was it known for a while whether he was dead or alive. He was sent to a prison farm and escaped, but was captured once more when he tried to cross the Danube.

Everett worked hard with seven other prisoners cutting the bars out of a window. The escape was not discovered until daybreak and within two days he was recaptured and returned to Heuberg and put in solitary confinement for thirty-one days. His fourth attempt was successful. With the aid of a friend he made it to the Swiss border, where he was directed to the Swiss military police who saw that he was taken to Berne and finally Paris.

Thomas Buffern from New York City, another aviator POW, joined the service and drove an ambulance for several months in Macedonia. He put in for the flying service and was accepted on June 15, 1918. He flew his share of patrols until May 6, 1918, when he was shot down behind enemy lines, only two kilometers from the front line. For weeks he was thought to be dead. Actually, he was interned at Trausnitz Castle at Landshut, Bavaria, where there were other American aviators. On one occasion he and several other POWs escaped from the fortress but were captured at the Austrian border fourteen days later.

Louis Leslie Byers of Philadelphia was shot down about July 18, 1918, near Marquises and confined in prison until the armistice.

Louis Charton, who was born in France and later became an American citizen, enlisted in the Foreign Legion in February 1917. He transferred to aviation and on February 10, 1917, after only two weeks of flying time, was shot down. He became very ill in prison camp and was subsequently interned in Switzerland until the end of the war.

Thomas Hitchcock was forced to the ground in German territory, wounded, placed in a German hospital, and later confined at a prison camp in Lechfeld. When Hitchcock, Herschel McKee, and Herman Whitmore were to be transferred to another camp, their planned escape was foiled. They did not give up but gave their food and maps to other prisoners. Once aboard their trains they asked many questions of their guard and even secured a guide to the area through which they were riding. Hitchcock studied the map carefully for bridges, rivers, and towns in the area about twenty miles from the Swiss border. The nearest point to the border was Brix. The guard became sleepy and a few stations later they made their break. Only Hitchcock was successful; McKee and Whitmore had to wait until after the armistice to be released.

American Walter Shaffe of Pennsylvania was shot down behind enemy lines.

Clarence Shoninger of New York City crashed and was believed dead, but it was learned that he was a POW. He also was released after the armistice.

Alan Winslow of Illinois, one of America's first great air heroes, was one of the fliers to regain his freedom. But one of his arms was amputated above the elbow in a German hospital. Jimmy Bach also returned from captivity.

Thirty-eight Americans served with the Lafayette Escadrille. Eight were killed in action. Two of the most famous aviators were Jimmy Doolittle of New York, who became a hero in the air during World War II, and Eddie Rickenbacker. Neither had to suffer time as a POW. Thus the aviators of World War I made quite a record for themselves.

Byron Farwell tells us that by the end of the war the 2d Division suffered the most killed (2,419) and most wounded (20,657), but captured the greatest number of the enemy (12,026). The 26th Division on the Western Front by the end of the war had engaged in seven major battles and took about 3,000 prisoners.[24]

Prisoners captured by combat patrols and as a result of aerial reconnaissance represented the main sources of intelligence information for both sides.[25] The Alabama soldiers of the 167th Infantry acquired a great deal of information, and Croix de Guerres were given to all members of a combat patrol that took two soldiers of the 77th Bavarian Infantry as prisoners.[26]

VARIOUS BATTLES

The Second Battle of the Marne on the Aisne River began on May 28 with the Ludendorf offensive. The first U.S. offensive operation of division strength in the war was at Belleau Wood and took 300 prisoners.

The battle of Cantigny, May 28–30, 1918, was the first division-size offensive action by the U.S. military in World War I and was its first victory. But more than that, it convinced the Allies of the Americans' ability to fight and persuaded them to keep the AEF intact and under Pershing's command, which he wanted from the beginning.

Two nights before the attack there was fear that American plans had been compromised. An engineer, Lieutenant Kendall, had moved forward with a work party. The men escaped, but not Kendall, who had maps on him. His grave was discovered in 1919 near Cantigny. What happened to him? Was he killed immediately or was he a POW before his death? These remain unanswered questions.

The Germans captured two Americans, but they were accidentally killed by American machine-gun fire; a German spy in an American uniform was also mistakenly killed. German soldiers captured in this sector provided valuable tactical information about their unit strength and positions from squad to company level.[27] During the battle, the 28th Infantry Regiment captured five German officers and 220 soldiers.[28] The costliest battle in the history of the U.S. Marine Corps was at Belleau Woods (eventually surpassed in the battle of Tarawa in November 1943).

On July 18–19, the 2d Division suffered largely in KIAs and wounded, but before relieved had captured 66 officers and 2,810 other men. It was on July 30 that Sergeant Joyce Kilmer was killed by a German sniper.

At the St. Mihiel offensive, September 2–6, 1918, many exhausted Germans surrendered. At Boullonville, Sergeant Harry Adams of the 89th Division followed a pair of Germans into a dugout. Firing his last two bullets, he demanded their surrender and to his amazement, 300 filed out, whom he brought to the rear. Coffman tell us that the sergeant turned the prisoners over to a French officer of an approaching infantry unit.[29] This incident of a large group of POWs preceded Sergeant York's capture of 132 POWs in the Argonne Forest on October 8, 1918. Private Clayton Slack captured ten prisoners, whom he marched back to an infantry unit he saw approaching and turned them over to their French officer. Between July 18 and November 11, the British seized about 385,000 POWs, of whom 188,000 were captured by the French and 44,000 by the Americans.[30]

THE WAR'S END

The Allies did not agree to repatriate German POWs until the end of the peace conference in June 1919. The last to release prisoners were the French, since they needed POWs for labor. Byron Farwell and Frederick Pierce's books give a wealth of information on prisoners as well as the war itself.

The peace conference opened in Paris on January 18, 1919, and on June 28, 1919, the Treaty of Versailles was signed by Germany and the Principal Allied Associated Powers. On September 1, 1919, the last American combat division departed from France. But on November 19, 1919, the U.S. Senate declined to sign the Versailles Treaty. The war was over, however, and the fighting had stopped. After the Versailles Treaty was finally signed, the stage was set for

World War II, the continuation of World War I as characterized by John Keegan.

NOTES

1. Herbert C. Fooks, *Prisoners of War* (Fredericksburg, Md.: Stowell, 1924).

2. Carl P. Dennett, *Prisoners of the Great War* (Boston: Houghton Mifflin, 1919).

3. John Keegan, *The First World War* (New York: Knopf, 1998), 3.

4. Keegan, *First World War,* 7–8.

5. Keegan, *First World War,* 9.

6. Cyril Falls, *The Great War* (New York: Putnam's, 1959), 259.

7. Martin Gilbert, *The First World War* (New York: Holt, 1994), 329.

8. Byron Farwell, *Over There: The United States in the Great War, 1917–1918* (New York: Norton, 1999), 53.

9. Farwell, *Over There,* 77.

10. Farwell, *Over There,* 107.

11. Farwell, *Over There,* 103.

12. Farwell, *Over There,* 114.

13. Dennett, *Prisoners,* 43.

14. Dennett, *Prisoners,* 176.

15. Dennett, *Prisoners,* 13.

16. Dennett, *Prisoners,* 13.

17. Dennett, *Prisoners,* 13–19.

18. Fooks, *Prisoners of War,* 97–98.

19. Clifford Milton Markle, *A Yankee Prisoner in Hunland* (New Haven: Yale University Press, 1922), 48.

20. Fooks, *Prisoners of War,* 4.

21. Fooks, *Prisoners of War,* 87–88.

22. Archibald Whitehouse, *Legion of the Lafayette* (Garden City, N.Y.: Doubleday, 1962), 293.

23. Whitehouse, *Legion of the Lafayette,* 297.

24. Farwell, *Over There,* 96.

25. Farwell, *Over There,* 114.

26. Farwell, *Over There*, 114.

27. Steven Light, "Doughboys' Mettle Forged at Cantigny," in "Battle of Cantigny," *Military History*, October 1993, 33.

28. "Doughboys'," 37.

29. Edward M. Coffman, *The War to End All Wars: The American Military Experience in World War I* (New York: Oxford University Press, 1968), 320.

30. Coffman, *War to End All Wars,* 259.

10

World War II: North Africa and Europe

As was the case with World War I, the United States did not enter World War II for a while. Consequently, many Germans and Italians were seized as prisoners of war by the Allies and Allied prisoners were captured by the enemy before the United States entered the war. The beginning hostilities in North Africa were the combined Afrika Korps under General Rommel and the Italians against the British forces. Italy's North African forces in 1940 were more numerous than the British, but Mussolini's troops were not aggressive. In August the offensive was initiated; the Germans had already marched into Poland in 1939 to start the war. The United States observed these developments without getting involved.

GENERAL ROMMEL

German troops landed in Africa under the leadership of General Rommel, and he began operations at the end of March 1941. Prime Minister Winston Churchill was determined to see Rommel defeated. What favored the British was the fact that the British navy ruled the Mediterranean from June 1940 to April 1941. The British captured 500 prisoners south of Sidi Barrani in early December 1940, and 20,000 POWs were later reported seized with their tanks, guns, and equipment.

At Sollum the Italians built a barbed wire enclosure to hold expected British prisoners, but ironically those interned there were Italian POWs. At the end of the first stage of the campaign, about 30,000 Italian POWs were captured. An Australian company captured Bardia and many Italians gave up because of lack of food and shelter, as well as simple exhaustion. Once the Italians surrendered, the Germans took over. The United States was still not involved.

Much of the failure of the Italians was their own fault. They proceeded too slowly and could not cope with the desert, which Alan Moorehead said beat them.[1] Rommel started digging in when he took over and prepared for what was to come. Churchill's hope was that British troops would eliminate Rommel, but certainly getting the United States into active participation would be an important advantage.[2] Then on December 7, 1941, the United States was attacked by Japan, and on December 11, 1941, both Germany and Italy declared war against the U.S. On the same day President Roosevelt asked Congress to declare war against these two nations.

The objective after North Africa was Sicily. Success in North Africa would pave the way to Sicily, but more importantly, according to Jackson, "the North African Campaign made Overlord possible."[3] In between North Africa and Overlord (the operational name for the Normandy invasion) would be many military operations involving battles, deaths, wounded, and the taking of POWs on both sides.

Operation Attila was the capture of North Africa. Operation Torch, under the leadership of General Patton, included three landings by different task forces in North Africa. Torch was strongly endorsed by Churchill and FDR. The invasion of Sicily was labeled Operation Husky, the invasion of Italy, Operation Avalanche, and the invasion of the Anzio beaches, thirty miles from Rome, Operation Shingle.

The Wehrmacht was the German army in World War II and the Afrika Korps was the branch under General Rommel that served in

North Africa. From it came the first German prisoners seized by the Allies and the American forces.

It might seem ironic, but a vast majority of these POWs were ultimately interned in the United States. Judith Gansberg's book was appropriately entitled *Stalag U.S.A.* Other prisoners would be interned in England, Canada, and even Ireland, a neutral nation.

OPERATION TORCH

Churchill's proposed Operation Torch did not win immediate approval from General Dwight Eisenhower and General George Marshall, but FDR approved it in July 1942. It did, however, give Eisenhower "what he wanted most, command of troops."[4] Torch was begun on November 8, with Major General Patton, as task force commander, taking a division and its supporting troops to Egypt. Three landings were made in the western center and eastern areas at Casablanca, Oran, and Algiers. The western task force consisted of Americans trained and organized by Patton. The U.S. Navy transported them to their destination. The other two forces were Anglo Americans whose transport would be supplied by the Royal Navy. Major General Fredendell commanded the army group of the center task force, and Major General Ryder was in charge of the assault force in the eastern sector.[5] Thus the Americans were active participants in the subsequent fighting and took a significant number of prisoners, as did the Germans.

In a February 26 offensive, General Von Arnum said he captured 25,000 Allied POWs, but he suffered more than 1,000 casualties. The last battle in which Rommel engaged had been costly for him, and his successor, General Von Arnum, also did not fare well. On March 9, Rommel left Africa and officially turned over his Afrika Korps to Von Arnum. Von Arnum himself was taken prisoner and sent to England. Finally he was interned with other German generals at Camp Clinton, Mississippi.

When Rommel captured Kasserine Pass, about 3,000 Americans were killed or wounded, and about 4,000 became POWs. But in reality this did not amount to much of a victory for General Rommel. By May, the Germans were forced into northeastern Tunisia and were abandoned by the Luftwaffe units that had hurriedly flown off to Sicily.

About two-thirds of the 238,000 POWs taken by Allied troops were Germans who had surrendered. After North Africa Rommel was involved in an Italian campaign and ultimately was assigned to building up the Atlantic wall described by Geoffrey Perret as "thousands of pillboxes and long rows of concrete teeth that snaked over the landscape for mile after mile across the approaches to the Reich."[6]

If Rommel had been captured in North Africa, he would have been quite a prize for the Allies and would not have been available for the assignments later given him by Hitler. He also might have been a survivor. With the problem of North Africa cleared away, the stage was set for Operation Husky and the tactics of George Patton. This military operation was accomplished by Patton's army and Montgomery's 8th Army.

General Patton's son-in-law, an army captain, was captured in North Africa. He was transported to Oflag 64 in Poland where toward the end of the war he was rescued by some of his father-in-law's troops. Many U.S. forces were wounded and killed in the operation, and Patton was severely criticized for what was considered a major tactical error on his part.

MAJOR JERRY SAGER

A group not mentioned much in connection with the North African campaign is the OSS (Office of Strategic Services, the predecessor of today's Central Intelligence Agency). A guerrilla unit under Major Jerry "Dapper" Sager led hit-and-run attacks against the Afrika

Korps. It consisted of Arabs and anti-Fascist Spanish refugees from their homeland after the bloody Spanish Civil War.[7] Major Sager was captured in March, thus terminating his operations against the enemy. He escaped but was later recaptured along with an American and a South African. He claimed to be a downed airman to give himself prisoner of war status and avoid being shot as a spy. He was flown to Italy and later to Stalag 111 in Germany reserved for Allied airmen. This stalag will be discussed later in the chapter. Sager maintained his pilot story and later escaped to the Soviet Union. In early 1945 he was repatriated to the United States. Thus he was a very fortunate OSS prisoner. He experienced success in his OSS career in early 1943 in the attempt for Trieste.[8] He was much more fortunate than other OSS agents, who were executed by the Germans in Europe and the Balkans.

The German Convention of 1929 defined POWs and excluded guerrillas, spies, and other irregular soldiers. OSS agents were well aware of this. Actually, the treatment of military prisoners was governed, at least on paper, for the first time in history by the Geneva Convention.[9] In World War I, neutral countries like Switzerland worked in conjunction with the International Committee of the Red Cross to assume informal responsibility in such matters.

OPERATION HUSKY

The objective of Operation Husky was to invade Sicily in the hope of knocking Italy out of the war. Allied planes attacked Sicilian ports on July 2 and an airfield on July 9, 1943. The final preinvasion bombing and airborne parachute and glider operations on Sicily took place on July 9, and the next day Husky's landings started. Palermo was captured on July 22, and on July 25 Mussolini's government fell and General Badoglio took over. From August 8 to August 11, the Germans evacuated Sicily, with Patton seizing San Fratello and Cesaro on August 8. Enemy casualties during the campaign of thirty-nine days numbered about 164,000, estimated as 32,000 Germans and 132,000 Italians, most of whom became POWs.[10]

Another type of evacuation that the Germans tried shortly after the Italians gave up was to seize trains of thousands of Allied POWs held in camps in northern Italy and send them to Germany. Many of these camps were surrounded before the POWs really knew what was happening, but about 10,000 of 75,000 British POWs successfully escaped. In Churchill's own words "mostly helped by the local population with civilian clothes, were guided to safety, thanks to risks taken by members of the Italian Resistance and simple people of the countryside."[11]

One group of escaped prisoners was led by Lieutenant-Colonel Denis Gibbs. These men marched 625 miles from the valley of the Po through mountainous country in Europe to a crossing over the Volturno River held by five divisions. The march was accomplished in fifty-three days, and Gibbs's diary describes many acts of kindness offered by local Italians.[12]

The novel *Von Ryan's Express,* which was made into a film featuring Frank Sinatra, describes an attempt by POWs originally held by the Italians to reach neutral territory on a stolen train. The author, David Westheimer, is someone who knew the railroad system in northern Italy. The novel shows British and American POWs being transported on a train going north to a prison camp in the interior of Germany. Under the American Colonel Ryan the men took control of the train and tried to get to the Swiss border. The author also wrote a personal memoir as a POW in an Italian camp. He had been a navigator aboard a plane that might have been the first bomber shot down attacking the Naples area in Italy and probably was the first ever shot down by an Italian fighter.

Westheimer was picked up in Naples Bay by Italian fishermen in a rowboat, and he and his comrades were held in a carboniere prison that was once a monastery outside the town of Poggio Martelo.[13] Next he was confined in a regular POW camp that was not in Germany. When his plane had been shot down on December 11, 1942, crew members were given uniforms marked with white paint and the letters P.G. for *prigioniere de guerre* on the left breast. The internment camp, Concentramento Prigionieri de Guerre, was about twenty-one miles east of Rome, some kilometers from Pescore on the Adriatic.[14]

AMERICAN POWS IN ITALY

Eventually all American POWs in Italy, numbering about 200, were interned at P.G. 21. The only exceptions were high-ranking officers, those in hospitals, and a few strays from other camps. When the Germans decided to move the POWs after Italy's collapse, they were packed into boxcars. Some escaped; some were recaptured in the hills. Several made it all the way home. A few disappeared and were never heard from again. After two days, the train reached Florence. Senior officers were not carefully guarded in the coaches, and some escaped. There was a brief stop at Bologne.

One officer wandered off and did not return, but Westheimer saw him thirty-six years later at a 98 Bomb Group reunion. He was a dentist in Atlanta. He had crossed the Pyrennes Mountains into Spain, accompanied by a guide and an escaping tank officer who had been in the same dormitory with the author at Rice Institute in 1937.

Westheimer jumped off the train at Balzano at the entrance to the Brenner Pass. He mingled with the soldiers during an air raid, but a German patrol captured him with some prisoners, and all of them were returned to the train station. A German officer informed him that if a soldier escaped, four POWs would be executed, ten if an officer escaped.

AMERICAN POWS IN GERMANY

The next stops were Innsbruck, Munich, and finally Stalag V11A as a temporary location until a permanent campsite was constructed at

Stalag 111. An army sergeant suggested that Westheimer not reveal his Jewish identity to play it safe. Hitler had decreed that Jewish American POWs be segregated for inclusion in Hitler's infamous Final Solution—death.

Stalag Luft 111 was located in Upper Silesia between Berlin and Breslau near the village of Sagan. Here the POWs played volleyball, grew gardens, and in some cases cooked for themselves. The camp was surrounded by high double barbed wire fences. It was situated in a carved out area of prime forest. It was not escape proof, however. Tunnels were built and from this stalag British POWs staged their successful Great Escape.

The men here had more control over their affairs than those in Italian or other German camps. They lived in small rooms and created a family atmosphere. There was a theater, and facilities were fairly good. For months Stalag Luft 111 was reserved for white personnel until it received its first African American officer, a P-51 pilot from the all-black 332d Fighter Group.

MINORITIES IN BATTLE

During World War II, a group of black pilots known as the Tuskegee Airmen demonstrated their ability and courage. As in the Civil War, when there was reluctance in the North to assign blacks to fighting units, this Tuskegee airmen group first had to fight against discrimination and segregation. The group saw sixty-six of their number killed and about thirty shot down and made POWs.[15] Another group that experienced difficulty in finding acceptance was the Nisei (second-generation Japanese American soldiers), who eventually distinguished themselves in battle in Italy and France.

The first Japanese blood was shed on September 29, and there were many more casualties in the Italian campaigns. Captain Saki Takahashe was known for taking about 175 POWs and probably killing the same number. Daniel Inouye lost an arm near the end of the war. Inouye later became famous as a distinguished senator from Hawaii. But full recognition of his and other Nisei's services was not given immediately.

DEFINITION OF TERMS

The Germans, building on their World War I experience, were well organized to receive Allied POWs. The German term Stalag was an abbreviated form for Stammlager—a permanent army camp for non-commissioned officers or enlisted men on a base from which labor detachments were sent out. An Oflag was a permanent officers camp and a Dalag was a transit camp. An airman's camp was a Luftlager or Luftwaffelager, and an airman's transit camp was a Dulag Luft, but all Luftwaffelager camps were known as Stalags. The American POW was a Kriegsgefanger, which the prisoners shortened to Kriegie.[16]

The Gestapo was Germany's secret police that interrogated prisoners when they were captured or recaptured. The Luftwaffe resented the Gestapo and jealously guarded its right to take charge of captured Allied POW airmen. When a prison camp was taken over by the Luftwaffe, conditions usually improved. Each camp was supposed to have one or more members of the Abwehr, the German military intelligence organization in World War II. Their primary duty was to question newly arrived POWs. But Heinrich Himmler was given complete charge of all POWs.[17] Foy states that "atrocities were committed by both sides during the war and that these massacres in particular were committed by a very small percentage of the German military forces."[18]

A very uncomfortable situation developed on August 26, 1944. Eight members of an American crew were shot down and captured near Hanover in northern Germany. Guarded by two German soldiers, the airmen boarded a train for a POW camp near Frankfurt am Main. Forced to halt because of a damaged truck, they were marched to a train on the other side of town. German civilians, including two women, yelled, "Beat them to death." A local naval official urged the civilians on and then emptied his gun into the prisoners, killing six. Two were hurt but managed to escape. They were recaptured by a German patrol and sent to a POW camp. This incident was kept quiet for some time. The two who had pledged silence broke it when a U.S. tribunal tried the perpetrators and sentenced seven civilians and the Nazi to death.

THE MALMEDY MASSACRE

Perhaps the greatest injustice was the Malmedy massacre of American POWs at the Baugnez crossroads in the Ardennes Forest in Belgium on December 17, 1944, the second day of fighting in the famous Battle of the Bulge. The killing was carried out by a German assault unit commanded by Colonel Joachim Peiper. He was a harsh, ruthless, and arrogant man who was on his way to fame for the Germans.[19] Very few Americans offered any resistance. A total of eighty-one soldiers were killed brutally. Eight soldiers were killed but not buried. Three survivors told the story to two newspapermen. The story, called the European Pearl Harbor, received maximum publicity. By late evening rumors of the shooting reached frontline divisions. One commanding officer reportedly said, "No krauts will be taken prisoners," and the noose was being fastened that night for Joachim Peiper. At his trial before the American military tribunal in Dachau in 1946, Colonel Peiper was sentenced to thirteen years in jail, and the Malmedy defendants were released on parole and then given probation. However, their movements were greatly restricted. Many Americans felt that justice was not served in this case.

OPERATION AVALANCHE

On August 15, Eisenhower outlined his plans for Avalanche, and September 9 was the date set for its beginning. The Salerno landings took place on September 9 as planned, with 1,078 killed, 1,561 wounded, and 589 missing, according to Sheppard.[20] While the Salerno battles were being fought, 600,000 Italians in the Balkans, Greece, and Crete gave up without resistance. Anyone willing to fight for the Germans would be accepted, but those not willing would become POWs for forced labor. Almost 500,000 Italian troops disappeared and Rommel's subordinate commanding officers rounded up 4,000 to be sent to Germany. Operations continued up the Italian peninsula, and on January 22 the VI Corps landed at Anzio. On June 4, Rome was captured.

THE OSS

As already noted, the OSS was active in early 1943 in North Africa until Major Sage was taken as a POW and managed a good cover story. Although his activities ended, those of the OSS did not. It secured some intelligence information for the Sicilian invasion; ironically, the Mafia provided intelligence information to Naval Intelligence.

In England, OSS teams of three—usually two officers and a radioman—received special training for missions in France to prepare for Operation Overlord. Others were getting ready for the invasions of Sicily and Italy and activities in Yugoslavia, Albania, and Greece. The idea behind all these efforts was to help train resistance efforts everywhere. The OSS soon realized it required its own trained navy and air force.[21] The later months of 1944 would be the decisive time for special missions and operations on a worldwide scale.[22] The created air force began to lose C-46s and consequently pilots found themselves picking up pilots and crew members forced to bail out of planes disabled in flight. Detachment 101 saved 25–35 percent of such airmen from becoming POWs. The era of air, land, and sea rescue helicopters had not yet arrived, although if it had, such missions might have been impossible because of the distance to the interior.

In Italy, on September 9, 1943, the invasion of Salerno, there was the McGregor Project. Captain Steven Rossetti was responsible for getting spies through enemy lines or from the inside of enemy lines back to friendly lines. He was accompanied by three Italian agents and was attacked by the Germans. The target was Naples, but they returned safely. The original plan was to contact an Italian officer of the chief of staff who had a brother in New York City and was available to help the OSS. A letter had been sent by an OSS team agent in Sicily who used as a courier an Italian POW who had surrendered to the Allies and was willing to perform the mission, which was in the POW's hometown. The so-called McGregor Project failed as well as the penetration of Italy during the difficult period between the Allied Sicily landings and Italy's secret surrender on September 2. Efficient communication was missing in this effort.[23]

Another task of the OSS was in the north and involved POWs. Many contacts had been made with thousands of escaped Allied POWs who regained their freedom when Italy surrendered. By winter these men were constantly relocating to avoid recapture by the Germans and Fascist mobile police.[24] It was the objective of the A Force of the OSS to collect these POWs and, with the help of guerrillas and the underground, get them out of Italy and into Switzerland where they would be interned in greater comfort.

Early in 1944, Colonel Florimund Duke, the head of the OSS Balkan desk in Washington, a forty-nine-year-old World War I pilot, volunteered for a dangerous mission with Major Alfred Suarez and Captain Guy Nunn. Suarez was a radio technician and veteran of the Spanish Civil War, and Nunn was a magazine writer who spoke fluent German and fairly good French.

Having passed a parachute-training course, Colonel Duke made the jump into Hungary in March and met no resistance. The men met too late, unfortunately, and accomplished nothing. On March 19 the three surrendered themselves as POWs with the cover story that they should have been dropped into Yugoslavia. They had simply parachuted into the wrong place. Getting rid of their money and radio, they gave themselves up to the Germans who, very suspicious of them, first moved them to a political prison in Vienna. The Germans threatened to execute them as spies, but they stuck to their cover story and insisted they were bona fide POWs since they were in uniform when captured and claimed protection under the Geneva Convention. After months of threats and intense interrogation, they were transferred to Colditz Castle. This infamous prison on the Mulde River between Leipzig and Dresden housed 350 Allied POWs, and the three Americans sat out the war there. Thus the OSS "sparrow mission" was a failure.

Most of the men imprisoned at Colditz had escaped from a lesser German prison. A naval lieutenant of the Fleet Air Arm who was a survivor of Malmedy had escaped from Stalag Luft III in the Great Escape of March 1944 and was recaptured and confined at Colditz.[25] Also at Colditz was Winston Churchill's nephew Giles Romilly. At first most POWs were from England and other European nations, but on the very last page of Reid's narrative he tells us that First Lieutenant John Winant of the U.S. Air Force arrived. Finally American POWs were joining the ranks of the Colditz internees.

There were two German officers who participated in a series of inspections and escaped from Allied authorities. One was Hauptmann, an airman who gave U.S. POW authorities much trouble and eventually escaped from Canada to the United States. The story is that he jumped from a train near the St. Lawrence River, stole a boat and crossed the river, and eventually reached the German consulate in New York. Later he was reported to have been shot down and killed somewhere on the Russian front.

LIEUTENANT JOHN KRIZAN

Another failed OSS mission was the Dawes mission. Its commander, Lieutenant Holt Green, and Lieutenant James Gaul were captured by the Germans and executed. OSS agent John Schwartz, alias U.S.

Army Lieutenant John Krizan, was more fortunate—he was released from a German prison camp in Vienna. Krizan had been interrogated by a Soviet NKVD officer with a Czech resistance fighter Maria Gubevico as interpreter just before release.[26] The former teacher, twenty-three years old, spoke fluent Czech, Russian, German, and Hungarian. She was closely associated with the underground and was later executed for her activities.

Krizan was captured after the "houseboat mission," and a week later he and his crew were transferred to Rasaucherlinder prison in Vienna rather than a POW camp. One day in February 1945, he was confronted with the pilot of his crew and immediately thought his cover had been blown. The pilot, however, claimed that Krizan was not in his drop. The Gestapo couldn't break Krizan down. The pilot was confronted with a slip of paper as evidence and charged as an OSS agent, but he claimed he didn't know what the OSS was and that he was expected to give the paper to a British officer.

Krizan and two American airmen were released as political prisoners on April 15, 1945. Krizan led the two to his underground contact and holed up with the other Americans until Vienna was captured by the Russians. He was returned to Bari by the USSR. Thus "another dead agent had come back to life."[27]

In 1944 the United States formally asked permission to deploy Americans on military missions to Czechoslovakia, Hungary, and Rumania to search for and repatriate downed airmen. It received the go-ahead and by the end of July 1944, Americans were flying into German-occupied Czechoslovakia to rescue downed crews gathered up by the partisans. The military mission was the official cover for the failing "Dawes," "houseboat," and "day" missions. The "Dawes mission," led by U.S. Navy Lieutenant Holt Green with Sergeant Joseph Horworth, a Slovak interpreter, and PFC Robert Brown, radio operator and aide to resistance in Slovakia, was to secure intelligence information. The purpose of "houseboat" was to get information also. Lieutenant Krigan, nom de guerre for a Czechoslovakian born in the United States, army Private John Schwartz, Lieutenant

Jerry Miren as a second agent, and navy radioman Specialist Charles Heller failed in their objective.

In Czechoslovakia in the summer of 1944, British Air Force teams gathered together a number of American airmen who had bailed out of their damaged planes and put them in Banaka Byatricee, a small city in the Slovakian mountains, and landed at an abandoned airfield.

On September 17, 1944, six OSS agents in American military uniforms got on three B-17s of the 15th Air Force Special Group at Bendise. The planes flew over the mountains and landed at an abandoned airfield and sixty men got off.[28] The number of Americans delivered was twenty-one POWs who escaped from prison camps.

THE EAGLE SQUADRON

Few American prisoners were caught in the early days of the war in France because there were no land battles. But quite a number of airmen were shot down and captured. In *Caged Eagles*, Vern Hougland writes that of 244 downed American fighter pilots and sixteen British officers who served in the three Eagle Squadrons, 108 lost their lives during the war. Forty-seven other Yankee Eagles became prisoners or evaded capture after coming down in enemy territory or were captured in neutral countries.[29] The first pilot to become a POW while still an Eagle Squadron member was William Hall of the 71st Squadron, who bailed out of his Hurricane near Lille, France, on July 7, 1941. A German doctor operated on his legs in the village of St. Omer. As the year progressed, three more men of the 71st Squadron became POWs. Bill Geiger was shot down off Dunkirk on September 17, 1941. He was picked up from his dinghy by Germans in the English Channel. On arriving at Dulag Luft, he was questioned at the Luftwaffe Intelligence Center at Frankfurt. Someone came to talk to him, but he was really an interrogator. Geiger was soon joined by another Eagle—Gilmore "Denny" Daniel, an Osage Indian from Oklahoma.[30]

Daniel was probably the youngest pilot to be shot down by Germans in World War II. He parachuted into the Dover Strait about five miles off the English coast on October 13, 1941, and then drifted in his dinghy about seventy-eight hours. He washed ashore in France and was taken by the Germans to a hospital at St. Omer where Hall had been a patient, and from which Douglas Bader (a British wing commander, a legless fighter pilot) had escaped. Daniel was transferred for interrogation purposes and placed with Geiger and Bill Nichols. At this time America was not yet at war with Germany.

One Eagle found himself interned in neutral Ireland—Roland E. "Bud" Wolf of Nebraska. His engine had quit on him and he landed in County Donegal. Later he was moved to an internment camp in County Kildare. There were no Americans there—only English, Canadians, Free French, Poles, and a New Zealander.[31] Adjacent to his camp was a German POW camp, but he saw little of the German POWs. Wolf escaped seven times during his twenty-two months there, but each time he was recaptured. His eighth attempt was successful. Ireland was not particularly sympathetic to the British war effort but remained neutral.

The first of the Eagle Squadron fighter pilots to be shot down by the Germans and escape successfully and return to his old unit was Oscar Cohen from Illinois.

In 1942 the Eagle Squadron was on its way to join the war effort in North Africa. Bix Bicksler of Ohio transferred to one of the desert American squadrons. Cliff Thorpe was shot down on September 15, 1942, and became a POW. The year 1942 brought a change of prison locations. Danny Daniel said that in January 1942, POWs were moved to Oflag IXA, Spangensberg castle, near the town of Kassel, for a few weeks, and then to Stalag Luft III at Sagan, later to Oflag XXIB at Schubun, a Polish village. There he joined another Eagle POW, Nat Marunz. He was interned there for a year and then sent back to Stalag Luft III. More Eagle Squadron pilots joined the ranks of the POWs. Casey Jones was at Sagan; Jackson Barrett "Barry" Mahan was shot down and drifted ashore where he was seized by the

Germans. He was the first American POW to become friendly with the Luftwaffe pilots, who took him to Paris and left him in a truck with a guard while they toured the cabarets. Fearful of the SS in Paris, they kept returning to the truck to give their prisoner champagne. Mahan ultimately was taken to Frankfurt for special interrogation.

The usual phony Red Cross form seeking information of a military nature was given to him. He was then sent to Stalag Luft III. From Hall's point of view, Stalag IXA had been a good POW camp.

On September 29, 1942, the Eagles were officially transferred from the RAF to the U.S. Army Air Force. Thus the only status change was that, if captured, the POWs were Americans.

Charles Cook of the 133 Squadron, a Californian and veteran Eagle, did not return from a mission on September 26, 1942. At 6:15 P.M. he was shot down near Brest, France, and became another candidate for Stalag Luft III. Also shot down near Brest was Robert E. Smith who, with the help of the French underground, got to a safe home in Toulouse where he met another Eagle. Both successfully reached the Spanish border.[32]

The Eagles were growing in numbers and in September 1943 were changed from the north compound to the new south compound. In June 1942 Charles Cook became the senior ranking officer. On March 24, 1944, news spread that eighty officers had escaped by a tunnel from the north compound (the Great Escape). Seventy-three were recaptured and escaped execution only due to fear of reprisals on American-held German POWs.

The year 1944 witnessed the single largest annual tally of Eagle POWs. Some were confined at Stalag Luft I at Barth near the Baltic sea 225 miles northwest of Sagan.

Robert Patterson's plane was hit on October 8, 1943, near the Dutch town of Onstusdde west of the German border. He was taken to Oflag Luft I in Frankfurt and then to Barth and finally joined later by Paul "Duke" Ellington of Oklahoma. The last Eagle captured in 1944 was Don Smith, the last Eagles to enter Stalag Luft III. The war was coming to an end in 1945 and the Sagan camp buzzed with rumors of a big move. Allied bombers were doing their job and the five camps with 2,000 in each dispersed their captives in Moosbug, Nurenberg, and Tienthorst, where they eagerly awaited their forthcoming liberation.

THE STALAGS

The stay in stalags was not a waste of time for some. Nicholas Katzenbach improved himself as a POW. As a navigator interned at Stalag Luft III, he set up a library with books supplied by the YMCA. He did a tremendous amount of reading and enabled others to do the same. Later he became attorney general of the United States.[33] Other stalags developed libraries and at many bases trades and languages were taught that would profit the POWs when they were repatriated.

At Stalag Luft I, Colonel Henry Spicer became known as the "Patrick Henry" of that stalag. His protests against German treatment made him very unpopular, and he was placed in solitary confinement under penalty of death until April 30, 1945. Stalag Luft I was reserved for air force officers until the Battle of the Bulge. One characteristic of this stalag was the segregation of Jewish Americans. The actual decision was made by the ranking senior Allied officer, according to First Lieutenant Sam Kalmas writing a letter in response to an article by Mitchell Bard in *Harbor Watch* (January 29, 2000). Kalmas stated that prior to the order for desegregation, many Jews attended High Holy Day services "right under the Nazis' noses." The tent in which the services were held was made available by Father Michael Carlton, a Roman Catholic priest and a British captain. This was done with the approval of the Nazis.

Another writer whose letter appeared in *Harbor Watch* on January 28, 2000, was a POW for over fifteen months at Stalag Luft I in Barth, Germany. His last days of being a POW were filled with apprehension because of Hitler's war against the Jews, but fortunately the Russians freed him and his fellow prisoners and shortly afterward they were flown out from a captured airfield by B-17s to Paris. General Eisenhower was responsible for the flight.

Another chaplain during World War II, assigned to the Rainbow Division, was captured during the Battle of the Bulge and was interned for several months in Stalag 12, where he said Mass every day. On March 31, he and the others were freed by American soldiers. Colonel Delmer Spivey entered Stalag Luft III in late July 1943, and with the aid of three lieutenants he appointed as historians, kept an accurate log of activities there. He devised a simple code and kept the notes well hidden until late January 1945, when the camp was evacuated and the notes retrieved.

Receptions given downed pilots varied, depending on the stage of the war and the attitude of the people who captured and had access to them.[34] Airmen always had a fear about what might happen to them if they landed or crashed near one of the targets just attacked.

One American chaplain was captured and brought to a camp that contained several hundred Americans. The German officer said in good English, "Chaplain, we have heard about you from Colonel Schmidt. We heard what you did for the wounded German prisoners who were in your hands. That is the most Christ-like act that I have ever heard of. Colonel Schmidt said that you were to have whatever you want. What do you want?"

Some German officers were appreciative and generous. The chaplain walked freely among the prisoners and took care of their needs, but when the time came to be taken to Sfax on the coast, he did not get the same consideration and was treated just like the other prisoners.

Captain Roland Sargent claimed he was an American flying officer after being shot down and taken prisoner. Having no ID, he was in real trouble. He was in Fresnes prison, which was also Gestapo headquarters. They called him a spy and the next day put him in a cell with two Americans. They were given little food. Then a fourth officer joined them, First Lieutenant David Whitehead, shot down with a British unit as an observer. He wasn't trusted and finally admitted he was an American paracommando captured on a sabotage mission in civilian clothing. There was talk in the prison that his comrades were being tortured.

One day Sargent was taken out and brought to an officer in a Luftwaffe uniform. He said he was trying to locate a certain Allied officer reported MIA after air raids over Europe. Sargent had to give his name, rank, and serial number but no other information. If he couldn't convince his interrogator, he would be at the mercy of the Gestapo. He was put on a train to Frankfurt and the main interrogation center located nearby. At last Sargent's mission was really over.

Tail gunner Alexander MacArthur received a letter from his brother in the Pacific. The Gestapo accepted him as a downed airman and sent him to the Luftwaffe interrogation center in Verona, Italy. Finally he was transferred to Stalag Luft III. Verona was only a branch office of Stalag Luft.

Persons who appeared to have valuable information and could not be isolated in solitary confinement were usually sent to the snake pit, a one-story building used as a station. Colonel Spivey experienced this. Fortunately, POWs sent there spent only a few days before being sent to the interrogation center.[35]

Its most prominent feature was called the cooler. There were 240 such confinement cells where prisoners received little food and were constantly harassed. "It was demoralizing that the Germans would often cite the prisoner's unit number, the location of the unit, the name of the commander or other notable personnel, the types of aircraft it possessed, the missions it had undertaken, possibly some of the missions planned for it, and a seemingly infinite list of other details that left the prisoner astonished and convinced that the Germans did in fact know everything they wanted to know."[36]

A similar incident was related by an air force pilot, a major, an instructor in the Fordham College Air Force ROTC unit. He and his crewmen were shot down over France and taken prisoner. The major gave only name, rank, and serial number when questioned. He was taken away and two days later summoned back by the same interrogator, who told the major his unit and the base from which he had flown in England. He knew that the major was married and was from Georgia and other personal information about him that could only be known by neighbors back in Georgia. The major tried to show no emotion or surprise but admitted to me and other students that he was astounded that the Germans could secure such information. A motion picture that showed how German intelligence officers pieced together bits of information from combat crews was *Target Unknown,* featuring Cornel Wilde.

Colonel Spivey was surprised by what his interrogator knew about him. Spivey was told about his mission objectives, which not even the crew knew about, and also was told the birthdates of his wife and child. There is no record showing that POWs knowingly revealed military secrets.[37] What happened at Dulag to POWs was only one of the elements that bonded POWs in Stalag Luft III.

When Brigadier General Arthur Vanaman was shot down and captured, he was the highest-ranking American officer in captivity. Later he assumed the role of senior ranking officer at Stalag Luft III.[38] At first Vanaman did not want to be assigned to a special camp near Dresden for generals and other VIP POWs. He was sent to the Air Ministry in Berlin, where he met someone he knew and then was sent to an air force prison camp, where he arrived in August 1944. His decision would ultimately prove profitable as his rank would be important to the safety and welfare of the prisoners.[39]

The Germans had much to gain through leniency because large numbers of their soldiers were POWs in the West, and German prisoners usually were well treated. As long as POWs on both sides didn't try to escape or cause trouble, privileges were given and restrictions relaxed, especially for the Germans. The treatment given German POWs in internment camps in the United States was very good.

Both General Vanaman and Colonel Spivey encouraged men to attend church services. This seemed to revive some religious feeling among POWs and fostered religious experiences as it did later in Vietnam. Robinson Risner, in *The Passing of the Night: Seven Years as a Prisoner of North Vietnam,*[40] noted the same effect religious services had on prisoners in Hanoi. The men had no chaplains and had to provide their own services. Colonel Spivey noted that one priest spoke to the east, center, and north compounds. Interestingly, when the Russians were approaching at the end of the conflict, the Germans tried to be nice to POWs. Vanaman and Spivey were smuggled into Switzerland, and liberation was on the way for the rest. Reunions were held every five years for Stalag Luft III, and in 1965, some of their German captors were invited to the reunion. General Spivey credited the Luftwaffe with good treatment afforded POWs, and most Stalag III POWs agreed.

Foy's book *For You the War Is Over* includes a list of all prison camps.[41] It is broken down into POW camps, camps for airmen, officers camps, civilian internee camps, and hospitals. The nearest town to each is mentioned. The table presented by Foy was based on information acquired in December 31, 1944, and was published by the American National Red Cross. Almost eighty locations were spread out in Denmark, Netherlands, Austria, Germany, Poland, Czechoslovakia, Hungary, Yugoslavia, and East Prussia. The estimated number of American POWs as of different specified dates is given on page 64. Most of the American POWs taken at Normandy (Operation Overlord, which was to drive toward Germany and end the conflict) were sent to Stalag XII-A at Limburg, east of the Rhine. Operation Overlord raised the morale of POWs.

An interesting sidelight on POWs concerns an Irish monsignor, Hugh O'Flaherty, leader of a network in Vatican City that helped POWs. The network aided almost 4,000 and prevented them from becoming POWs—among them, 1,695 British, 429 Russians, 185 Americans, and 22 from other countries.[42] A motion picture was made about this program and O'Flaherty was played by Gregory Peck. The aftermath of the Normandy landings in June 1944 naturally brought more prisoners to both sides as well as many wounded and deaths.

CAPTURES AND SURRENDERS

At Utah Beach, Lieutenant Richard Winters captured six German soldiers and later twelve more; Lieutenant Rebarchek with his men took some Germans not able to fight. Captain George Moby killed some Germans who resisted and captured others who surrendered. Then troops were sent into a flooded area where more Germans surrendered without resistance. Captain L. Johnson led a patrol of paratroopers down a causeway to a beach and saw a number of German soldiers waving a white flag. They were older men and not good soldiers. About fifty of them were enclosed within barbed wire fencing. Sergeant Harrison Summers, with fifteen men, was sent to capture a barracks of soldiers whom he turned over to his men.

At Omaha Beach, Sergeant Lewis took five prisoners. At Pointe-de-Hoc, the Rangers had a tough time making contact with each other, and both sides took prisoners. The British at Sword Beach had many POWs. Reportedly, the Northwind offensive was a failure in a Rhineland battle. The Germans never got near Strasbourg; there were casualties on both sides and the 7th Army processed 5,985 German POWs. On February 9, Chaplain Father Donald Murphy noted in his diary that a GI outpost let its soldiers fall asleep, and all were captured by the Germans, including two lieutenants. All these prisoner seizures were reported, and while they seem to represent small numbers, the numbers increased rapidly as the Allies marched toward Germany. After mid-April, some 325,000 troops plus 30 generals in the Ruhr pocket surrendered.

One unbelievable incident concerned Captain John Cobb of the 82d Airborne on the day the Ruhr pocket surrendered. He was in charge of a temporary prisoner compound when a German ranking officer requested to see him and asked to be allowed to join the

United States with volunteers when a war against Russia began. The prisoner was quite surprised to learn that Americans had no such intentions toward Russia.[43]

Almost half a million German POWs were distributed throughout the United States in 511 POW camps. Life in different camps was not the same, but essentially the treatment was good and certainly much better than it was in German camps. There was no equivalent of the Gestapo's browbeating of prisoners. A point that Arnold Krammer makes at the outset of his book is that not all German POWs were Nazis and thus it was necessary to separate the Nazis from the non-Nazis.

German officers were not required to work and often would wander freely within fifty miles of the camps in some areas. There were plots to escape by officers and enlisted men, but their main problem was being thousands of miles from their homeland. The nearest countries to which they could flee were Mexico in the south and Canada to the north, which also held POWs.

Almost all who escaped were captured and returned to military authorities, often by local people and one or more civilians. Only one, by the name of Gaertner, remained unaccounted for in October 1984. In that month and year someone called Krammer—whose book had been published in 1979—and praised his accuracy in writing about conditions in a POW camp. Krammer immediately knew he was talking to an ex-POW. The caller identified himself as a former POW in New Mexico, the last German fugitive to escape from Camp Denning in September 1945. He had been on the run for almost forty years. Krammer immediately addressed him as Mr. Gaertner who laughed and said, "Hello, Professor Krammer." The public was amazed when it learned about him.

A SURFEIT OF POWs

In May 1943, when the Afrika Korps was defeated, countless POWs were transported to the United States. The numbers greatly increased when German POWs from the Sicilian and Italian campaigns could not be adequately cared for by British camps. After September 1943, POWs were accepted from every battlefield in Europe, and these men were more fortunate than those confined in North Africa.[44] The War Department decided in late 1944 against taking any more POWs, but this was temporary and the final contingent of POWs—3,000—arrived May 13, 1945, a few days after V-E Day.

Initially Britain had been receiving large numbers of German and Italian POWs and tried to win U.S. cooperation, which was not forthcoming. Finally, in August 1942, a breakthrough was accomplished: the U.S. government reluctantly took 50,000. In North Africa, Montgomery and Patton were piling up POWs. The question was how many could the Americans take to alleviate the situation in England. One of the first problems was a lack of interpreters, so the only practical solution was to use English-speaking POWs to interpret and help run the camps. The lack of interpreters was caused to some extent by a prevailing attitude in the educational system not to teach Italian and German in high schools. Getting German teachers was particularly difficult. The two main ports of entry for ships with POWs were Camp Shanks, New York, and Norfolk, Virginia. Then the POWs were transported by train to various camps.

Krammer gives a diagram of the standard layout for a group of 5,000 as well as a map showing distribution of the major POW camps in the United States as of June 1944. The appendix lists forty of the forty-eight states that had prison camps. There were none listed in Montana, Nevada, North Dakota, and Vermont. The map shows a camp in Connecticut and New Hampshire, but perhaps they were not considered "major camps," and Minnesota and South Dakota were not listed on the map.

Different camps segregated officers and enlisted men, but officers were permitted to have enlisted men serve as their orderlies and aides-de-camp. Needless to say, these enlisted men fared much

better than others. One main exception was Camp Clinton, Mississippi, and a few others, to accommodate forty German generals
and three admirals held in the United States during the war.[45] One
reason advanced for this arrangement was the possibility that after
repatriation some might be the leaders of the new government.
German priests and ministers were granted some of the same privileges.[46] One general was a real prize, Jürgen von Arnum, Rommel's successor to the Afrika Korps.

POWs were permitted by article 43 of the Geneva Convention to
form an organization that provided them with spokespersons for
grievances and requests. They usually were the highest-ranking personnel, as in Allied POW camps. If there was good internal discipline, escapes and arrests were unlikely. In limited cases a parole
system was based on word of honor for the Germans.

There were, of course, exceptions. In one case, Private Clarence
Bertucci, a guard at Fort Douglas in Utah, went berserk and machine-
gunned eight German POWs in their sleep. The guard had twice been
given summary court-martials and sentenced to hard labor and also
had been in several hospitals. Poor judgment had been exercised in
employing him as a guard, but in considering the large number of
POW camps in the country (and there had been no precedent for
them), they were run quite well.

Many POWs were used as laborers in local businesses and on local farms. Pay received could be used in the camp PX. The quantity
and quality of food was good, educational programs became available, and sports and recreational facilities were also available. Many
educational programs served to help POWs after repatriation in post-
war jobs.

The POW labor program helped the status of industrial and farm
labor. The theme of Lewis and Mehwa's book—not just for World
War II but also previous wars—was on the use of German POWs in
the United States and how they alleviated labor shortages. In some
cases, they were not readily accepted by unions, but difficulties were
ultimately worked out.

ESCAPEES

The most interesting part of Krammer's book discusses the subject of escapes. Because camps were located in isolated areas, there weren't many mass escapes. Giving POWs good conditions and the right to control themselves did help the situation, of course. The real problem after escape was "no place to go,"[47] the aforementioned POW, who was never caught, being a real rarity.

The earliest recorded escape, November 5, 1942, involved POWs on the way from Cincinnati, Ohio, to Tennessee; they were caught two days later.[48] Submarine officers were usually efficient and quick thinking. While a demonstration was taking place, twenty-five escaped through a 250-foot tunnel.[49] Ironically, the name of the camp commandant was Colonel William Holden (the actor William Holden played an important role in the film *Stalag 17*). The submariners' escape was called the "Papago Park escape." Three U-boat captains led the escape and managed to get 130 miles to the Mexican border and 40 miles into the interior before they were recaptured by Mexican authorities and returned to the camp at Fort Ord, California. An escape of 500 Germans had been foiled.

POWs never lost the desire to escape. Major Tilmer Kuo was transferred to Alva, Oklahoma, a site reserved for difficult cases. About 65 percent of the escapees were successful "getting through, under, or over the stockade fence."[50] Shooting them was always a last resort. By the end of the war, fifty-six men had put their lives on the line trying to escape and were shot.[51]

Three German submariners in Tennessee were drawing water from a pump and were ordered "to git" by a mountain woman who then shot one of them. She expressed horror and sorrow when informed of their identity and commented, "I thought they wuz Yankees."

How were escape attempts punished? Article 45 of the Geneva Convention did not permit collective punishment, which the Japanese often employed. Extra work and confinement were allowed. General treatment was motivated by the hope that the same courtesies would be granted to the more than 90,000 American POWs in German hands. As already mentioned, the higher-up Germans, thought to be the possible leaders of the new German government, were treated better. Ultimately, many German POWs, like the Hessians in the Revolutionary War, did not desire repatriation. The difference was that our government didn't demand repatriation in the Revolutionary War, but now it had to. Perhaps the last line of Krammer's book expressed the feeling best. A Houston reporter said to a former POW in Texas, a one-time Afrika Korps corporal, "You must have had it pretty easy." The comment made by the POW was "I'll tell you, pal, if there is ever another war, get on the side that isn't American, then get captured by the Americans—you'll have it made."

ITALIAN POWs

So far German POWs and American POWs have been discussed. What about Italian prisoners? More than 53,000 Italian POWs were confined in the United States. POWs who complained were given their special national foods, so they were treated as well as the Germans. Fort Missoula in western Montana housed many Italians. About 1,600 Italian nationals were interned at Fort Missoula, and many of them had sons in the armed forces of the United States. Once the Italians arrived at Missoula, they divided along generational lines with the older, longtime residents becoming very bitter. The younger men were largely sailors taken in American ports in the spring of 1941 who saw Missoula as a pleasant and safe place to sit out the war. They called the area Bella Vista. Many of the internees were former musicians, singers, and dancers removed from a cruise ship captured in the Panama Canal Zone.

Many internees, however, were civilians who were labeled "enemy aliens." When President Roosevelt signed an executive order, it affected not only Japanese on the West Coast but also many Italians, putting them out of work. Many Italian fishermen were put out of work among others, and many had to relocate on their own. In addition, 264 Italian soldiers had been captured in North Africa, Sicily, and Italy.

In March 1941, Italian ships in American ports remained there, having been seized by our government. The men aboard were transported to Ellis Island and the Italian media here called foul. America was not yet at war with Italy.

Twenty of twenty-eight ships were sabotaged by their crews. Two hundred Italians were charged and about a thousand were confined at Ellis Island. Later, in May 1941, many were sent to Fort Missoula in Montana. Bart Benedetti wrote a book about conditions there, which were not bad.

There were workers of all kinds among them and they used their talents well. They had barbers, carpenters, laborers, and they built their own barracks. No one was ever missing; they felt at home making their own food. The only trouble ever encountered with them concerned food—they rejected a good amount of beef, preferring their own cooking oil.

There was plenty of time for recreational purposes—playing bocci and soccer. One ship had excellent cooks and there were waiters, cooks, and other workers taken from their jobs at the New York World's Fair.

The Italians had good relations with their captors. The main problems were boredom and anxiety about their families. Unfortunately there were three suicides. Some were paroled and allowed to work outside as chefs and housekeepers. As the war raged on, some joined the U.S. military through the draft or enlistment to become citizens. How many finally settled in the country is not known.

In March 1941, FDR faced the problem of aliens and what to do about them. Italian Americans on the West Coast suffered the most; many were California fishermen. Included in this group was the father of the baseball player Joe DiMaggio. Many were taken from their homes and jobs. Civil rights for them were denied. This was largely due to executive order 9006. General DeWitt started the movement for such an order. For this he was sometimes called General Dim Wit. It even got to the point that posters were used to discourage people from speaking Italian.

The real hero who emerged from this fiasco was Attorney General Francis Biddle, who fought the government on this issue. Finally Italians were no longer considered enemies.

Classic examples of injustice included Enzio Pinza and a famous Italian professor. Pinza was confined at Ellis Island without formal charges but later released. The Italian professor from San Antonio, Texas, was arrested but later released and sent to teach Italian to high-ranking military officials at Stanford.

In 1983 governmental archival information was found that revealed that the Italians and Japanese had been confined for racial, not military reasons. In November 1999, Representatives Eliot Engle and Rick Lazio fought to publicize this information and champion the cause for these people. The measures taken by the U.S. government represented a blot on its record and had no constitutional basis.

NOTES

1. Alan Moorehead, *The March to Tunisia: The North African War, 1940–1943* (New York: Harper & Row, 1967).

2. I.S.O. Playfair, *The Mediterranean and the Middle East,* vol. 3, *September 1941 to September 1942* (London: Her Majesty's Stationery Office, 1960), 373.

3. W. G. F. Jackson, *The Battle for Italy* (New York: Harper & Row, 1967), 1.

4. Geoffrey Perret, *A Country Made by War* (New York: Random House, 1989), 384.

5. Jackson, *Battle for Italy,* 276.

6. Perret, *Country Made by War*, 415.

7. Edward Hymoff, *The OSS in World War II* (New York: Ballantine, 1972), 101.

8. Hymoff, *OSS in World War II*, 101.

9. Ronald H. Bailey, *Prisoners of War* (Alexandria, Va.: Time and Life Books, 1981), 9.

10. G. A. Sheppard, *The Italian Campaign, 1943–1945* (New York: Praeger, 1968), 139.

11. Sir Winston Churchill, *The Second World War*, 6 vols. (London: Cassell, 1948–1953), 5:167, 139.

12. D. L. A. Gibbs, *Apennine Journey* (Gale & Polden).

13. David Westheimer, *Sitting It Out: A World War II POW Memoir* (Houston: Rice University Press, 1992), 32.

14. Westheimer, *Sitting It Out,* 43.

15. Christine Coleman, *Black History Month,* February 24, 2000.

16. David A. Foy, *For You the War Is Over* (New York: Stein & Day, 1984).

17. Foy, *For You the War Is Over,* 27.

18. Foy, *For You the War Is Over,* 230.

19. Charles Whiting, *Massacre at Malmedy* (New York: Stein & Day, 1971), 23.

20. Sheppard, *Italian Campaign.*

21. Hymoff, *OSS in World War II*, 114.

22. Hymoff, *OSS in World War II*, 145.

23. Hymoff, *OSS In World War II*, 168.

24. Hymoff, *OSS in World War II*, 178–79.

25. P. R. Reid, *The Colditz Story* (Philadelphia: Lippincott, 1953), 37.

26. Hymoff, *OSS in World War II*, 183.

27. Hymoff, *OSS in World War II,* 227.

28. Hymoff, *OSS in World War II,* 186.

29. Vern Hougland, *Caged Eagles* (Blue Ridge Summit, Pa.: Tab Aero, 1992), 1.

30. Hougland, *Caged Eagles,* 22.

31. Hougland, *Caged Eagles,* 23.

32. Hougland, *Caged Eagles,* 95.

33. Bailey, *Prisoners of War*, 24.

34. Arthur A. Durand, *Stalag Luft III* (Baton Rouge: Louisiana State University Press, 1988), 53.

35. Durand, *Stalag Luft III,* 61.

36. Durand, *Stalag Luft III*, 67.

37. Durand, *Stalag Luft III*, 70.

38. Durand, *Stalag Luft III*, 71.

39. Durand, *Stalag Luft III*, 124.

40. Robinson Risner, *The Passing of the Night: Seven Years as a Prisoner of North Vietnam* (New York: Random House, 1973).

41. Foy, *For You the War Is Over,* 62–63.

42. Bailey, *Prisoners of War*, 80.

43. Stephen Ambrose, *The Victors: Eisenhower and His Boys: The Men of World War II* (New York: Simon & Schuster, 1998), 338.

44. Judith Gansberg, *Stalag U.S.A.* (New York: Crowell, 1971), 12.

45. Arnold Krammer, *Nazi Prisoners of War in America* (New York: Stein & Day, 1979, 33.

46. Krammer, *Nazi Prisoners of War*, 34.

47. Krammer, *Nazi Prisoners of War*, 115.

48. Krammer, *Nazi Prisoners of War*, 116.

49. Krammer, *Nazi Prisoners of War*, 119.

50. Krammer, *Nazi Prisoners of War*, 120.

51. Krammer, *Nazi Prisoners of War*, 126.

World War II: The Pacific Theater

The Japanese attack on Pearl Harbor surprised citizens and many government officials, but some have always said that it was no surprise to military authorities and high-ranking government leaders: something was on the verge of happening. Renowned historian John Toland revealed in his book *Infamy* (1982) new evidence that by December 4, FDR and some of his advisers had intelligence that Japanese carriers were on the way to Hawaii. The burning question was, Did FDR really know about the oncoming conflict? Toland ultimately said, "In any case, the Pearl Harbor disaster was not simply the result of American errors of omission and commission."[1]

Despite this ongoing controversy among historians, the fact remains that Japan attacked the United States, which was not militarily prepared for this tragic moment. The Japanese found easy targets because Major General Lewis Brereton's seventy P-40 fighters were on the field with the B-17s. These planes and the navy ships in the harbor were destroyed. The title of the book, *At Dawn We Slept,* is appropriate.

THE INFLUENCE OF JAPANESE CULTURE

Japan's culture was quite different from that of the Germans, and this difference had a great effect on relationships concerning prisoners of war. Many Japanese died who could have surrendered and lived. Unfortunately they had no real choice because of the pressures imposed on them by their culture and their military leaders. Suicide was the proper alternative for them rather than surrender. This was a part of their honor and being. Consequently, Americans did not take many prisoners. The Japanese thought it was shameful for prisoners to surrender, and Japanese soldiers inflicted barbaric tortures on American (and other Allied) prisoners.

Japanese soldiers, much like the black soldiers of the Civil War, fought to the death, but with different motivation. Black soldiers did not want to commit suicide but feared what might happen to them if captured by Confederates. On the part of the Japanese, the war was a *War without Mercy*, the title of a book by John W. Dower. The common observation of Western war correspondents was that fighting in the Pacific was more atrocious than fighting in the European theater of operations.[2]

Another main problem was that obtaining information from Japan about U.S. POWs was difficult, whereas it was more readily obtained from the Germans. Moreover, Japanese internment camps were not administered as well as German camps, and in the final analysis, the Geneva Convention meant nothing at all to the Japanese.

History had seen the development of issues about POWs from Professor Leiber's "Instructions for the Government of Armies of the United States in the Field, our Civil War," the 1874 Brussels Declaration concerning the Laws and Customs of War on Land, the Hague Peace Conference in 1907, and the Fourth Hague Convention in 1907. This last remained in operation until the Geneva Prisoner of War Convention in 1929, which was the relevant convention on POW treatment in World War II. Some revision resulted from World War II experiences, but there has always been the problem of how to enforce such measures. The Japanese, and subsequently the North Korean and North Vietnamese Communists, and Saddam Hussein's government, did not pay serious attention to international directives.

Thus at the very beginning of hostilities with Japan, there were extreme difficulties. The Americans generally followed the directives, but the Japanese did not.

ENSIGN KAZUO SAKAMAKI

The very first POW taken by American forces in the Pacific was Ensign Kazuo Sakamaki, whose midget submarine was ten miles off the Pearl Harbor coast very early on December 7, 1941. There were four other subs as well, and their objective was to torpedo American destroyers or battleships.

The mission failed miserably. Sakamaki's gyroscope did not function properly and he hit a coral reef three times and was forced to surface. An American destroyer saw his sub and fired on him. He wasn't hit, but his sub was blasted off the reef and Sakamaki was rendered unconscious. Reviving, he tried to get his sub going, but it flooded and filled with smoke and fumes that again rendered him and his warrant officer unconscious.

Soon both woke up and Sakamaki, after opening the hatch and observing that they weren't far from the shore, made one more futile effort but grounded again on a coral reef. He ordered his warrant officer to abandon the sub, which he would try to blow up. He leaped into the water, but the sub failed to blow up. His warrant officer drowned and he himself fell unconscious on the beach, where the next morning he was found by an American soldier. Sakamaki was interrogated at Fort Shafter and sent to a POW camp in the United States.

Sakamaki died at eighty-one, but not before he had visited the Admiral Nimitz Museum in Fredericksburg, Texas, in 1991, where his minisub was on display. A fellow Japanese navy veteran commented that although Sakamaki wrote his memoirs and had them published in the United States, he had always maintained a low profile because he had a lot of feelings he could not put into words about his becoming the first Japanese POW at a time when falling into the hands of the enemy was shameful.[3]

A footnote appears in John Toland's book *The Rising Sun*[4] that refers to the activities of miniature submarines. Toland accounts for six times when minisubs were used by the Japanese: Pearl Harbor, the Sydney Harbor, Madagascar (May 31, 1942), west of the Mindanao Sea (January 5, 1942), and twice at Guadalcanal (November 23; October 7, 1942). All missions were failures. By the end of the war there were 230 minisubs, but none had seen any service and no damage was inflicted by them.

Two days after Pearl Harbor, on December 10, 1941, Guam fell, and the Japanese enjoyed a string of conquests. On December 21, General Wainwright had to start his defensive planning. On that night, Japanese troops landed in the Lingayen Gulf, located on the western coast of Luzon, and on December 22 their invasion began against an unprepared Philippine army.

GEOGRAPHY OF THE PHILIPPINE ISLANDS AND JAPAN

The Philippine archipelago comprises over 7,000 islands. Luzon is the northernmost and largest; the southernmost is Mindanao, which is also large. In between are located smaller islands, some of which are Negros, Ceo Boho, Leyte, Panay, Samar, and Mindoro. As the number of POWs increased rapidly, camps were situated on these islands. On the island of Luzon were Cabanatuan, Bilibud, O'Donnell, Los Baños, and San Tomas, all of which were Japanese prison camps and will be discussed later in this chapter.

The infamous Bataan Death March began on April 12, 1942. Brigadier General Edward King was the commanding officer on Bataan who had to surrender his forces to the enemy. This involved more than 10,000 American and 65,000 Filipino soldiers. Many died on their forced march to Camp O'Donnell. Another move for many POWs was to Cabanatuan. There were fewer than

1,000 survivors of the march.[5] One of those interviewed claimed he was captured and had not surrendered. Donald Knox's *Death March* describes many of the atrocities committed by the Japanese. When Japan surrendered in August 1945, 4,000 Bataan survivors were still alive.

Japan is also an island nation, consisting of Kyushu, Skiloku, Honshu, and Hokaido. Honshu is the largest island and has such cities as Tokyo, Hiroshima, Nagasaki, and Yokohama. All of these islands had Japanese prison camps. POW camps were also located in Korea, on the island of Formosa (now known as Taiwan, Republic of China), the mainland of China, and Manchuria.

General Wainwright had serious manpower problems when the Japanese invaded Luzon. The Philippine Scouts, the 26th Cavalry, represented his only trained group and thus he had to order this unit to prevent the Japanese from advancing beyond their beachhead. Colonel Clinton Pierce had the unenviable task of commanding this unit. He could see the invasion fleet and he started a delaying action, which he hoped would enable Wainwright to have more time to organize. Perret calls this "one of the finest delaying actions of the war."[6]

AMERICAN DEFEATS

The Japanese forces were outflanking the American soldiers, who finally had to fall back. Lieutenant General Homma was successful in his invasion of Luzon, and the Japanese were simply too much for American forces because of their numbers, naval firepower, and fighter planes, which strafed the American soldiers. Wainwright's men were defeated. For military reasons and to stop the killing of his men, Wainwright offered to surrender the fortified islands at the entrance to Manila Bay.

This meant that thousands of men in the army and navy became immediate prisoners of war with their existing stores and equipment, but the Japanese did not stop fighting. General Homma intended the complete destruction of all Americans and Filipinos. He wasn't satisfied with taking prisoners. Wainwright found it necessary to go to Homma rather than have Homma come to him. The threat was made that if all the troops in the north and south did not surrender, Wainwright would be forced to witness the shooting of ten American officers every day until there was a complete surrender. Wainwright himself was not recognized as an official prisoner of war until all opposition stopped. As soon as this happened, he would be considered a POW and he and his staff officers would be sent to a prison camp for senior officers at Tarlac.

At the Luzon force surrender by Major General King on April 9, 1942, almost 10,000 American troops became POWs, which was a record for American forces in a single engagement with a foreign enemy, and of this group 6,000 to 7,000 died as POWs.[7]

On March 11, 1942 General MacArthur was ordered by President Truman to leave Corregidor for Australia. Wainwright became the commander and the "fall guy." If MacArthur had been there, he might have become a POW. General Rommel was spared this in North Africa, when General Von Arnum took over there and became a POW.

MacArthur's leaving was bitterly resented by Brigadier General Brougher, who became a POW and said, "A foul trick of deception has been played on a large group of Americans by a Commander-in-Chief and small staff who are now eating steak and eggs in Australia, God damn them!"[8] Did Brougher know that President Truman had ordered MacArthur to go to Australia?

During the withdrawal in Luzon in December 1941, many small units of MacArthur's forces, which were proceeding to Bataan, became separated from their unit and this spared them from becoming POWs. They became the nucleus of guerrilla groups to fight in the Philippines and represented a powerful influence there. The commander of this group, called the USAFFE Guerrillas, was Lieutenant Colonel Byles Merrill.

Author E. Bartell Kerr relates individual instances of Americans captured by the Japanese elsewhere. December 1941 saw the first capture of Americans by Japanese in such places as China, Guam, and Wake Island. As a result of this, Tokyo saw fit to establish a prisoner of war bureau.

By December 8, early in the morning, two navy river gunboats, the USS *Wake* and the British HMS *Petrel*, were sailing on the Whangpoo River near the Shanghai waterfront. Both ships were ordered to surrender. The British ship was shelled and sank while the U.S. gunboat surrendered. Thus the first American POWs of World War II were seized and subsequently taken to a former Chinese hospital where they were interned with survivors of the British ship. All were treated well, although a few guards slapped some POWs, for which they were censured. That incident seemed to prevent future incidents. The men had to fill out certain forms stating that they would not escape, but everything else was done in conformity with principles of the Geneva Convention. The POWs held at the Shanghai Naval Prison Camp represented the few to be given good treatment.

At Peking and Tientsen there were 204 marines whose commanding officers had surrendered without offering resistance. The American Unit at Guam was defeated on December 10. Its governor, a U.S. Navy man, signed a surrender once he was assured that the rights of the navy people there would be guaranteed, and that all would be treated humanely. Marine John Podebesny was one of a group of forty Americans ordered to strip. He defied the order and was immediately bayoneted to death. Needless to say, those remaining complied and were sent with other persons to a nearby church for internment for a month.

On December 23, Wake Island was seized. The officers were placed in a building and well treated, but not so the enlisted men and civilians. As the Japanese resorted to ill treatment, the Swiss government got into the act to protect U.S. interests and especially POWs in Japan and territories occupied by Japan.

JAPANESE TREATMENT OF AMERICAN POWs

In the last week in December, General Tojo, prime minister and minister of war, assumed all responsibilities for POW camps. It took him a month to state whether the Japanese government would live up to the Geneva Convention, and subsequently he proved to be a callous, cruel, and unfeeling individual. Four hundred POWs started their journey to Japan and became the first POWs to reach the Japanese home islands. This destination was Shikoku.

The Japanese in charge of transporting the Wake Island POWs were ruthless. A notice was posted for benefit of the POWs, which cited the rules. Violating any rules would result in death. The morning of January 12, 1942, they began their voyage to Shanghai, China. At Yokohama, the POWs were cleaned up after having been subjected to crowded and poor conditions on board ship, but the real reason for this was Japanese propaganda. There they were exposed to Japanese newsmen and photographers.

This trip was tragic. Five Americans were charged with breaking the rules, and Captain Saito read an execution order. All were beheaded and their bodies thrown into the water. They were listed as MIA, and the rest of the prisoners were not informed about their fate. The survivors did not learn what really happened until the end of the war.

The navy delivered the POWs to an army guard detail that marched them to a camp within a week where they were joined by marines from Peking and Tientsen. In a letter to the Swiss government the Japanese did not give all the true details. The American POWs there numbered about 1,400.

In Java, in early March, about 1,100 Americans were seized. The first of three American ships to succumb to the Japanese navy off the coast of Java was the USS *Houston,* on the night of February 28, 1942. Many of the survivors, about 350, were picked up by Japanese ships and taken to shore, and then to the town of Serang. Other survivors made it to the beach on rafts and floats, but they were turned over by Java to Japan and they also ended up in Serang.

At the city of Makassar in northeastern Java on Celebes Island, the Japanese held more than 3,000 allied POWs, mainly of nationalities other than American. There were about 200 survivors of the U.S. submarine *Perch*, and a sunken destroyer, the USS *Papi*. The submarine had been scuttled by its men. The small number of Americans in Java remained there until the Japanese decided what to do with them, but for reasons unknown, most Americans stayed there until the end of the war. They were never reported as POWs but simply as MIAs.

One other important event was an attempted escape in Woosing camp in China. The instigator was Commander C. D. Smith, former captain of the captured USS *Wake*. He was joined by four others. After two weeks of preparation, on March 11 the five began their escape and headed north to the Yangtze River but failed to cross when they were refused help by a Chinese boatman. They were recaptured by Chinese soldiers who were a part of the Japanese puppet government. Returned to their former camp, they were found guilty of desertion and sentenced to different prison terms.

The greatest number of POWs came from Bataan and Corregidor and formed the nucleus of the POWs on the Bataan Death March. These men, as they moved along the road, saw the bodies of many Filipinos and Americans along the way. Remaining behind in the hospital were about 800 wounded and sick along with their medical personnel.

Sixty-five nurses were christened the "angels of Bataan and Corregidor." Later they were separated from the other captives and interned in Santo Tomas for the duration of the war. Theirs is yet another story, told by Elizabeth Norman in her book *We Band of Angels*.

WOMEN IN THE WAR

Many people before the Gulf War insisted that women should not have combat roles in the military. Barbara Ehrenreich, in her review of Norman's book on the American nurses captured by the Japanese, cites these women as real role models and specifically makes the point that critics "seem not to have heard of Major Rhonda Cornum" and her experiences as a captive in the Iraqi war.[9]

At the surrender of Bataan, the nurses were taken to Corregidor, where they cared for the wounded and sick until Wainwright's surrender in May. The nurses, who were officers, thus became prisoners of war and were brought to an internment camp in Manila. As officers, they were subjected as POWs to the same horrible conditions as other POWs, and they conducted themselves valiantly. None of them were raped, beaten, or molested, according to the book reviewer. Unfortunately, these nurses were never given any major medals, which they certainly deserved. Their efforts were recognized to some extent when Eleanor Roosevelt referred to them in a Washington ceremony by rank rather than by the usual "Miss."

THE DEATH MARCH

The Death March preceded the confinement at Camp O'Donnell and other POW camps distributed among the Philippine Islands, Japan itself, Korea, mainland China, and Formosa.

The best primary sources for the Death March were written by experienced officers who endured its rigors and subsequent confinement and survived. These survivors wrote their personal memoirs or expressed them through experienced editors. Survivors include Lieutenant-General Jonathan Wainwright, Colonel Irwin Alexander, Colonel William Brady, and Lieutenant Colonel William Dyess, who wrote the first revelation of the atrocities of the Death March. These, of course, represent only some of the firsthand accounts. There are also histories by Gavan Daws, E. Bartlett Kerr, and Donald Knox, which were drawn upon heavily for this chapter.

The Death March began on April 10, 1942, and it ended at Camp O'Donnell. Much happened between its beginning and end. When

General King surrendered his forces on Luzon on April 9, almost 10,000 American troops became prisoners and represented the largest number of Americans who ever surrendered in a single engagement with an enemy.[10] For the first time in the history of the United States, generals were forced to walk for many miles to their internment. General King was one who was allowed to proceed to Camp O'Donnell in a car.

Along the route, Japanese soldiers committed countless atrocities on both Americans and Filipinos. Some West Point officers had their fingers cut off so the Japanese could take their rings. One captain who had Japanese money on him was decapitated, and Filipino prisoners were subjected to mass killings.[11] The Japanese senior officer responsible for many POW deaths was Nara Akira, a general who had been trained before the war at Fort Benning, Georgia. General Homma's men were never punished for mistreatment of a POW, nor was Captain Tsuneyoshu Yoshio, camp commander at O'Donnell.

Colonel Alexander described many of the events of the journey. Artillery fire nearby unfortunately killed one American and wounded another while destroying a Japanese battery.[12]

The worst single incident of the Death March took place on April 12 near Balanga. It was here that the Japanese killed 400 Filipino soldiers and NCOs of the 91st Division for no reason at all, "hacking them to pieces with their swords."[13]

Many of the men were weak, half starved, and sick with beriberi. Irving's account points out that the Japanese captors made no distinction between officers and enlisted POWs.[14] One Catholic chaplain was so sick he had to be helped by three priests. The Japanese showed no compassion, but the chaplain was helped by the Filipinos and managed to survive and return to a small parish back in Ohio.

Men who were slow in getting started after short rests were killed. Along the treacherous route some Filipino civilians tried to help or give some food or water to prisoners without putting themselves into grave danger. One young American was bayoneted to death for "breaking the water line." Reaching O'Donnell would be an achievement, but then some prisoners, when slated to be sent to confinement areas in Japan or other areas, had to endure another terrible experience, traveling in the ships later called the Death Ships. Colonel Alexander, General Wainwright, and other high-ranking officers experienced such voyages.

The Death Ships, also called the Hell Ships, were somewhat reminiscent of the prison ships in New York harbor during the Revolutionary War. Men were crowded in the holds, water and food were scarce, and there was no provision for sanitary facilities.

LIEUTENANT COLONEL DYESS

The story of Lieutenant Colonel Dyess includes the atrocities of the Death March and his unusual escape from his place of confinement after the march. His details of the march were censored by the War Department, after it initially gave permission to a newspaper to print them. The government changed its opinion three days later, forbidding any release of information of Dyess's prison experiences and escape.

Dyess's grandfather had been captured by Federal forces during the Civil War while scouting Union lines in Pennsylvania and confined as a POW in Chicago. He refused parole because he would have to promise not to take up arms against the North, which he was unwilling to do.[15]

Dyess relates the details of his capture. When fleeing along the road, he and his fellow pilots were found by a unit of three Japanese tanks. He witnessed a number of atrocities. He did not see the actual decapitation of an air force captain, but he had seen the body and "in the year to come there would be enough killing of American and Filipino soldier prisoners to represent . . . a mountain of dead."[16] They were marched from southern Luzon to the north, given no food, and

many were buried alive. After a twenty-one-hour march from Cabanatuan they arrived at Orani. At Lubad, close to San Tomas, some
civilians were clubbed or beaten to death when they tried to give the
POWs food.

At San Fernando, the POWs were placed in a barbed wire compound. Headed for Camp O'Donnell, they were packed in boxcars
on a train. The final trip was a seven-mile hike to O'Donnell.

The Japanese captain who addressed them said that they were not
prisoners of war but enemies of Nippon and not to be treated as
POWs of an honorable war. No medicines were given the sick and
many Americans died. The Japanese forced many Americans and
Filipinos into labor gangs. At first, no religious services were permitted, but later Protestant and Catholic chaplains who were prisoners were allowed to conduct services.

Many prisoners came from Corregidor, but most of those who had
surrendered were sent to Cabanatuan, including Dyess. Previously a
number of generals and full colonels were sent to Japan and Formosa
to work as slaves in factories or on farms. Many German POWs contributed to the labor force in the United States, but their conditions
were much better than what Americans were subject to in Japan,
Formosa, and Korea.

In late October 1942, a number of POWs were sent to Japan for
factory labor and Dyess knew that escape from Japan was almost
impossible. He was willing to go anywhere but to Japan. He was put
in a boxcar and shipped to Manila, stayed at Old Bilibud about a
day or so, and then marched through the streets of Manila. He arrived at the docks in the late evening. He had no idea about his destination.

He was sent to Davao, in the Phillipines, and was put to work.
Everyone worked there regardless of rank, age, enlisted or officer
personnel; even chaplains were required to work. Dyess says that the
Filipinos there were "the greatest bunch of murderers and cut-
throats."[17] Dyess started planning his escape and a decision was
made not to kill any Japanese in the process for fear of retaliation

against other POWs. Dyess had to make his way through dense jungle and his account ended with the line, "We were fighting men once more."[18]

The sad fact about the information Dyess gave MacArthur in Australia was that the government wouldn't release its Filipino guerrillas, who had helped considerably in the successful escape. Once the details of the escape and the Death March were released, the news horrified the world. It was quite clear that Japan, while claiming that it would abide by the Geneva Convention principles, was not doing so. The International Red Cross was never allowed to visit POW camps and often parcels were never delivered to the POWs. The same was true for mail. The plan of executing remaining POWs by a shooting squad when one escaped was undoubtedly a major consideration for the government to suppress Dyess's story.

VARIOUS WAR INCIDENTS

One ironic tale told by Ronald Spector concerned Captain Sidney Stewart. On April 10, a Japanese soldier demanded Stewart's bottle of sleeping pills. He asked if they were all right to which Stewart said yes. The Japanese swallowed two handfuls, which killed him in minutes. Thus the officer had "achieved a small revenge." Spector took this accident directly from Stewart's *Give Us This Day*, the personal memoir of his experiences.

Incidents involving airplane and submarine attacks on ships carrying prisoners to Japan were very tragic. The *Shinyo Maru* was sunk by an American sub. Only a small group of POWs survived and were rescued by the Allies. The Death Ships were not marked in any way that they contained POWs, a factor that would have spared many American lives.

After Bataan and Corregidor fell, the Japanese continued their drive to take all islands in the Pacific area. The very next day after

Pearl Harbor, simultaneous attacks were made on many islands of the Pacific and Japanese control of Southeast Asia depended on the success of these invasions. Like Hitler who wanted complete control of all of Europe, the Japanese objective was complete control of all of Asia.

All these islands would have to be retaken to fulfill General MacArthur's promise that he would return. The army and marines, with the help of the navy with its bombardment capabilities, fighter pilots, and transportation facilities for army and marine ground personnel and their equipment, would provide the necessary ingredient for military success. Not merely ground personnel became prisoners but also army, navy, and marine flying personnel. Some submarine personnel were taken as well. All this meant more casualties and prisoners on both sides.

MacArthur's plan for the taking of the Philippines, and before that the other islands, was essentially an island-hopping tactic. This was called Operation Cartwheel, a complicated campaign that involved many phases and represented a combined army–navy effort led by MacArthur and the naval forces. This operation demanded great resources in ships and planes, especially after the bloody battles in Papua and Guadalcanal. The Japanese lost the largest naval battle in history at Leyte. The results were the loss of the Japanese fleet and much of its air power; this meant, according to Dyess, certain defeat for the Japanese forces.[19] The battle of Okinawa was another American victory in which many Japanese died, and only eight POWs were taken.

The capture of Arawe and Cape Gloucester on New Britain at the end of 1943 was a part of the MacArthur–Admiral Halsey operation to isolate Rabaul. By the end of March 1943, MacArthur and Halsey received their orders from the Joint Chiefs of Staff to begin their advance on Rabaul. Rabaul was on the Gazelle Peninsula in the northeast part of New Britain Island. It was the most important Japanese airbase in the southwest Pacific and had an internment camp for prisoners of war.

Located in the prison camp, Tobera, was a mixture of different nationalities. Of about eighty-five Americans, seventeen survived the ordeal. Twelve died of different diseases or illnesses and their fate remains unknown. About thirty-five were executed. The favorite form of punishment, as already noted, was decapitation. On one occasion a POW was shot to death as he tried an escape. Tobera was ruthlessly administered and had a very bad reputation.

MAJOR "PAPPY" BOYINGTON

Some POWs were sent to Japan and a good number survived. One such person was "Pappy" Boyington, a Marine Corps major and fighter pilot of the Black Sheep Squadron. Major Boyington was leading a fighting sweep about December 17, 1943, and four Zeroes followed him down as his fuel tanks ignited. He parachuted out of his plane at a low altitude. He landed in the water and was strafed but not hit. About five miles from shore he was picked up by a Japanese submarine. His disappearance greatly disturbed the American public and the Marine Corps. It was not a good beginning for 1944.

He was placed on a truck and taken into town for his first interrogation. As a POW he was helped by Eddie Hondo, a Hawaiian who had renounced his American citizenship. He had joined the Japanese navy as an interpreter in 1942 and arrived in Rabaul, August 1943. He gave good advice to Boyington when the Japanese left the room for a break.

Lieutenant John Arbuckle, a PBY pilot who was also shot down and captured in December 1943, joined Boyington. The policy of the Imperial Navy to execute POWs was questioned, but Tokyo instructed Rabaul headquarters not to send any more prisoners to the homeland. (A study of documents in Australian archives on war crimes investigations at Rabaul revealed mass executions of Allied POWs from 1942 to 1944.)[20]

Orders came, however, for Hondo to escort POW Boyington to Japan. Hondo and six POWs were released from the Rabaul naval prison. Their plane landed at Truk and then Hondo and the POWs arrived in Japan aboard a DC-3 transport plane. All the POWs survived their internment. They had been confined in a suburb of Yokohama. Boyington had been treated well in the submarine that originally picked him up and managed fairly well as a POW in Japan.

During his last four months of confinement there were daily bombings from B-29s. The Japanese colonel in charge of the camp didn't want to release the prisoners because a surrender had not been signed, so American visitors were sent back to their ships where they got help from the marines. Harold Stassen, a former governor of Minnesota, was there and recognized Boyington.[21] The prisoners took showers, were issued new clothes, were received by medical doctors, and were fed well. President Truman later presented the Congressional Medal of Honor to Boyington.

Hondo was arrested by the U.S. Army Counter Intelligence Corps in Japan after the war. He turned himself in and was sent to Guam where he translated for the war crimes trial. When it was confirmed that he had renounced his American citizenship in 1941, he couldn't be tried for treason. Boyington had given him a watch, and after a few months at home he received a letter from the War Crimes Commission personnel in Tokyo. It told Boyington that an interpreter there had claimed a watch was given him by Boyington which, of course, was confirmed by Boyington.

At Boyington's confinement center very few POWs died. That there was no notification that this group was alive was a flagrant violation of the Geneva Convention. The Japanese excuse was that in Japanese there are different meanings for the terms prisoner and captive.[22]

POW CAMPS IN THE PHILIPPINES

At Camp O'Donnell, where the Death March terminated, there was a partially completed airfield about eight miles west of the Manila railroad line at Caprao. The Japanese decided to confine prisoners taken at Bataan at O'Donnell until the surrender of Corregidor. A high barbed wire fence surrounded O'Donnell that had the usual gun towers. Outside the stockade there was high grass in every direction growing on a rolling plain that had very few trees.

At this camp, high-ranking officers were segregated from the other prisoners and moved to a camp nearby. According to Colonel Alexander, O'Donnell was divided into three sections — the Japanese had the middle section along the east and west highways for their headquarters, barracks, and storehouses; the Filipinos were confined in an enclosure that could accommodate 5,000; finally, the north side had an enclosure that would hold 10,000 Americans over whom General King had charge. General King established a hospital that was under the care of American personnel, but medical supplies were seriously lacking. Unfortunately, many patients did not survive. In the first forty days there were about a thousand deaths, and the death rate for the Filipinos was even worse.

In June 1942, many were transferred from O'Donnell to an unknown camp that would become known as Camp Cabanatuan. Although it was at a different location, the struggle for survival continued. Because of the surrender of Filipino laborers in the camp, contacts were made by mail and messages between prisoners and well-to-do friends of theirs in Manila. This meant getting more food, which probably alleviated the death rate. A German priest visited them, probably due to the archbishop of Manila. The German priest had a German passport, which undoubtedly helped the situation, but at the end of the war he was arrested and executed by the Japanese.

In October 1942, 3,000 prisoners were moved to Mindanao, the largest island in the southern Philippines. On this island was located the Davao prison camp, which housed about 2,000 American prisoners who tended large farms there. It was surrounded by swamp and impenetrable jungle and seemed to be escape proof, but, as previously mentioned, Colonel Dyess and two others escaped in April of 1943.

Cabanatuan City was about 100 miles north of Manila on the central plain. An underground system was developed from Cabanatuan to Manila, where there were many fearless people devoted to the American cause. The system enabled messages, money, and food to be had to make things easier for prisoners, and because of this, thousands of Americans were saved. The recapture of Cabanatuan by the American Rangers will be discussed later in the chapter.

O'Donnell was an intermediate prison for most soldiers before transfer to Cabanatuan and then to Bilibud, although some spent considerable time at O'Donnell. Some of the Death Ships that were torpedoed or bombed by U.S. forces were supposed to transport POWs to Japan. According to Colonel Alexander's account of prisoner experiences, the prison ships held 68,068 POWs, of whom 22,000 lost their lives. This number takes into account only those killed by U.S. attacks. Many lost their lives at sea because of lack of food, water, and medical care.[23]

Of about 9,000 American prisoners who made it to O'Donnell, 1,547 died and it is believed that ten or twelve were executed. The last known POW death occurred in November 1942. Most who survived were sent to Cabanatuan between May and July 1942.[24]

Two other important camps were Los Baños and Santo Tomas on Luzon, and the populations there consisted largely of civilians. Many Americans were sent directly to Santo Tomas under protective custody.[25] This camp was established on January 4, 1942. Santo Tomas was a former university and held people of many different nationalities and many members of religious orders.

The Los Baños population of prisoners contained a mixture of people. Many civilians were taken from their homes in 1942 and placed in this camp, which had been an agricultural college. The civilians were warned that the Japanese were trying to starve them to death. There were so many Catholic priests and nuns, as well as

Protestant missionaries, in the camp that the section in which they resided became known as Vatican City.[26] This camp existed from May 1943 to January 29, 1945. Los Baños was thirty miles east of Manila and well behind enemy lines on February 23, 1945. It was accessible only by air and by water across an inland lake, Laguna de Bay.

MacArthur was not merely interested in retaking the many islands initially captured by the Japanese, but had great concern for the people at the prison camps. There was a fear of reprisal against American prisoners before the end of the war; consequently, plans were drawn up for daring rescue raids for civilians and military personnel in such places as Santo Tomas, Los Baños, and Cabanatuan. Dropping the atomic bombs severely reduced the morale of all the Japanese.

PERSONNEL LOSSES

The Doolittle Raid took the Japanese by storm, but POWs captured as a result of it suffered considerably. This was the first attack on Japan itself. The Japanese captured eight crewmen, tortured them, and beat them. Three were executed and five sentenced to life imprisonment. In 1943 and 1944 Americans experienced more success in the war. Japanese soldiers were told to commit suicide rather than surrender, but this was not always the case, and some prisoners were taken. By the time MacArthur was planning his return to the Philippines, the United States had knowledge of the locations of POW and internment camps on Luzon. Many of these locations would be designated on pilots' maps. Gavin Daws says that MacArthur also knew what was happening on the water[27] (the Death Ships) and seems to find some fault with MacArthur on this point.

During the Battle of Midway, two months after the Doolittle Raid, three airmen were picked out of the water. But instead of being taken prisoner, two were thrown overboard and weighed down, and the third was killed with a fire ax. In different areas pilots were shot, beheaded, and bayoneted. Raids over Japan resulted in 200 men dead, killed in firebombing; almost 100 flyers were killed horribly.

According to intelligence information, there were no POWs in Hiroshima, one target of the atomic bomb, but U.S. intelligence was erroneous. There were some Americans in various locations and although some survived, others were killed by the Japanese. Nagasaki also had some POWs who were killed.

JAPANESE AMERICAN POWs

When the first U.S. torpedo boat and landing craft in Tokyo Bay came cruising down the channel of the POW camp at Oman, hundreds of Americans climbed on top of the wharf pilings to shout with joy. Frank Fujita dove in and swam out and almost drowned. Fujita wrote a book about his experiences as a POW.

He was called "Foo" for short and was a Texan of Japanese descent serving as a combat soldier. His battalion was overwhelmed by the enemy and surrendered on March 8, three months after the start of the war. He was a POW for two and a half years and endured the Death March and Death Ships. About 6,000 Japanese Americans saw military service, most of them in Italy. Only two Japanese were captured by the Japanese, one of whom was Foo in Java; the other was Richard Sakakida in the Philippines.

Foo got a message to Major Gregory "Pappy" Boyington that he wanted to see him. Boyington had been shot down and captured near Rabaul in December 1943. Foo was discharged but in December 1948 reenlisted, giving up his 100 percent disability. He was a reservist and was called to active duty during the Korean War.

Fortunately, Foo's family was not subjected to confinement at a "relocation center." He was held as a POW about eight blocks away from the Imperial Palace and maintained a secret diary. In

June 1943, the Japanese learned he was half Japanese and in October 1943, he was transferred to Omari POW camp near Tokyo. The U.S. Navy liberated him and his fellow POWs on August 29, 1945.

The second Japanese American POW, Master Sergeant Richard Sakakida, fought in Bataan and Corregidor, spied on Japan, and served as an interpreter and a double agent. He provided vital information until MacArthur's return in 1944. He was wounded when accompanying retreating Japanese and escaped in 1945. He was wounded again and emerged from a hiding place as he shouted, "Don't shoot me. I am an American."

Although it happened much earlier in the war, in 1942 there was another unusual and interesting story about an American marine, Guy Gabaldon, who was brought up by a Japanese family. A Japanese mother and father took in the young boy who was a classmate of their sons. The two Japanese Americans served in the army in the Italian campaign. They were American born—Nisei.

Gabaldon joined the marines to fight in the Pacific, and he spoke fluent Japanese. In a beach landing on Saipan he advanced with his comrades while battleship cannons were firing over their heads into Japanese positions. He had to kill Japanese machine gunners, and in further action on the island rounded up Japanese holdouts by talking to them in Japanese. He helped save many women and children and took almost 1,000 prisoners.

General Matsu, running low on food and ammunition, reminded his men that there was no dishonor in death. He had a special map for an attack at 0700. When he was captured with the map, he was put under guard while one marine took the map but was killed by a sniper. Gabaldon received permission to speak to the last remaining Japanese. The major general spoke to his men, who threw down their weapons. The general himself committed suicide as civilians and his men paraded by. This episode was built into the motion picture *Hell to Eternity,* which starred Jeffrey Hunter and also had Vic Damone and David Janssen in minor roles.

AMERICAN RESCUE ATTEMPTS

American forces made three daring, heroic moves to rescue military and civilian prisoners of war. The first involved POWs held at Cabanatuan and took place on the night of January 30, 1945. The rescuers included Filipino guerrillas, the Rangers, and the Alamo Scouts.

By January 30, 1945, about 511 POWs, mainly Americans, managed to survive thirty-three months of captivity. Earlier there had been as many as 12,000 Americans in the stockade under poor conditions, but thousands had been shipped off to Japan and Manchuria to provide slave labor for Japanese war production. Approximately 26,000 other American POWs had been killed by Japanese guards or died of starvation, disease, or maltreatment. Of the 511 Americans remaining, some were blind, unable to walk, or missing arms or legs.[28]

Seventy-five miles northeast of Cabanatuan, MacArthur's forces stormed ashore at Linguyen Gulf. Fear that the Japanese would slaughter helpless people was a strong motivation for the Cabanatuan raid. Three months later, Colonel Mucci and his Rangers reached Plateros.

The land around the POW camp was flat and treeless, so more intelligence was necessary for a successful day raid. Disguised as Filipinos, Lieutenant Nellis and his Alamo Scouts checked out the area concerning the gate entrance and other relevant information for Colonel Mucci.[29]

The guards at Cabanatuan were just as cruel as those at O'Donnell. Four who tried to escape were recaptured, tied to posts, and beaten with fists and clubs. They were forced to dig their own graves and then executed by a firing squad. The next day an announcement was made by Colonel Shigei, the commandant, that ten POWs would be killed for every one escapee. The commandant's order did not discourage escapes by those who could no longer endure the atrocities. Two other Americans tried escapes and were beaten badly. Then others were lined up with them and shot.

As already noted, MacArthur had heard about POW atrocities on the Death March and at prison camps from Dyess and the two officers with him, Navy Lieutenant Commander Melvyn McCoy and Army Major Stephen Mednick. They had pulled off their daring, hair-raising escape from Davao on Mindanao.

Through swamps, jungles, and up and down mountains they made their way to a coastal town, guerrilla headquarters. In late June 1943, Australia sent the submarine *Thresher* to pick up Dyess, Mednick, and McCoy while others had to wait. The final decision not to release reports of the Death March and brutalities at O'Donnell was made by President Roosevelt, which originally greatly disturbed MacArthur. The media, however, finally were permitted to report the details.

At the beginning of 1944, MacArthur started pulling together plans for his return. A new type of force had to be established to accomplish some of his ideas—a six-week training course to train those who would be called the Alamo Scouts. There were two rehearsal missions for the attack on Cebu. The thirty-three-year-old Pearl Harbor survivor and West Point graduate, Colonel Mucci, was assigned to prepare the men for the mission. The men of this Ranger Battalion would number about 570. Mucci encouraged married men to transfer, but most of them decided to remain. No one really knew what lay ahead.

THE CABANATUAN RAID

The American guerrilla chief, Major Bob Latham, briefed General Krueger's intelligence chief in late January 1945. He had crucial information on the POWs and was rushed to see Colonel Horton White.[30] The number of Japanese in the area was staggering and he recommended a crash operation to rescue the POWs.

Before noon the next day, Colonel Mucci met in White's tent with Latham and three Alamo Scouts and thus the stage was set for the Cabanatuan raid. A tremendous amount of coordination was necessary among the Rangers, the Alamo Scouts, and the Filipino guerrillas.

Church services, Protestant and Catholic, were held after the briefing, and Mucci insisted that all go to church and "swear to God that you'll die if need be rather than let harm come to our POWs."[31]

The Alamo Scouts represented a top secret echelon created for special missions in the South Pacific. Many of its operations were kept secret for more than fifty years, and some still are. MacArthur put General Walter Krueger, commander of the U.S. 6th Army, in charge of them. This special task force would engage in very dangerous missions, the first of which was to rescue POWs at Cabanatuan where there were many survivors of Bataan and the Death March. The story of this rescue group has been told by many authors, perhaps the most recent being *Ghost Soldiers* by Hampton Sides. This writer starts his book by narrating some of the cruelest atrocities, including a massacre of American troops at a camp on Palawan Island in December 1944.

General Krueger would do things his way and the army way. Some of the recruits washed out. The final selection of the Alamo Scouts would consist of four 6-man teams. Their training was difficult, and the creation of the group actually preceded that of the Rangers.

The first mission about which so much is known and for which the Scouts became famous was the rescue of POWs at Cabanatuan. As already mentioned, to get intelligence information, two Scouts dressed as Filipino farmers, crawled on their stomachs on the outskirts of the camp, and gained valuable information for the operation. Later the Scouts planned a massive campaign for the invasion of Japan, but this mission never got started because the atomic bombs brought about Japan's surrender. After the war, the Scouts were dismantled, their activities being declassified many years later.

Two important Filipino guerrilla commanders who contributed to the success of the mission at Cabanatuan were Juan Pajata and Eduardo Joson. Many of the liberated POWs had been confined for almost three years. Only one American was killed in the raid, Dr. James Fisher.

Sides describes the deeds of "High Pockets"—Claire Phillips—an American woman who pretended to be Italian and ran a cabaret in Manila where she was very popular with the Japanese. Needless to say, her espionage ring was very helpful toward the cause of the prisoners.

The U.S. 547th Night Fighter Squadron was to provide air cover. They were to fly low to distract the Japanese soldiers while the Rangers were proceeding to the stockade; other P-61s would patrol Luzon's skies to seek out and destroy Japanese trucks, as well as vehicles and tanks that might join the Japanese camp forces when the shooting began.

The evening of January 27, every Ranger studied air reconnaissance photos of the camp. Lapham's guerrillas, having spied on the camp for months, provided many details that would serve as guides and gave flank protection to the Rangers. Never before had such an operation been planned. Shortly after dawn on January 30, the Rangers were treated to a magnificent breakfast by the villagers, and just before 9:30 A.M. Mucci gave the final orders. A final briefing was given and the Rangers were ready.

The Rangers fired on the Japanese troops and threw hand grenades. Unfortunately, some POWs were confused. Waiting on the north shore were wheeled carts for the rescued prisoners, and P-61s eliminated Japanese trucks and tanks. The liberated POWs reached the 42nd Evacuation Hospital and just before noon on February 1, a jeep arrived from which MacArthur emerged. Mucci was heaped with praise, but he emphasized that success was really due to the Scouts, Rangers, and guerrillas.

A total of 516 POWs were rescued by the Rangers, who lost only two men killed, one of whom was their battalion surgeon. One POW died at the gate of the camp only a few seconds from freedom, and another POW was accidentally left in the camp. His later rescue was another amazing story. MacArthur said of the operation, "No other incident of the campaign has given me such personal satisfaction." General Walter Krueger said in the spring of 1944, "I wouldn't take the whole damn Japanese army for one Alamo Scout."[32]

One interesting event narrated in Breuer's book concerned an army sergeant and a Catholic priest he was rescuing. Staff Sergeant August Stern was carrying a POW piggy back from the highway and suddenly found himself wading in mud. He tripped but didn't drop his man. He shouted some profanity and his POW said, "I'm a Catholic, Chaplain Kennedy. I'm a Catholic, priest." The sergeant apologized and the priest replied, "That's okay, I understand. There's a time and place for everything. I guess this is it."

A former Alamo Scout, Master Sergeant Galen Kittleson, holds the distinction of being the only American soldier involved in three major assaults on enemy POW stockades: the first two in World War II—a raid in New Guinea to free Dutch POWs and at Cabanatuan; and the Green Beret raid on Sontay in North Vietnam.

SANTO TOMAS

The second successful raid by American forces took place on February 7 at Santo Tomas. Previously a Dominican University, it was converted to a prison camp holding foreign nationals from all over the world. It became known as STIC (the Santo Tomas Internment Center). One-fourth of almost 3,800 internees were children under eighteen and another fourth were people over sixty, mainly men. Many of these had been interned originally on the island of Cebu. Conditions for Britishers and other Allied nationals were terrible.

The internees elected a committee under the leadership of Father McCarthy, a Maryknoll priest, to establish some order, and on May 16 permission was given for the prisoners to move to Cebu Junior College. This was much better for the prisoners, but in December 1942 all Cebu internees were put in trucks and driven to a wharf where they boarded a freighter. Below the decks to the afterhold, conditions were very cramped. Filipinos were added later and on December 19 the ship reached Manila. The people were driven to Santo Tomas and were the first provincial visitors to arrive there.[33]

Elizabeth Norman, in her book *We Band of Angels,* describes Santo Tomas quite well. Located in the middle of the camp was a main building three stories high and a block and a half long. This building was a large quadrangle built around two interior courtyards. The central dormitory was for men only and to the left was a gymnasium. Behind the main building the women were assigned to the annex sleeping quarters with their children. To the left of this "compound within a compound" was the area reserved for the Dominican priests.[34]

The head of Santo Tomas was a civilian who allowed the creation of two management boards. The talents and skills of internees were used to help all internees survive the ordeal. Nurses captured in Manila were assigned to the camp hospital. From the outset, therefore, things didn't seem too bad in this prison.

Three internees successfully escaped but were recaptured and beaten seriously. They were given courts-martial and sentenced to death. There were, of course, some internees who wouldn't work, drank and smuggled liquor, and stole. Fortunately, their number was small.

Although doctors and nurses were available, medical and food supplies were lacking, and an underground smuggling operation was used to get these items. This dangerous operation was run by fearless Catholic priests. Norman describes the nurses' response to having to bow to Japanese guards. A plan was devised for nurses to pass guards at repeated intervals and thus as one bow was completed and returned, another nurse would walk by. It got to the point that Japanese guards would turn their backs when they saw them coming.[35]

Major changes came during the first week of 1944, when control was transferred from the Japanese Bureau of External Affairs to the

War Prisoners Department of the Imperial Japanese Army. Santo Tomas was due for radical changes. The boards of management were eliminated and new restrictions put into effect. Fewer rations and more harassment were on the agenda. By February 1, it was truly a prison camp.

By now, things were going badly for the Japanese in the war. MacArthur ordered the 1st Cavalry Division to kill the Japanese and go to Manila to free the Santo Tomas internees. The cavalrymen were joined by guerrillas who led them to the gates of Santo Tomas.

On the morning of February 3, Santo Tomas people could hear the shelling of the city and low-flying reconnaissance aircraft. Those in Santo Tomas knew that something was definitely in the wind and the Japanese ordered all to stay inside. On February 7, MacArthur arrived at the front gates and liberation was at hand. The Japanese wanted free passage and were now begging for this concession. MacArthur then turned to Major General Swing to plan the rescue of Los Baños, about forty-two miles from Manila.

Of the ninety-nine army and navy nurses who went to war on December 8, 1941, sixteen were still alive in 1998.[36]

LOS BAÑOS

The third successful rescue attempt took place at Los Baños on February 23, 1945, a day its resident prisoners would never forget. This was the most dramatic rescue of the three—one without precedent that was accomplished by the 11th Airborne Division and Filipino guerrillas. The rescue is vividly described in *The Angels Came at Seven,* a pamphlet by Father William McCarthy, the Maryknoll priest who had been a POW and leader on Cebu Island.

Father McCarthy was held prisoner in five different camps. He was confined for thirty-four months, twenty-one of them at Los Baños. In his opening paragraph he states, "I'm well aware that soldiers are not commonly thought of as angels, but to the 2,158

prisoners in Los Baños Concentration Camp, the hard-bitten soldiers of the Eleventh Airborne Division will always be remembered as Angels of Liberation."[37]

Other dramatic events happened the same day, including the rais-
ing of the American flag by six marines on Iwo Jima's Mount
Suribachi. The Los Baños escapade represented a humanitarian di-
version.[38] A cross section of society was present in the Los Baños
camp: priests, Protestant missionaries, and civilians of the Philippines taken from their homes in 1942 and placed on the grounds of
an agricultural college. At the outset they were well treated, but
conditions changed when Lieutenant Sadacki Konishi took over as
commandant.

Internees realized that something was up when planes started flying over at an altitude of 500 feet and dropped scores of figures in
parachutes. The angels of the U.S. 11th Airborne Division landed at
dawn. The name of the camp was changed to Camp Freedom. The
Japanese executive committee said it would take over at 0500 and
left enough food for two months to keep the internees in the camp,
but Lieutenant Konishi returned, so Camp Freedom was no more.

Los Baños was about thirty miles southeast of Manila and well
behind enemy lines on February 23, 1945, and accessible only by air
and water. At 0700 hours, U.S. infantry and artillery units moved
across the San Juan River to attack Japanese positions at Lecherra
Hill; fifty-two amphibious tractors landed near Mayondong point
and moved toward Los Baños. A company of paratroopers landed a
few hundred yards from Los Baños Internment Camp. It was ironic
that the only fatalities came during the diversionary attack fifteen
miles from Los Baños.[39]

Radio operator Sergeant John Fulton had been sent by the plan-
ners of the raid to hide with Romeo Espino to maintain radio contact
with the 11th Airborne Headquarters. The urgency of the rescue mission was pointed out by the message that Colonel Price (Romeo Espino), guerrilla leader, gave to Fulton. As was pointed out previously, General MacArthur had chosen General Joseph Swing,

sometimes called the "Patton of the Pacific," to receive the surrender of the Japanese ground forces six months after Los Baños. General Swing had been Eisenhower's airborne adviser for six weeks during the battles for North Africa and Sicily.

A young lieutenant, "Fly" Flanagan, later wrote a military history of the 11th. He was a participant in the Los Baños action and later rose to the rank of lieutenant general.

As in the case of the previous rescues, this operation was extremely well planned and the paratroopers did a magnificent job. Many of the civilians they rescued were Catholic missionary priests, nuns, and Protestant ministers, as well as women, children, and old men.

One young soldier received a hug and said, "Hold on, sister." Later he found out she was a nun. Another nun, Sister Mary Trinita, was questioned intensively and refused to sign a confession; she was ultimately transferred to Los Baños in early January 1945. Another soldier carried out a baby. By 11:00, the camp was cleared and almost everyone assembled at the beach.

The ruthless, cruel Major General Masatoshi Fujishige, a former commandant near Los Baños, admitted his guilt at his war crimes trial and received the death penalty. On June 24, 1946, Lieutenant Konishi was accused of four counts of murder, found guilty, and hanged. A Maryknoll nun, Sister Theresa, later reported that before his death he converted to Christianity.[40] Sister Miriam Louise Kraeger returned after the war to Baquio and wrote about those days in Manila in 1943 and 1944. Twelve navy nurses were the only military prisoners on the roster of the Los Baños internees. Flanagan tells us that only eighty-one military women were held as POWs in World War II. The two main Catholic orders that had prisoners were the Maryknollers and Jesuits and Jesuit Scholastics who were studying to be priests.

At the sight of the descending parachutists, a Maryknoll nun joyously proclaimed, "Parachutes! Parachutes! Americans!" The parachutists made a textbook landing. Sister Marie went to a window to offer a play-by-play account and a Jesuit priest shouted to her to take refuge before she was killed.[41] Said Douglas MacArthur, "Nothing could be more satisfying to a soldier's heart than this rescue. I am deeply grateful. God was certainly with us today."

Father McCarthy reported that one Sunday morning as he was saying Mass, Lieutenant Kodi, commandant at Los Baños, arrived. Later that day Kodi sent a note to the priest to report to his office. Father McCarthy was asked through an interpreter some general questions and then came the surprising question "Do you have enough Mass supplies?" Father McCarthy answered that all the priests were short of wine. Three days later a guard delivered six bottles of wine to the chapel. That was quite a shock, but soon the lieutenant was reassigned.[42]

Freed from Los Baños Camp, Father McCarthy intended to resume his mission work in Cebu City but was recalled by his superiors to the United States for a rest. He and his fellow priests were truly saints who had been rescued by the angels of the 11th Airborne.

Many high-ranking Japanese were tried for their atrocities and sentenced to death. They seemed to suffer more than those convicted in the war crimes trials for German officials.

Aboard the battleship *Missouri*, on September 21, 1945, General Douglas MacArthur accepted the surrender of the Japanese government representatives. It was fitting that General Jonathan Wainwright was brought by MacArthur to witness the occasion.

RELOCATION CENTERS

Today, the creation of American relocation centers for Japanese civilians is viewed as a violation of their constitutional rights. Americans of German descent were not subject to relocation, although some of Italian descent suffered.

The man responsible for establishing the relocation centers was Lieutenant General John De Witt, the commander of the Western Defense Command and the 4th Army. Martial law was never declared, and while these events were happening, the Japanese were trying to establish their loyalty. James Sakamoto said, "This is our country, we were born here and raised here, have made our homes here . . . we are ready to give our lives, if necessary, to defend the United States.[43]

Immediately after Pearl Harbor, General De Witt started cracking down on Japanese nationals on the West Coast and then on U.S. citizens of Japanese descent either born here or naturalized. At the time, many people did not view this action as a violation of their civil rights, and though De Witt's order could have been overturned by President Roosevelt, it wasn't. A case actually went to the U.S. Supreme Court (*Toyesboro Korematsu v. United States* or *Duncan v. Kohanomoku*). The Supreme Court defended the position of the U.S. government.

In early 1942, almost 112,000 men, women, and children, representing the entire population of Japanese Americans from California, Oregon, and Washington, were shipped off to relection centers. According to Roger Daniels, almost eight out of ten lived in the Pacific coast states; three-fourths of Japanese Americans resided in California.[44]

Agreeing with De Witt was the California attorney general, Earl Warren, who was preparing to run for governor. Daniels remarks that here was a man who should have stood for justice and later was elevated to the Supreme Court. On January 21, 1945, Major General Pratt assumed command of the Western Defense Command and ended the total exclusion from the West Coast of loyal Japanese American citizens. But the harm had already been done. These American citizens by birth and naturalization were not technically prisoners of war. But they had become, for all practical purposes, prisoners of war.

It is ironic that on the same day that General De Witt said "a Jap is a Jap," 2,686 newly enlisted Nisei arrived at Camp Shelby from Hawaii, and men of the 100th Infantry Battalion and 442nd Regimental Central Team had performed admirably in the Italian campaign.

California, Utah, Arizona, Colorado, Idaho, Arkansas, and

Wyoming were the principal states that contained relocation camps. About 73 percent who were interned because of their race were born American citizens. Many Americans, both military and civilian, were concerned about these people and made certain they didn't starve.

President Roosevelt's Executive Order 9066, February 19, 1942, affected German and Italian nationals living in the restricted areas and many were granted individual hearings. There were ten relocation centers—two in Arizona, two in Arkansas, two in California, and one each in Utah, Colorado, Wyoming, and Idaho. Korematsu, who became involved with the Supreme Court, refused to be evacuated. Three dissenters—Owen Roberts, Robert Jackson, and Frank Murphy—were in the same category, and Justice Hugo Black rejected a charge of racial prejudice.

Many felt then and and still feel today that the presence of these citizens on the coast did not represent a "clear and present danger" to the security of the nation. None of them had been involved in espionage cases or acts of sabotage, and although attempts were made to rectify the wrongs done, the creation of the relocation centers represents to many a blot on the history the United States, and extends to Italian Americans as well.

ITALIAN POWs IN AMERICA

In his book on prisoners of war, Arnold Krammer focuses chiefly on German POWs in the United States but also supplies information on Italian POWs. When it was learned that Germans doing postal work (under supervision of American army personnel) had secretly opened sealed letters at Camp Hearne, Texas, the postal facilities were changed to Fort Meade, Maryland, where Italian POWs took over the job.[45] At an Arizona camp, many Italian POWs volunteered to fight against the Nazis in October 1943, but their requests were turned down by the War Department.[46] Krammer further states that by the spring of 1946 the expectations were that 49,784 Italians (as well as 36,170 Germans and 5,080 Japanese) would be repatriated. Unfortunately progress was very slow.

Italian POWs who did not meet certain requirements were sent to large detention centers such as Fort Lincoln and Fort Missoula in Montana and Crystal City, Texas. Thus not all Italian POWs were interned in Fort Missoula.

In 1945 a center for Italian POWs in Umbarger, Texas, showed the spirit of Christmas in a special way. This center was in the Texas Panhandle's high plains. Nine Italian POWs made a great impact on St. Mary's Catholic Church there. Interned at Hereford Military Reservation and Reception Center, these nine men used their talents to paint religious portraits. The leader of the group was twenty-four-year-old Franco Di Bello. An art exposition was held that included 220 paintings, woodcarvings, and sculptures. Di Bello would become an Italian general in the future, and helping him in the art exposition was a professional artist who had painted church frescoes in Geneva and Turin. The artwork was accomplished in forty-one working days and was officially dedicated on December 8.

The Italians were not the only artists. German POWs confined at Algoma, Iowa, also contributed their efforts. Sergeant Eduard Kaib, age twenty-three, created a Nativity scene. Before being repatriated, he and three other POWs began working on a sixty-foot crèche. Kaib refused to sell it to Marshall Field's department store but gave it to the community of Algoma, Iowa.[47]

NOTES

1. Ronald H. Spector, *Eagle against the Sun* (New York: Free Press, 1985), 971.

2. John W. Dower, *War without Mercy* (New York: Pantheon, 1986), 10.

3. Richard Goldstein, *New York Times,* December 21, 1999.

4. John Toland, *The Rising Sun: Decline and Fall of the Japanese Em-

pire (New York: Random House, 1976), 867.

5. Interview by John Cervone, "Remembering the Bataan Death March," *Military History,* December 1999, 31.

6. Geoffrey Perret, *A Country Made by War* (New York: Random House, 1989), 367.

7. Donald Knox, *Death March* (New York: Harcourt Brace Jovanovich, 1981), xi.

8. W. E. Brougher, *South to Bataan, North to Mukden* (Athens: University of Georgia Press, 1972), 32.

9. *New York Times Book Review,* Sunday, May 23, 1999.

10. Knox, *Death March,* xi.

11. Gavan Daws, *Prisoners of the Japanese: POWs of World War II in the Pacific* (New York: Morrow, 1994), 75.

12. Alexander's chapter in *Surviving Bataan and Beyond,* ed. Dominic Caraccilo (Mechanics, Pa: Stackpole, 1999), 27

13. Spector, *Eagle against the Sun,* 397.

14. Alexander in *Surviving Bataan and Beyond,* 33

15. William E. Dyess, *The Dyess Story: The Eye-Witness Account of the Death March and the Narrative of the Experiences in Japanese Prison Camps and of Eventual Escape,* ed. Charles Leavelle (New York: Putnam's, 1944), 13.

16. Dyess, *Dyess Story,* 71.

17. Dyess, *Dyess Story,* 156.

18. Dyess, *Dyess Story,* 182.

19. Dyess, *Dyess Story,* 517.

20. Henry Sakaida, *The Siege of Rabaul* (St. Paul, Minn.: Phalanx, 1996), 21.

21. Gregory "Pappy" Boyington, *Baa Baa Black Sheep* (New York: Arno, 1958), 343.

22. Boyington, *Baa Baa Black Sheep,* 275.

23. Alexander, 11–20.

24. Alexander, n. 255.

25. Frederic H. Stevens, *Santo Tomas Internment Camp* (New York: Stratford House, 1946), 7.

26. Anthony Arthur, *Deliverance at Los Baños* (New York: St. Martin's, 1985), 2.

27. Gavan Daws, *Prisoners of the Japanese: POWs of World War II in*

the Pacific (New York: Morrow, 1994), 296.

28. William B. Bruer, *Retaking the Philippines* (New York: St. Martin's, 1986), 1.

29. Bruer, *Retaking the Philippines*, 5.

30. Bruer, *Retaking the Philippines*, 161.

31. Bruer, *Retaking the Philippines*, 166.

32. Forrest Bryant Johnson, *Hour of Redemption: The Ranger Raid on Cabanatuan* (New York: Manor, 1978), 113.

33. Stevens, *Santo Tomas Internment Camp*, 309.

34. Elizabeth M. Norman, *We Band of Angels* (New York: Pocket Books, 1999), 14.

35. Norman, *We Band of Angels*, 188.

36. Norman, *We Band of Angels*, 16.

37. W. McCarthy, *The Angels Came at Seven* (New York: Maryknoll Fathers, 1980), 3.

38. Arthur, *Deliverance at Los Baños*, xiii.

39. Arthur, *Deliverance at Los Baños*, 147.

40. Arthur, *Deliverance at Los Baños*, 261.

41. Bruer, *Retaking the Philippines*, 175.

42. McCarthy, *Angels Came at Seven*, 5, 9.

43. Roger Daniels, *Concentration Camps USA: Japanese Americans and World War II* (Hinsdale, Ill.: Dryden, 1971), 1.

44. Daniels, *Concentration Camps U.S.A.*, 48.

45. Arnold Krammer, *Nazi Prisoners of War in America* (New York: Stein & Day, 1979), 178.

46. Krammer, *Nazi Prisoners of War*, 217.

47. Marion Amborg, "Gift of Peace," *St. Anthony Messenger,* December 2001, 18–22.

12

The Korean War

The U.S. military authorities sent to Korea when World War II ended were not particularly enthusiastic about their assignment to dismantle the Japanese regime. Civil unrest prevailed, and the U.S. military presence from 1945 to 1949 seemed to inflame the situation. The withdrawal of U.S. forces signaled disengagement, especially after Secretary of Defense Dean Acheson excluded South Korea from the U.S. security sphere in Asia. This stance, however, was not maintained for long.[1]

President Truman called the events in Korea a police action, not a war. "Police action," the "war we didn't win," and the "forgotten war" are some of the labels given to this conflict. The United States received the approval of the United Nations resolution to act in response to the Communist invasion of North Korea. At that time the Soviet Union did not belong to the Security Council. General Douglas MacArthur was named commander in chief of the U.N. forces.

On January 13, 1950, the Soviet delegate, Yakov Malik, protested the U.N. refusal to seat Communist China in the United Nations instead of the Nationalists (Taiwan). He was absent on June 25 when the U.N. resolution condemned the North Korean attack on South Korea. As Matthew Ridgeway says, "The U.N. intervention in Korea was a fluke of history made possible by the unique accident of the Russian boycott."[2] The hostile North Korean action started on the morning of June 25, 1950.

U.S. INVOLVEMENT IN THE KOREAN WAR

The reality of the war is that it needlessly took the lives of many on both sides. Its termination was delayed chiefly by prisoner of war issues that seemed almost insoluble. Often it was a temptation to use the term U.S. forces instead of U.N. forces. Although the American contribution was the largest, sixteen other nations were involved in the war effort, with Turkey, Australia, Britain, and Canada supplying combat troops.

The 24th Division was commanded by General William Dean, who knew Korea well. On June 30, 1950, however, the infantry was not in good shape.[3] The North Korean People's Army (NKPA) started advancing south on July 5. The fighting had really begun and about 185 were killed, wounded, captured, or missing. In a battle on a ridge south of Chosen, U.S. troops discovered six dead American POWs. Their hands were tied behind their backs and they had been shot in the back of the head. Thus North Korean war atrocities started early, a sign of things to come.[4]

On June 30, two rifle battalions of the U.S. Infantry Division were airlifted from the island of Kyushu to Pusan, Korea, under General William Dean.[5] On July 13, the 25th Division landed at Pusan and General Walton Walker, commander of the 8th Army, was named commander of all U.N. forces in Korea

GENERAL WILLIAM DEAN

When the NKPA blockaded an important highway in July 1950, General Dean turned his jeep by mistake to the south and was confronted by a NKPA block. He and his aide, pilot Arthur Clarke, abandoned the jeep and took to the hills along with stragglers who wanted to reach friendly lines once night came. Dean fell down an embankment and, meeting up with a lieutenant, wandered for a few days. An enemy patrol surprised them and they became separated.

Dean wandered for thirty-six days and was finally captured in a village thirty-five miles south of Taeju by civilians. He was turned over to the police on August 25. He was the NKPA's highest-ranking POW enemy officer, but his capture was kept a secret until December 18, 1951. He was repatriated on September 3, 1953.

Dean was never confined as a POW in an official POW camp. In his book he says that "the final twenty months of my captivity in North Korea were in sharp contrast to the first sixteen, and I'm convinced that Wilfred Burchett, deliberately or otherwise, was principally responsible for this change."[6] Dean felt that Burchett was primarily responsible for his captors' changed attitude and policy toward him. Dean was never tortured and the treatment he received improved. His imprisonment is not typical because he was separated from other prisoners.[7] Dean was probably the only one to have kind words for Burchett. Burchett worked for British newspapers before World War II and was a representative of a large London newspaper in the Pacific theater of operations. He was an Australian who seemed to be out of touch with the free world and reality.

At Dean's first military interrogation there were no reporters present. He couldn't be tricked into providing any information on what was to come, especially about the Inchon landing.

POW ISSUES

By autumn of 1950, after the Inchon success, the United Nations held almost 60,000 POWs. A rehabilitation program was directed by a marine colonel aided by a civilian, Major Osborn, whose objective was to introduce the ways of the free world to the prisoners.

These POWs were asked if they would like religious services. None wanted Buddhist services, but many asked for Christian services. The second Sunday, forty-five attended a Catholic Mass and 165 attended Protestant services. When 500 were moved to Pusan, however, the whole operation was terminated. It was quite clear that only a few desired to return to North Korea and a strong pattern of anti-Communism prevailed. The men were confined behind barbed wire with other POWs near Pusan and also on the island of Koje-do; some were on Cheju-do. More information is available about Koje-do, probably because there was so much trouble there; less information is to be found about Cheju-do, where most non-Communist POWs were confined, since there was less trouble. Both these islands are located off the coast of South Korea.

The prisoner of war issue at Panmunjom escalated to a breaking point. The Korean cease-fire came on July 27, 1953, and the repatriation of POWs began on September 4. But then came a war of words over enforced repatriation of POWs never before seen in the annals of war.

In late September 1950, the 24th Infantry resumed its advance and on the way liberated ninety-seven haggard POWs from their compounds, which were abandoned by the NKPA. On September 21, an important prisoner of the NKPA was taken by U.S. cavalry: the chief of staff of the NKPA, a colonel. He supplied important intelligence information, and on September 27, men of the 1st Cavalry Division moved north near Suwan. The NKPA forces began to disintegrate with tens of thousands of its men pouring into POW cages hastily constructed by the 8th Army and the X Corps.[8] Their numbers were becoming problematic, the main difficulty being what to do with them in the event of a retreat.

The North Koreans claimed that they would live up to the Geneva Convention principles on POW treatment, but many did not do so. Americans followed the rules. As Stokesburg says, "There were holes in the Geneva Convention through which it was possible to drive a truck, perhaps all the way to victory."[9]

AIR FORCE FIGHTING

The first major activities of the U.S. Air Force, even though it put everything in the air, were restricted. Near the coastal city of Pusan there was an attempt to gain time for the army's 24th Infantry Division, being boxed into a corner. The Pusan perimeter was a six-week series of actions that started on the evening of July 31, when General Walker's army retreated and crossed the Naktong River going east. The battle of Pusan consisted of a number of crises for the 8th Army.

U.S. F-80 Shooting Stars were fighting off enemy aircraft and bombing and strafing North Koreans and their artillery front lines, but restrictions were imposed on them, including minimum periods of time over target areas before returning to Japan. Some viewed this as highly unrealistic and impractical.

Thus arose the necessity for airfields in Korea at the outset of the war. The F-80s were not as effective as the Communist MIG-15s, but they were soon replaced by the famous F-86 fighter and fighter-bomber. In August-September 1950, the United States began establishing airbases in the south to improve its defense capability. It wanted the enemy to feel its power. The navy got into the act by bringing the carriers *Valley Forge* and *Triumph* to the Yellow Sea.[10] The major enemy airfields located at Pyongyang and Yonpo became prime targets for air force and navy aircraft.

On July 18–19, fighters and bombers reduced the airfields' capabilities considerably, but by July 21, the North Korean air force was no longer a serious problem. The network of airfields was greatly enlarged in the coming years, and this helped U.S. bomber missions in the far north and close-support missions for army and marine land units.

Each U.S. airfield was called a K-site. The 80th Fighter-Bomber Squadron and the 51st Fighter-Interceptor Squadron would ultimately be located at K-13 in Suwon. This increase meant more POW fliers would be added to the growing numbers of army land forces. The K-13 airfield was not far from actual enemy territory in flying time and presented a 4,000-foot runway strip. This meant that fighters and fighter-bombers from K-sites farther south could land at K-13 and the pilots could be debriefed there while their aircraft were refueled. Ted Williams, baseball star and marine pilot, was one such pilot.

Good seaports were lacking in both North Korea and South Korea. At the southern tip of the peninsula was Pusan, where the U.S. Army Prisoner of War Headquarters was first located. On October 7, the 8th Fighter-Bomber Group and the 35th Squadron arrived at Suwon (K-13), and on October 25, the last fighter-bomber squadron, the 80th. The runway was in bad shape, which necessitated a return to Kimpo on October 30. With reorganization plans, the 5th Air Force Headquarters moved to Seoul, and the 80th went back to Suwon about December 4. By January 1953, K-13 had been built up considerably. More K-sites were spread out and by June 1, 1952, there were thirteen in South Korea.[11]

WAR CRIMES

Blair reports that around August 15, 1950, fifteen captured American soldiers were crowded into a valley and machine-gunned. Fortunately, a few wounded escaped by faking death. This incident prompted MacArthur's warning to the Communists that officers would be held responsible for their actions at the end of the conflict and subjected to war crimes trials, as had the Japanese and Germans at the end of World War II. Blair, however, seems to think that the North Koreans were acting independently at lower levels rather than as a matter of policy.[12] Later it became apparent that this was not the case because of U.N. shock at the low number of POWs taken by the Communists. It was soon learned that the Communists made a habit of killing POWs when they retreated.

Bevin Alexander supplies details of the October 20 massacre near the Sunchon Tunnel, as do Ray Appleman and Albert Biderman. Frank Allen, assistant commander of the 1st Cavalry Division, and his men found a sad and sickening sight: the bodies of American POWs around a railroad tunnel near Myongucham about five miles northwest of Sunchon.

Two trains, each carrying about 150 American POWs, left Pyongyang on October 17. The POWs were fixing heavily broken trucks as they proceeded. The men were survivors of 370 Americans whom the North Koreans had marched north from Seoul after the Inchon landing. Each day five or six Americans died of different causes and their bodies were taken off the train; a few Americans managed to escape.

On October 29, during a parachute drop, the second of the two trains stayed in the tunnel. That evening the North Korean guards removed about 100 Americans and separated them into three groups for the evening meal. As they waited for their food, they were shot. Some American survivors faked their deaths and the train left that night. General Allen and his men originally found twenty-three American escapees, some of whom were wounded. Two died during the night. This tunnel massacre was the "Malmedy massacre" of Korea. A third massacre occurred at Kujang-dong on December 21, 1951. Here some thirty American POWs were shot and bayoneted to death as reprisals against air force strafing of their trains.[13] These massacres heightened animosity toward the North Koreans.

Before the Inchon landing, only some 1,000 North Korean POWs were held, but afterward numbers rose and within two months almost 130,000 POWs were under U.N. control. First they were held near Pusan under South Korean control, but later they were transferred to Koje-do Island over the course of the winter. This would set the stage for further trouble at Koje-do, for which the Chinese higher-ups would really be responsible.

CHINESE TROOPS IN NORTH KOREA

For some time it was not known that large numbers of Chinese troops had invaded Korea. The first ROK forces reached the Yalu on October 25, and some captured Chinese POWs were sent to the Americans. On October 25, the ROK 1st Division captured a Chinese soldier, and the next day more were taken.[14] By the end of the month, twenty-five Chinese POWs were captured, but it seemed that the U.N. command "could not bring itself to recognize the simple truth that the Chinese had entered the Korean War in force."[15] On October 26, the CIA received results of the 8th Army interrogators for the first Chinese POWs taken at Unsan. The report, unfortunately, was sent forward with little priority.

Early November CIA reports, however, were changing their tune as an estimated 30,000–40,000 Chinese were already in Korea and many more over the Manchurian border were ready to cross. Between October 13 and October 25, MacArthur's staff didn't receive much intelligence information about the presence or movement of such forces, but they were there, and Hastings poses the question, "Who were these fanatical hordes?" He notes conservative writers who still say that if MacArthur had been given more support, and perhaps not removed by President Truman, there might not have been a Vietnam, but he considers this highly unlikely.

MacArthur's intelligence about Chinese and North Korean intentions was poor and faulty. He didn't have much faith in the CIA and preferred his own intelligence sources. There were no successful covert U.N. operations in North Korea.

AMERICAN POWs

On November 30, 1950, the Chinese captured marine Andrew Condon in Hellfire Valley with fifty Americans in the Chosen River campaign and treated them well. Unfortunately, Condon turned out to help the Communist cause.

The worst atrocities on U.S. POWs were committed by the North Koreans in transit or at special compounds outside Pyongyang— "Pak's palace," the caves, and camp 9 at Kangdong. When the Chinese took over camp 5 in the spring of 1951, conditions improved. Marine Andrew Condon was one of the infamous prisoners to side with the Communists.

By the summer of 1951, there was a new Chinese policy for POWs under more organized Chinese arrangements. British and

American officers were transferred to a new camp 2 about a hundred miles into the mountains. In camp 5, Father Emil Kapaun, a POW and Catholic chaplain of the U.S. 1st Cavalry, died. One thing the Chinese wanted to destroy was religious faith.

Hastings describes an incident at NCO prisoner of war camp 4. Lieutenant Thornton, U.S. Navy, noticed that black POWs were separated from whites. One of the best-loved POWs was Captain John Stanley, who said, "I am an American, not a Negro."[16] Nobody ever escaped from a Yalu camp. At the end of the fighting only 13 percent of the marines versus 38 percent of the army survived.[17] Then, of course, there were the twenty-one who refused repatriation.

At one point, General MacArthur wanted all enemy POWs to be confined in the United States, as had been done with most German POWs in World War II, but the idea was rejected by the U.S. government. It would have been a massive operation, although such a move might have prevented the Koje-do incident. Prison camps had to be located in South Korea and offshore islands.

The Communists established a system of permanent POW camps in 1951 along the Yalu River, which separated Communist North Korea from Communist Manchuria. There were a few other camps throughout North Korea. Maps were given to pilots on combat missions in North Korea that located known POW camp areas, and these locations were included in the briefings given by intelligence officers, especially when a target was close to a camp area.

PHASES OF POW TREATMENT
IN CHINESE COMMUNIST CAMPS

Albert Biderman's *March to Calumny* includes the timetable of the establishment of Chinese Communist POW camps. The first phase was June-September 1950. During this phase, POWs received fair treatment in most cases. Food was sufficient and first aid and hospitalization of sick and wounded were provided. The POWs were moved by train from Seoul to Pyongyang and later to Mampojin. There were some severe threats and some isolated and capricious acts of mistreatment.

The second phase extended from September 15 to mid-November 1950, a period of defeat for North Korea. The good treatment ended in September as U.N. forces advanced to the Yalu; then came the surprise entrance of Chinese troops into Korea. They took over the POW barracks, ousting the POWs. Their food was curtailed, and they were subjected to many brutalities. The first death marches occurred and the weather became severely cold.

The third period involved confinement in temporary camps from November 1950 to March 1951. Masses of new POWs arrived and about two of every three captured in the summer did not survive the ordeal. Group punishments were enforced and brainwashing began to be used. Some men successfully resisted. Army Sergeant Lloyd Pate was captured on January 1, 1951, and joined a two-month Death March north to camp 5, arriving on March 5. For resisting brainwashing, he and his men were court-martialed and tortured; he survived and was repatriated. He later served two tours of duty in Vietnam.[18]

The fourth phase, March-June 1951, witnessed the establishment of permanent camps along a fifty-mile stretch next to the Yalu. The Chinese treated prisoners better than the North Koreans had, as part of an intensified approach to brainwashing.

The next phase, July 1951 to May 1952, involved compulsory indoctrination and a marked improvement in POW treatment. Following this came a controversy about the repatriation procedure, May 1952 to April 1953.

The final phase was from April 20, 1953, to September 6, 1953. Operation Little Switch started on April 20, and an agreement was signed on July 27 that ended the fighting. Operation Big Switch began on August 3 and ended on September 6, 1953.

The Communists were distrusted because of atrocities and because they took advantage of certain situations. During Little

Switch, the war was still on and the Communists moved troops and supplies in trucks marked POW or Red Cross to avoid being bombed.

THE BATTLE OF CHOSEN RESERVOIR

In December 1950, air support for U.N. troops at the Battle of Chosen Reservoir was very limited because of the weather. On December 9 the weather improved, but this did not mean that all problems would be solved. First Lieutenant Ozzie Vom Orde and his platoon left the Kate-ri perimeter at about 2:00 P.M. on December 8 with most of the materials required for fixing up a bridge. The next day, with much better weather, Vom Orde and First Lieutenant Dave Peppin of D Company looked the situation over very carefully. The concrete apron bridge seemed to be seventy or eighty feet, and the blown gap about eighteen to twenty feet. At about 1:00 P.M. the rigs arrived at the bridge, but Vom Orde and Peppin discovered to their dismay that the bridge span was five feet too short. Vom Orde was equal to the task, however, and outlined a plan to construct a wooden abutment on a small ledge four feet below the surface on the far side of the gap. With the help of Chinese prisoners, the structure was finished.[19] Technically, this was not in conformity with Geneva Convention principles, but it was nothing like what happened a year later on December 21, 1951: the Kujang-dong train massacre. There were well-documented reports on atrocities committed on American POWs in Korea.

In July 1951, Lieutenant John Kaelsch, a U.S. Navy helicopter pilot, tried to rescue a downed marine flier, but Kaelsch himself was shot down. The mission was a double failure—he did not help the marine and Kaelsch and his crew and the injured pilot became POWs. Kaelsch died as a POW and was posthumously awarded the Medal of Honor.[20] Another recipient of the Medal of Honor was Thomas Hudner, who tried to rescue pilot Jesse Brown near the

Chosen Reservoir. Unfortunately Brown's rescue was not successful. Brown had the distinction of being the navy's first African
American pilot.[21]

TRUCES AND REPATRIATION

Truce teams met and argued first at Kaesong, not Panmunjom.
Conversations went on for two years. A peace pact was worked
out, but the Communists used the delaying tactics that came to be
a part of their regular modus operandi. They insisted that all U.N.
forces be withdrawn before a truce was signed, which was completely unacceptable to U.N. forces. Surprisingly, an agenda was
neverthless agreed on, but one item, the proposed POW exchange,
dragged on for another nineteen months. The chief issue was
forced repatriation of 5,000 POWs who did not wish to return to
Communist control. There were about 13,200 prisoners in U.N.
compounds, but the Communists accounted for only 11,559 allied
POWs.[22]

The U.N. problem called for those POWs not selecting repatriation to be released and paroled. This meant some type of screening
was necessary and then the fireworks really started.

Operation Little Switch began in late April at Panmunjom. More
than 6,000 sick and disabled Communists were exchanged for 684
Allied prisoners. After Little Switch, newsmen were given sensational stories by POWs. Finally, on July 10, 1953, a document was
signed at Panmunjom that ended the hostilities and led to Operation
Big Switch. Once again it was truly amazing that the Communists
agreed to such an exchange.

Admiral Turner Joy was the first chief of the U.N. truce team, and
the U.S. position on voluntary repatriation of POWs "had cost us
over a year of war."[23]

Joy tells the story of Communist techniques in his book. His
successor at Panmunjom, General Harrison, set down three choices

for the Communists, all of which they rejected. Consequently, he declared an indefinite recess and said that the U.N. Command would do whatever it deemed necessary. This total impasse lasted one year and three months after the start of the truce talks. Little Switch was an accomplishment. Hermes tells us, "The U.N. returned 5,194 North Koreans and 1,034 Chinese POWs plus 446 civilian internees. In exchange the U.N.C. got 471 ROK soldiers, 149 Americans, 32 British, 15 Turks, and 17 other U.N. prisoners."[24]

UNCRC\UNRC

At Panmunjom, on April 26, truce talks resumed, but there remained the problem of neutral nations. The stage was set for the Neutral Nations Repatriation Commission (UNCRC), similar to an Indian proposal in the United Nations in the fall.

During the Revolutionary War, thousands of Hessian (and some British) soldiers decided to stay in the United States, which was not a problem. Why did so many Korean and Chinese prisoners refuse repatriation? Where had the Chinese soldiers who invaded Korea come from, and why? These questions will be answered in the section on Cheju-do Island and the Koje-do riots.

The UNRC consisted of five nations: Poland and Czechoslovakia, classified as pro-Communist; Switzerland and Sweden, classified as pro-American and more democratic, and India, the closest to a neutral position. Some had doubts about India's neutrality, and Syngman Rhee didn't help matters when he refused to permit Indian troops on Korean soil.

The next problem facing the United Nations was logistics and how to deal with the coming explanations and Rhee's attitude. The solution was to establish the United Nations Command Repatriation Group (UNCRG), headed by Brigadier General A. H. Hamblen, starting on September 1, 1953. His deputy commander and chief of staff was Colonel Ward Ryan, former commanding officer of the U.N. Command POW camp 2 near Pusan.

As already noted, the Republic of Korea under Rhee's leadership refused to allow Indian troops to set foot on Korean soil. This necessitated "one of the largest helicopter operations in military history."[25] The mission of the UNCRG "was to insure that all POWs have an opportunity to exercise full freedom of choice, to insure that the efforts of the Communist explainers be not coercive, and to explain to the non-repatriated UNC prisoners their rights and their freedom of choice."[26]

The Indian custodian forces completed taking custody of non-repatriated POWs by September 24. The call went out to the armed forces to supply officers and enlisted men to serve as workers and observers at the explanation sessions. It was also necessary to hire Department of the Army (DAC) translators. Thus civilians, army, navy, air force, and marines would be involved. These people were given a brief orientation at Pusan at the army POW headquarters and then sent to different POW compounds. The main concentration of anti-Communist Chinese POWs was on Cheju-do Island off the southern corner of the Korean peninsula. Both Chinese and North Koreans were held at Koje-do, where there were many difficulties and confrontations.

KOJE-DO

U.N. forces made some indoctrination efforts but never to the same extent as the Chinese, who used starvation as one method. The Communists began their brainwashing techniques in April 1951 in some of the Yalu prison camps, according to William White in his book *The Captives of Korea*. It was not an easy task to separate POWs into Communist and non-Communist camps, just as it was difficult to separate German Nazis and non-Nazis during World War II. There were deaths in both Communist and non-Communist camps, and the

U.N. certainly did not want to be held responsible for such deaths. By early 1951, almost 25,000 Chinese were confined, out of a total of 170,000. Not many wished repatriation and this seemed to be the eternal problem while other armistice issues were agreed on. No POW lists were given to Geneva, which was a major hang-up for U.N. negotiators.

In four compounds on Koje-do Chinese POWs were willing to be screened, and many were anti-Communists. Many Korean and Chinese interpreters were flown to Koje-do in anticipation of what was to come when POWs arrived there. White gives a breakdown as follows: compound 1, 6,900, 85 percent chose not to be repatriated; compound 2, over 90 percent chose not to be repatriated; in compound 3 there were 253 militant Communists. These statistics were hard to take at Panmunjom, for the Chinese Communists were "seriously losing face." Koje-do's Korean compounds were under such tight Communist control that the screening process was completely rejected.[27] Colonel Robinette, former Koje-do commander, said that the POWs there had gathered a multiplicity of homemade weapons. The Communists were ruthless with anyone showing inclinations to nonrepatriation, often trying and hanging them. Koje-do was ripe for serious difficulties. President Truman insisted that there would be no enforced repatriation.

Then began a frightening development that was unknown at the time. Trained Communist agents deliberately got themselves captured so they would be sent to Koje-do and cause internal strife. These were dangerous assignments because being uncovered in the wrong compounds could mean death. One of the U.N.'s sources of information was a Soviet officer of Korean ancestry who joined the U.N. side and told his story. Even if Communist manpower could have taken over the island, the Communists would still have the problem of escaping the island. Although the decision to put the POWs on offshore islands was a wise choice, some feel MacArthur's original idea to bring them to the United States might have been better.

THE DODD INCIDENT

On May 7, 1952, the Dodd incident took place. It was a small, planned move. Korean Private Pak Sung Hyong and his organization instigated the riots. When the revolt wasn't successful, fearing for his life, he came over to the U.N. side.

When General Dodd was seized and taken prisoner by the Communists, the U.N. command structure was shocked. General Van Fleet ordered troops from Pusan to Koje-do, and Brigadier General Charles Colson took command of the POW camp from Dodd, whom Van Fleet formally relieved. Colson arrived May 8 and warned that if Dodd was not released unharmed before a certain deadline, U.N. troops would invade the compound and free Dodd by force with tanks, if possible. The view was that "a General's life is no more precious than the life of a common soldier and that each is asked to risk his life every day."[28]

The 87th Airborne Combat Team was sent to reinforce General Boatner's troops, and it entered the compounds on June 10. In an hour and a half the resistance folded. The barricades were destroyed and 150 POWs were killed or wounded. Control was returned to the U.N. forces. One American lost his life and thirteen were wounded. Dodd and Colson were reduced in rank, a measure some considered unjust and uncalled for, but which all the higher-ups approved. There are those who view Dodd's going into the camp unarmed a courageous act and that although it might have been somewhat imprudent, he should not have been punished for it.

A major riot broke out in December 1952 at Pongam-do. A mass breakout resulted in 854 dead and 100 or more wounded. A Communist report that came into the U.N.'s hands clearly proved the willingness of the Communists to sacrifice the lives of their own prisoners for propaganda purposes.[29]

Cheju-do was the first offshore island proposed for a prison camp site in early 1951 but was rejected. Some think it probably would have been a better location than Koje-do. Little information has been published about the details of the explanation sessions held at Munsan-ni. White relates that the first explanations were held on October 15 and that the team of representatives, interpreters, and observers consisted of seventy-five Americans, fifty ROK officers, and fifty Chinese Americans under Chen Yi, who had a master's degree from the University of Chicago. Certainly the U.N. wanted to protect the Chinese anti-Communist forces whose relatives might suffer if they were identified. Press cameras and tape recorders were barred from explanation areas, but UNRC members were free to take whatever pictures they wanted. White says that the Czechs and Polish sneaked candid shots,[30] but others report that this was not done in their presence.

THE EXPLANATION SESSIONS

When a prisoner of war entered the tent, there were usually three Communist explainers who would stand, bow, and smile. Almost always the prisoner would spit on them and on the first morning would leave immediately. There were four main points of emphasis: (1) Come back, all is forgiven; (2) We soon will rule all Asia, so be on the winning side; (3) Back in your homeland we are building a wonderful new way of life; (4) Please come home for the motherland needs her son.[31]

The prisoner could ask any questions. Once he made his decision, he would choose or refuse repatriation. If he didn't want repatriation, he would exit through the door from which he entered; if he chose repatriation, he would exit the door near the Communists. There was some difficulty with the term "repatriation." To some, the Chinese translation "going home" meant Taiwan, not the mainland.

White says that the POWs were given light folding chairs just opposite the small table of the Communist explainers. After a prisoner picked up a chair and threw it at the explaining team, a chair was no longer supplied. The POW simply stood in the center of the tent while an explainer spoke to him. There was a small chair next to the Communist table and this was usually occupied by a young Chinese boy who was an interpreter, in case English was spoken.

OBSERVERS

Paul Garvey of the U.S. Information Service said that each POW was accompanied on the first day by an Indian guard on either side in case there was any violence. Garvey, of course, could not have observed all sessions. I was quite surprised years later to learn that such a reporter was permitted by the Communists. As a U.S. officer, I had legal status as an observer to be present with an interpreter. Were the brief written reports of observers all shown or made available to Garvey or the press media? I doubt that very much, but I can't be sure. The press of both sides were often in Colonel Robinette's tent, according to White, but generally they wandered through the area searching for violence, easy to find. Many POWs were disruptive—throwing a chair or yelling. One POW grabbed a bench to throw at the Communists and the Polish officers wanted him to be court-martialed. Colonel Robinette, sitting as an observer, thought it was "like listening to a series of Patrick Henrys, each shouting for liberty or death."[32] Those who chose repatriation rushed through the Communist door and in some cases were considered to have been hidden agents. This became a known fact when some of the repatriates became explainers in future sessions.

When I was selected to be an observer (along with a major who was a combat pilot), I was informed of this assignment at 9:00 A.M. and told to be prepared to leave on a flight at 9:30 for the U.S. Army POW Command Headquarters at Pusan. The training and briefing sessions for observers had already ended, so we were latecomers. At first my status was in doubt. Was I an observer for the North Korean or Chinese anti-Communist POWs? There was also the possibility that I would be assigned to the team dealing with the so-called American POWs called turncoats. On the next day I was happy to learn that I was assigned to the anti-Communist Chinese POWs and not the twenty-one turncoats. The next problem was to get me and my interpreter to Cheju-do Island. A U.S. Navy LST picked us up at the beach at Pusan and brought us to Cheju-do.

On Cheju-do the observers and their interpreters were brought into the POW compounds to be introduced as people who would be present at the explanation sessions to protect their interests. At first we were supposed to be some type of defense counsel, but unfortunately our high-ranking officers yielded on this point at Panmunjom and said we would act only as observers. The main purpose of the UNRC was to see that there would be no forced repatriation, as previously stated.

On the first day that explanation sessions were held, there were so many who did not choose repatriation that it was embarrassing to the Communists. Consequently they found some reason for not continuing the sessions the next day. I do not recall how many days passed before the sessions resumed, but they finally did.

Back at Cheju-do there were representatives from Taiwan who spoke to the prisoners from outside the compound. This was to reassure them that the United States would support them. Our presence inside the compounds (observers and interpreters) was designed to accomplish that also. We were not allowed to carry firearms while we visited the POW compounds. The reason for this precaution was probably what happened at Koje-do, but many of us (perhaps the vast majority) did not know about the events that took place on Koje-do. Probably the high-ranking officers had some knowledge of those events.

In the compound when a group of prisoners was brought to us, I was always offered a cup of tea which I accepted. I declined the offer of cigarettes which caused a small problem because the Chinese

POWs couldn't believe that an American officer didn't smoke. My interpreter had to teach me how to say in Chinese "thank you, I don't smoke."

One very important fact I learned from POWs to whom I spoke on Cheju-do was that many of them who were peasants were taken from the mainland and literally impressed into the Chinese army and transported to Korea. They were often placed in the front lines without any weapons and ordered to rush in masses toward the battlefield with Communist soldiers behind them. If they refused they were shot in the back, but there was always hope they would be captured, a much better alternative to being shot in the back. It was certainly understandable that there would be countless Chinese POWs who did not want to go back to Communist control.

As I mentioned earlier, when I was on Cheju-do, things were under U.N. control. We were told, however, that sometimes bodies of POWs were found in the compounds and the supposition was that in some way they were probably found to be pro-Communist. Those who managed to hide such sentiments and arrive at Panmunjom to attend an explanation session were undoubtedly candidates for repatriation and, as mentioned previously, some became explainers in subsequent sessions.

PERSONAL MEMOIRS

I recall vividly two personal experiences at the explanation sessions. Some sessions were very simple. The prisoner would be brought in, spoken to, and would make a decision and generally leave to return, hopefully, to Taiwan. In all the sessions I attended, the Communists failed to persuade any POWs to be repatriated. They left via the door they entered, but some sessions were not so simple.

In one session the communist explainer stated that the two Catholic chaplains who had worked among them on Cheju-do were nothing more than CIA agents planted among them to cause trouble. As my interpreter was translating for me, I became infuriated by these lies. My job was to observe, not criticize or comment. But since I knew the two chaplains, Father Sullivan, a Franciscan, and Father Coffey, a Maryknoller, both of whom spoke Chinese fluently, I felt obligated to interrupt, even though it was illegal for me to do so. I stood up and called the Chinese explainer a fraud and said that when he called these priests CIA agents, he "was way out in left field." My statement caused considerable confusion because the very young boy doing the interpreting could not translate it. My interpreter immediately consulted with me and then urged me to continue using baseball slang or any English slang to confuse the boy more. I felt sorry for the boy because he was taking a verbal beating from his Communist bosses for his inability to translate my slang.

The Indian chairman ordered the prisoner to be removed from the tent. The correct exit was used. Then I was ordered to keep quiet. The Indian chairman said that I had no right to say anything and that I was only an observer. He was right, of course, and outside the tent after the session he bitterly complained about me to an army lieutenant colonel, who told me off. The colonel told me to "shut up and not cause an international situation." Actually, his language was quite crude. I saluted him and said, "Yes, sir," but quickly added that the Communist was a liar and we were supposed to protect the POWs. Today it seems ironic to me that the Communists had the nerve to make such an assertion when I later discovered, upon my research for this chapter, that the Communists sent their own trained agents into camps at Koje-do to cause trouble.

The next day another incident happened that almost brought the same colonel down on me. A prisoner was ushered into the tent by the same Indian guard who was at least six-six. From my first year of teaching American history I recalled the impressment issue of the War of 1812, when the British illegally removed both naturalized and native-born Americans from U.S. vessels on the high

seas, even within sight of the American shore, to serve in the
British navy.

One prisoner walked to the table at which the Communists were
seated and gave them a smart military salute. It was quite a surprise
to me and also the Communists, all of whom rose quickly from their
seats to acknowledge the greeting from someone they apparently
thought was a good candidate for repatriation. The POW approached
the table and then quickly withdrew from his sleeve an iron peg usually used to secure one corner of a large squadron tent to the ground.
The POW hit one of the Communists over the head and brought
some blood to his forehead. Needless to say, pandemonium and
chaos ensued.

The Indian chairman promptly summoned an Indian guard, who
picked up the POW with one arm and started to remove him from the
tent. But the guard was going to take the wrong exit. I ran to the exit
to block his way. I shouted "Taiwan! Taiwan!" and pointed to the
other exit. The Indian chairman recognized the problem and ordered
the guard to take the POW out the proper exit.

First aid was administered to the injured Communist outside the
tent on the Communist side while the members of the UNRC and my
interpreter and I were standing outside the tent on the other side. The
same colonel who had chastised me the previous day appeared on
the scene with fire in his eyes blazing at me. I immediately claimed
I had done nothing wrong and the Indian chairman explained the
whole situation, which absolved me.

I did not fraternize with any of the UNRC representatives but the
Swiss and Swedish representatives were very friendly. I cannot say
this for the Polish and Czechoslovakian officers, who avoided us
completely. I had a form on which I was supposed to record the
names of all the team members but met with resistance almost immediately when I asked for the name of the young Polish officer. He
wouldn't talk to me and shrugged his shoulders as if to say he didn't
understand me. I knew that he spoke French because I heard him
speaking French to the Swiss and Swedish officers. I said "Votre

nom, s'il vous plait?" The Polish officer disregarded me but went directly to the Czech officer, an older person, to converse quietly with him. After about five minutes the Polish officer approached me and gave me his name. I knew then who was the real boss! Many of us at Munsan-ni called the explanations operation persuasion, but nowhere else have I ever seen such a label in print.

The UNCREG story was unique in the annals of war. Explanations were given to more than 29,999 POWs and there were no precedents that could be used as guidelines because nothing like this had ever happened before. Similar delaying tactics on the part of the Communists were used in the Vietnam War at the Paris Peace Conference.

AMERICANS WHO COLLABORATED WITH THE ENEMY

The conduct of many American POWs left much to be desired. Stokesbury says, "It was the young, the immature, the restless, who sank into apathy, died or turned their coats."[33] This became evident from an examination of the backgrounds of the infamous twenty-one. The author also points out that survival and behavior were better among the British and Turkish prisoners as well as among American marines. Thus a new code of conduct was necessary for American servicemen. Some POWs turned into animals who stole from fellow prisoners and, in some cases, threw their fellow comrades out into the cold to hasten their death. Others acted in a progressive manner and seemed to accept Communist teachings, while others tried to play it cool by taking a middle ground.

The U.S. Army concluded that about 425 POWs could easily be tried for acts ranging from giving aid and comfort to the enemy to actual murders. About half of these men became civilians and thus were removed from military jurisdiction. Thirty-five went before boards of inquiry, and fourteen were tried by military court-martial.

Needless to say, the trials were not popular and were widely scruti-nized in the media. In the Mexican War, there had been speedy trials for the San Patrícios and some judgments for the traitorous men who had deserted and entered the ranks of the Mexican army to take ac-tive participation against U.S. forces. There was ample justification for the courts-martial held, even though they were hastily convened to mete out punishment.

The U.N. forces were embarrassed in September 1951, when Koje-do pro-Communist POWs tried fifteen POWs and executed them be-fore a "people's court" in the prison camp. Their only offense was that they were anti-Communist and wanted to go to Taiwan.

Kinkead, in his book *In Every War but One,* maintained that one of every three American POWs in Korea was guilty of some type of collaboration with the enemy. Unfortunately this book does not in-clude a bibliography of the author's sources, but previous articles of his contained some that were good and valid. Bad things were done that were proven beyond all doubt in other articles, government doc-uments, and books that must be considered, but Kinkead's writings did not help matters back in the United States.

Biderman *(March to Calumny)* answers Kinkead's book. He maintains that nowhere in his book does Kinkead say what propor-tion of POWs actually collaborated.[34]

Another criticism of Kinkead's book is that it is misleading about strengths and weaknesses "characteristically American,"[35] in that it de-picts POWs as inept targets of exploitation,[36] that marches were major causes of POW fatalities,[37] and that only two men were actually tried on charges at their return. Thus Biderman and Kinkead are at odds with each other. In some points Kinkead seems to contradict himself.

The most notorious case was that of Sergeant James Gallagher, convicted at a court-martial for killing two sick POWs by throwing them out into the snow. The specifications against him were as fol-lows: (1) two POWs were ejected out into the cold, (2) a third POW, name unknown, was murdered by being struck about the body and forcibly suspended from a hook on the wall, being left to hang with his feet off the ground, and thereafter forcibly being put from his place of shelter and exposed to extremely cold weather. The prisoner was sick, infirm from dysentery, and unable to help himself.[38] This brings back horrible memories from the Civil War when Americans were fighting Americans.

In his book, Kinkead classified collaborators in different groups, stating that 13 percent of POWs were outright collaborators. A second group collaborated to get special benefits. The third group, the smallest, were those who accepted Communism. The vast majority of POWs, three out of four, chose what seemed to be the path of least resistance. They were not traitors but played it cool and represented the fourth group. The author considered the first three groups collaborators.

Where did the twenty-one turncoats belong? The author's tendency leaned to the third group. Some may point to the fear of court-martial as probably the main motivation for their actions, which they knew to be wrong and that court-martial would have been deserved in each case. Brief biographies are supplied, and readers may draw their own judgment.

HIDDEN HEROES

Kinkead calls the true heroes of the prison camps the reactionaries who maintained their integrity and personal honor during their confinement.[39] These were mature men who could work well with all troops, could handle problems adequately, and could sabotage indoctrination attempts quietly. Some of them did not return.

Captain Emil Kapaun, the Franciscan Catholic chaplain mentioned previously, belonged to this heroic group. He did everything he could to help POWs, physically and spiritually, in different POW camps. In the winter of 1950–1951, Father Kapaun was in the Pyoklong POW camp. Sharing his food with hungry POWs, he himself was slowly starving. He had dysentery and limped because of a blood clot in his leg. In this weakened condition he comforted and nursed sick POWs and ultimately succumbed to his condition.

Father Kapaun served as an army chaplain in Burma in World War II, was separated at the end of the war, but returned to active duty in Korea. He was in the 8th Cavalry Regiment and served in the front lines. Both he and someone named Dr. Anderson were captured, and Kapaun visited nearby camps and helped soldiers of all denominations.

Throughout the winter his health declined considerably. He was taken to a POW hospital by his Communist guards but died on May 6, 1951. Lieutenant Ralph Nardella told of his martyrdom more than two years later and Father Kapaun received the Bronze Star and DSC posthumously for heroism. His medals, at the request of his parents, were given to his religious superior.[40] Another well-decorated hero about whom nothing was said for almost two years was Sergeant Hiroshi Mujamura. On October 24, 1951, near Taejon-ni, he performed valiantly against the enemy. He threw grenades and fired his carbine against enemy troops. He dressed the wounds of two soldiers hit by shrapnel and in hand-to-hand combat killed ten. He also destroyed a heavy machine gun. He was fighting fiercely when he was taken prisoner by an enemy soldier who said in English that they (the enemy) didn't hurt prisoners, which, of course, was not always true, but Mujamura was one of the lucky ones. When Mujamura was repatriated and passed through Freedom Village, he was introduced by Brigadier General Ralph Osborne and told he had been awarded the Medal of Honor. His citation had the date December 21, 1951 on it, but it had been classified "top secret" to protect him as a POW. "None of the recipients have learned about the honor quite the way that he did."[41] Mujamura was also included in Edward Murphy's *Korean War Heroes*.

MEDALS OF HONOR

In the Korean War, 131 Medals of Honor were awarded to both prisoners of war and nonprisoners. Included in the group of POWs was General Dean and a Lieutenant Kleps. Several other Medal of Honor recipients had been POWs.

Lieutenant James Stone, who ended up at Officers Camp 2 on the Yalu River, got his release at Freedom Valley. This was also kept secret to prevent retaliation while he was a POW.[42]

Sergeant Raye Duke, veteran of World War II, was ordered to leave his men at Chosen and then he ordered his men to leave him. He was shot and listed as MIA, but in late 1951 his family was told he had been captured and died in a North Korean POW camp. In 1954 he was given the Medal of Honor.

Master Sergeant Benjamin Wilson, a veteran of Pearl Harbor, requested combat duty when the Korean War started, which he got at Inchon. He also earned a Medal of Honor.

Two officers, Lieutenant Enoch and Lieutenant Quinn, broke under threat and admitted participation in bacteriological warfare. They were told that they were war criminals who could be tried and convicted. Joining the scene at this time was Wilfred Burchett, an Australian pro-Communist journalist, who was given a copy of Enoch's germ warfare confession. He was present in North Korea to cover the Communist side of the war for *Ce Soir,* the Paris counterpart of the *Daily Worker.* Some literary polishing of the so-called confessions was done by Burchett and his cohort Alan Winnington. These two pro-Communist writers coauthored *Koje Unscreened* and *Plain Perfidy*, both published in Peking.

In summer 1952, Captain Theodore Harris, commander of a B-28 reconnaissance plane, bombed a bridge near Sinuju in North Korea and was shot down by a MIG-15. As a prisoner, he confessed nothing. Kept on public display and questioned nightly, he refused to give information and was subsequently transferred to an interrogation camp thirty miles from Pyongyang.[43] White's book gives a fair comparison of the treatment and behavior of POWs on both sides.

THE TWENTY-ONE TURNCOATS

Kinkead's book *In Every War but One* showed the shocking behavior of the average POWs stemming from poor discipline and defects of character. It represented a stinging indictment of the home training of children, education, physical fitness, and religiousness of many Americans. It seemed to make hits on all minority groups. Biderman in his *March to Calumny* declared that by strictly legal criteria only ten out of 4,000 POWs were guilty of collaboration. In reality many allegations and recriminations of American repatriates against one another didn't really involve true collaboration but were simply selfish criminal conduct.[44] The American press tended to consider the twenty-one turncoats as innocent victims[45] and not real traitors. Although Kinkead was extremely harsh on POW behavior, much can still be learned from his book. Biderman's book, as already mentioned, is a strong contrast to Kinkead's.

Among the twenty-one turncoats there were sixteen Protestants, four Roman Catholics, and one Greek Catholic. There were three African Americans and the rest were white. All except one were native-born and only one was from a large city. There seemed to be no single answer to why they refused repatriation except for Virginia Pasley's suggestion that all of them had done something wrong and couldn't face up to it.[46]

One common denominator among the twenty-one was the lack of good education, although one of them could speak a few languages. One was a draftee and the rest were enlisted men. Their ranks ranged from one sergeant to private, private first class, and corporal. On the issue of court-martial, some feel that they could have gotten off with a special or summary court-martial, as opposed to a general court-martial, which is the most serious.

Thirty-six American fliers signed germ warfare confessions in Korea, all officers with good educations and high IQs. What explains their behavior? Marine Colonel Frank Schwable claimed he was brought to that point by cold, endless repetition, illness, loneliness, and systematic degradation. What is the breaking point physically and mentally for a POW? In Vietnam, air force, navy, and marine pilots suffered terribly, as shall be discussed in the next chapter, but most were able to endure the hardships. The twenty-one turncoats in Korea did not undergo any torture.

In the Pueblo incident after the Korean conflict, Commander Bucher surrendered his ship and men to the Communists without resistance. All eventually were returned, but Bucher was castigated for his surrender and subjected to court-martial. He was finally absolved by the secretary of defense, but his career was ruined as a result of the event.

BIOGRAPHIES OF THE TWENTY-ONE

Evidence against the twenty-one turncoats was given by many returned POWs who witnessed their actions in the prison camps and suffered as a result of them. Let us now take a brief look at the backgrounds of the twenty-one.

- Scott Bush had an education up to the eighth grade and a low IQ. A devoted student of Communism, he tried to convert fellow prisoners to his thinking, for which he received better food, medical care, and a job as a librarian.
- PFC Otto Bell had an eighth-grade education and a low IQ. He attended Communist indoctrination meetings and tried to convert others. He made propaganda recordings and signed peace petitions for which he was rewarded with a job of mail orderly.
- PFC Aaron Wilson participated in indoctrination and propaganda activities. He received better food and more freedom than other POWs. He had a low IQ and an eighth-grade education.
- Private Samuel Hawkins finished his third year of high school and had a low average IQ. He collaborated with the Communists and informed on fellow prisoners. He tried to persuade others to accept Communism and was made a mail clerk by the Chinese.

- Corporal Rufus Douglas had an average IQ and completed one semester of college. He wrote articles for the Communists, made propaganda broadcasts, and informed on his fellow prisoners. His rewards included better living quarters, better food, and duties involving recreation, mail, and sanitation.
- PFC Lewis Griggs wrote articles for the Communists, preached their philosophy, made propaganda recordings, and was an informer who collaborated in every way possible with his captors. His IQ was average and he had had two years of high school.
- PFC Morris Wills was guilty of the same offenses as Douglas and received many favors and a great degree of freedom. He had two years of high school and an IQ of 106.
- Private Richard Tenneson's conduct was similar to that of Wills, Douglas, and Hawkins. His chief rewards consisted of liquor and marijuana.
- PFC John Dunn was a high school graduate with an average IQ. He lectured for the Communists and wrote articles for the *Daily Worker* of London. He openly collaborated and became a camp librarian.
- Sergeant Richard Cordon had two years of high school and a high IQ. He wrote pro-Communist articles and informed on his fellow prisoners. He received better living conditions, better food, and medical treatment. He lived and worked at Chinese headquarters at two different camps.
- PFC William Corvart had three years of high school and an average IQ. He wrote articles and made propaganda recordings but received no special or regular duties. He was convinced that collaboration would make his life better.
- PFC Lowell Skinner had an average IQ and an eighth-grade education. He wrote articles, made propaganda broadcasts, and got better clothing, food, and medical attention.
- Corporal La Rance Sullivan had three years of high school and an average IQ. He wrote articles, made propaganda recordings,

and tried to convert fellow prisoners, for which he was put in charge of POWs.

- PFC William White was given the position of mailman for informing on fellow prisoners. He willingly accepted Communism and tried to influence others. He had an average IQ and four years of high school.

- Corporal Harold Webb had a low average IQ and a ninth-grade education. He was made a camp librarian for informing on fellow prisoners, writing propaganda articles, and making recordings.

- PFC Clarence Adams had three years of high school and an average IQ. He voluntarily collaborated and informed on fellow prisoners.

- PFC Arlie Pate had an average IQ and a ninth-grade education. He was appointed to the camp newspaper, wrote articles, made recordings, and informed on others. He received better food, clothing, and medical attention and had a large degree of freedom.

- Corporal Howard Adams had three and a half years of college and an average IQ. He wrote for the camp newspaper and kept Communists informed of POW activities. He received a Bronze Star for heroism in World War II and reenlisted in 1948.

- Corporal Andrew Fortuna had two years of high school and an average IQ. He was paid by the Chinese to write articles in the camp newspaper and was chosen as a public address announcer because of his reliability.

- Private James Veneres was a high school graduate and had an above average IQ. He lectured on Communism, led study groups, and tried to convert other POWs, for which he was made a librarian.

- Corporal Albert Belhomme was born in Belgium. He enlisted, wrote for the Communists, and created slogans for Communist camp posters. He had a European education and a high IQ. He was very knowledgeable and spoke a few languages.

The author who put all this information together did a marvelous research job and made clear the reasons for their staying—they knew what they were guilty of and didn't want to face the music. There are still some, however, who would like to give them the benefit of the doubt. All twenty-one had refused to come to any explanations, a fact that was revealed later.

CODE OF CONDUCT FOR POWS

The need for a special code of conduct for POWs became very necessary, but didn't come until a few years later. In World War II a pamphlet was distributed to members of the armed forces on the rights of POWs. The pamphlet, however, didn't spell out a code of conduct. It was in 1955 that such a code was drawn up, but it was far from adequate and had to be revised for the Vietnamese conflict. Would it have done any good if it had been published and distributed to servicemen in Korea?

The Korean War pointlessly took many lives on both sides mainly because of the intransigence of the Communist negotiations at Panmunjom, which unfortunately was continued during the Vietnam War and posed a great problem for Henry Kissinger in Paris at his secret meetings with Le Duc Tho and at the Peace Conference itself.

An important point made in William Vatcher's book is often overlooked in writings on the repatriation demands of the Communists. He mentions that Edwin D. Dickinson, an authority on international law writing in the *New York Times* (December 7, 1952), tried to correct a false notion about repatriation. He says that asylum can be granted in an unlimited way to POWs in the absence of a treaty, and he cites article 14 of the Universal Declaration of Human Rights adopted by the General Assembly of the United Nations in 1948.[47] Joy's book about the Communists is perhaps the best way to end this subject. The Communists "lied, they blustered, they became vindictive, they welshed, they twisted, distorted and denied truth, they delayed, they threatened."[48] Vatcher says, "It is significant that the Communists have never in their history fulfilled a pledge or kept a promise in regard to the return, repatriation, or even a full accounting of civilians or military personnel."[49] He further states that when a documented account of Korean atrocities was released after the signing of an armistice agreement, "The account makes Edgar Allen Poe's horror stories seem completely innocuous."[50]

The uniqueness of the Korean War remains in the element of the explanation sessions. Secretary of State Dean Acheson from the very beginning did not consider Korea important and later expressed the idea that the Geneva Convention principles should be strictly enforced. This would have meant no explanation sessions and perhaps an almost endless war.[51]

The idea of permitting POWs to make a choice was offered in the Capitol by Brigadier General Robert McClure, the army's chief of psychological warfare. It did not satisfy the Communists, but it was a move in the right direction that the Communists ultimately accepted.

Before the explanation sessions the screening process (trying to separate Communists and anti-Communists) had caused considerable trouble on the repatriation issue. Some disorder occurred, and on Koje-do the Communists either refused to participate or claimed there could not be any screening without violence.[52] Of the POWs on Koje-do, 30,484 expressed the desire for repatriation. The explanations ultimately required the presence of a representative from each member nation of the UNRC as well as one from the detaining country. These representatives were the observers.

MIAs

But what about the many POWs not accounted for, the MIAs? To get the Communists to agree to talk about this problem wasn't easy, as it would be regarding Vietnam MIAs years later.

Intensive talks about this problem took place at a meeting in Hawaii in 1987, well after the conclusion of the Korean conflict. The results were frustrating for the U.S., but they seemed, to some extent, to open the door. More than 8,100 U.S. and U.N. personnel were listed as MIA. The North Koreans turned over 208 sets of remains across the Demilitarized Zone, but nothing was really settled on a permanent basis.

In January 1986, the team that tried to recover remains of POWs was disbanded. *The New York Times* carried reports of these events. What compounded the problem of the mystery of the American prisoners were sightings of American prisoners supposedly held by North Korea. A defector claimed he had seen such prisoners in a top secret prison camp, Oh Young Nam, near Pyongyang. The defector was a thirty-two-year-old former police officer who had escaped to China and then went to Korea. There was also some talk of American POWs sent to Russia. This was denied by the North Koreans, but some historians claim that information on this subject could not be released for fear of a nuclear war with Russia and/or China.

The Associated Press on February 27, 2000, carried an article stating that the Pentagon had received the memoirs of a Russian émigré, which included a statement that a dozen Americans from World War II and Korea were being held in Siberian labor camps. Former President Boris Yeltsin admitted in 1992 that the Soviets captured a dozen U.S. airmen after their planes had been shot down. The Kremlin denied this charge. Thus the mystery continues, as does the mystery of MIAs in the Vietnam conflict.

A major continuing error in Kinkead's book was denying Communist reliance on terror as a means of control. The book stereotypes American soldiers as slovenly and stupid malcontents who should not be in the country or stationed on one's soil, who was a poor representative of his country.[53] Biderman took issue with this statement. Actually Kinkead wrote his book with the help of Defense Department officials and Kinkead and Biderman's books disagree considerably.

Many years later a tunnel was discovered under the Demilitarized Zone between North and South Korea by U.S. and South Korean military engineers. It was located in a remote mountainous area near the border and was the fourth one found since 1974. Conjecture was that it was built for an invasion.

NOTES

1. Harry Summers, "The Korean War: A Fresh Perspective," *Military History,* April 1996, 24–25.

2. Matthew B. Ridgway, *The Korean War* (Garden City, N.Y.: Doubleday, 1967), 56.

3. Clay Blair, *The Forgotten War: America in Korea, 1950–1953* (New York: Time Books, 1987), 113.

4. Ridgway, *Korean War*, 113.

5. S. L. A. Marshall, *The Military History of the Korean War* (New York: Franklin Watts, 1963).

6. William F. Dean, *General Dean's Story* (New York: Viking, 1954), 244.

7. Eugene Kinkead, *In Every War but One* (New York: Norton), 1959.

8. Ridgway, *Korean War,* 31.

9. James Stokesburg, *A Short History of the Korean War* (New York: Morrow, 1988), 181.

10. Edwin P. Hoyt, *The Pusan Perimeter* (New York: Stein & Day, 1985), 97.

11. Robert Frank Futrell, *The United States Air Force in Korea, 1950–1953* (New York: USAF Historical Division, Research Studies Institute/Duell, Sloan, and Pearce, 1961).

12. Blair, *Forgotten War*, 56.

13. Albert Biderman, *March to Calumny* (New York: Macmillan, 1963), 119.

14. Max Hastings, *The Korean War* (New York: Simon & Schuster, 1987), 130.

15. Hastings, *Korean War*, 131.

16. Hastings, *Korean War*, 298.

17. Hastings, *Korean War*, 304.

18. Kevin Dwyer, "A Test of Courage," *American Legion Magazine,* September 2000, 48.

19. Joe Sugarmen, "Breakout from Chosen," *Air and Space Smithsonian,* July 2000.

20. John Sotham, "The Heroes," *Air and Space Smithsonian,* July 2000.

21. *Air and Space Smithsonian,* July 2000, 38–39.

22. Samuel L. Marshall, *The Military History of the Korean War* (New York: Franklin Watts, 1963), 79.

23. C. Turner Joy, *How Communists Negotiate* (New York: Macmillan, 1955), 152; James F. Schnabel and Robert J. Watson, *The History of the Joint Chiefs of Staff: The Joint Chiefs of Staff and National Policy* (Washington, D.C.: Government Printing Office, 1979), 3:680.

24. Walter G. Hermes, *Truce, Tent, and Fighting Front* (Washington, D.C.: Office of the Chief of Military History, United States Army, 1966), 2:964–67; Bevin Alexander, *Korea: The First War We Lost* (New York: Hippocrene, 1986), 473.

25. *The UNCREG Story, Munsan-ni, Korea*, 1 September–December 1953, pamphlet issued by Headquarters UNCREG, 4.

26. *UNCREG Story,* 4.

27. William White, *The Captives of Korea: An Unofficial White Paper on the Treatment of War Prisoners* (New York: Scribner's, 1957), 188.

28. White, *Captives of Korea,* 213.

29. Ridgway, *Korean War,* 216.

30. White, *Captives of Korea,* 281.

31. White, *Captives of Korea,* 284.

32. White, *Captives of Korea,* 303.

33. James Stokesbury, *A Short History of the Korean War* (New York: Morrow, 1988), 192.

34. Biderman, *March to Calumny,* 39.

35. Biderman, *March to Calumny,* 45.

36. Biderman, *March to Calumny,* 73.

37. Biderman, *March to Calumny,* 104.

38. Eugene Kinkead, *In Every War but One* (New York: Norton, 1959), 70.

39. Kinkead, *In Every War but One,* 132.

40. Ray Bird, "Not Any Battlefield Heroes, but Sustained Bravery of Another Sort," *Military History,* 28, 30, 86–87.

41. Edward Hymoff, "For More Than Two Years, His Medal of Honor Was a Tightly Guarded Secret," *Military History,* April 1996, 12, 66, 68.

42. Edward F. Murphy, *Korean War Heroes* (Novato, Calif.: Presidio, 1992), 210.

43. White, *Captives of Korea*, 179.

44. Biderman, *March to Calumny*, 205.

45. Biderman, *March to Calumny*, 225.

46. Virginia Pasley, *Twenty-One Stayed: The Story of the American GIs Who Chose Communist China—Who They Were and Why They Stayed* (New York: Farrer, Straus & Cudahy, 1955), 16.

47. Hal Vatcher, *Mutiny on Koje Island* (Rutland, Vt.: Tuttle, 1965).

48. Joy, *How Communists Negotiate*, 146.

49. Vatcher, *Mutiny on Koje Island*, 117.

50. Vatcher, *Mutiny on Koje Island*, 126.

51. Dean Acheson, *Present at the Creation* (New York: Norton, 1973), 619.

52. Schnabel and Watson, *History of the Joint Chiefs,* 3:759.

53. Kinkead, *In Every War but One*, 122.

13

The Vietnam War

In the Vietnam War the United States again faced the Communists as the enemy and again the conflict was not an official war. Our main objective was containing Communism, which meant protecting South Vietnam from Communist tyranny and rule. In a film broadcast on the History Channel, *Courage under Fire*, Walter Cronkite posed the questions of how and why we got involved in the conflict, which he says is the only war we ever lost.

In Vietnam, soldiers and marines fought in land battles, and the navy, army, air force, and marines in the air, so once again our forces were subjected to the possibility of becoming POWs. In this conflict we saw for the first time the combat use of army and marine helicopters.

North Vietnam originally fought the colonial imperialism of the French, who thought they could control the situation in Indo-China, but their air power was very limited in jungle areas. The North Vietnamese built up arsenals with the aid of the Communists, and a large siege began on March 13, 1954. The French didn't stand a chance and the battle of Dien Ben Phu was called the Verdun of Vietnam back in France. It lasted fifty-five days and marked the end of the French experience in Vietnam.

U.S. INVOLVEMENT IN VIETNAM BEGINS

John F. Kennedy said that the Vietnamese would have to win by themselves but the United States would help. Defense Secretary Richard McNamara fully supported the South Vietnamese with equipment, supplies, and an advisory group of military officers. President Johnson continued this commitment after JFK was assassinated, and so too did Richard Nixon. Johnson and Nixon got into the act later when they and McNamara started selecting targets and/or delayed certain actions, which the Communists took advantage of. Some felt they should have left military decisions in the hands of military decision makers, remembering what happened with James Madison in the War of 1812.

U.S. military personnel in Vietnam ran the risk of becoming prisoners. In September 1967, Americans were not just advising but actually fighting, and with the alleged attacks on two navy ships, the war would be greatly escalated. ("Alleged" attacks because the Gulf of Tonkin incident is still controversial.)

The first combat troops were ordered to Vietnam in the spring of 1965 and by the end of 1968 more than 500,000 were there, according to Dan Rather, reporting in the film *Courage under Fire*.

NORTH VIETNAM REFUSES TO ACCEPT POW STATUS

In late 1965 and during the next seven years the U.S. government constantly pressured Hanoi to guarantee the rights of POWs. The North Vietnamese, however, refused to accept the status of captives as POWs because they considered U.S. pilots criminals who could be convicted under the principles established by the Nuremberg war crimes trials. Officially the United States was not engaged in war. Of course, it could have voiced the same complaint in Korea about the Chinese Communist so-called volunteers who were brought into Korea where they didn't belong.[1]

In the early summer of 1966, Communist campaigns began calling for war crime trials for captured airmen. This was in retaliation for increased U.S. attacks against Hanoi's oil facilities. In a mild form of counterretaliation, President Johnson sent warnings to nations throughout the world, but a group of Washington senators who had protested the president's policies appealed to Hanoi and warned of actual physical retaliation because of public demands. These efforts were successful because Hanoi put an end to its popular campaign for war crime trials.

Many accounts have been written about the Vietnam War, but two authors have reflected the background and land battles thoroughly: William Morrison in *The Elephant and the Tiger* and Stanley Karnow in *Vietnam: A History*. Morrison's book bears the subtitle *The Full Story of the Vietnam War* and the jacket copy on Karnow's book says, "The First Complete Account of Vietnam at War." However, both books say very little about prisoner of war problems that permeated the conflict. The indexes in these books do not include the term "prisoner of war," and there is a scarcity of information on POWs.

PRISON CAMPS

American POWs were held in different camps in North Vietnam, or in jungle camps in South Vietnam near border areas of Cambodia and Laos, two nations the United States was not supposed to be involved with. Americans who were held in South Vietnam near border areas were in places under the dominant control of North Vietnam forces. During the so-called secret war in Laos, the CIA operated three organizations: Air America, Continental Air Services, and Byrd and Sons.

Within fifty miles of the city of Hanoi there were six prison camps: Briarpatch, Sontay, Faith, Skidmore D-1, Rockpike, and Dogpatch in the northern mountains about five miles from the

Chinese border.[2] In Hanoi there were four prison camps: the Plantation, the Zoo, the Hilton, and Alcatraz. These, of course, were names given by the prisoners and not the North Vietnamese.

The Hilton, the Hanoi Hilton as it was often called, was the Hoa Lo prison, North Vietnam's main penitentiary and administrative headquarters for the country's entire prison system. Thick concrete walls about sixteen feet high surrounded the prison grounds and on top of them would be found broken bottles and jagged glass, which discouraged escapees. Barbed wire was used as well as electrified wires. At the four corners were located guard towers on top of the walls.

The Hanoi Hilton had four main divisions: Camp Unity, the Las Vegas area, Heartbreak Hotel, and New Guy Village. Heartbreak Hotel was a receiving station. Cu Loc prison was what the prisoners called the Zoo.

Other prison camps were not as organized. These were the jungle camps that bordered the adjoining countries of Cambodia and Laos. Rod Calvin, in *First Heroes*, gives examples of the presence of POWs in Laos, but not much more information about the camps and people in them. Mark Sauter and Tom Sanders say that there was one mysterious POW camp in North Vietnam's Ba Vi mountain.[3] No U.S. POWs ever returned from Laos and Cambodia alive.[4]

The PAVN was very reluctant to permit MIA recovery teams into Laos because it might hinder its operations along the Ho Chi Minh trail. This trail extended through the Annamite Mountains in North and South Vietnam, Laos, and Cambodia, and afforded the Communists a military supply route necessary to conquer the South once the Americans withdrew their forces. The Pathet Lao—the Communist Lao government—maintained that it had captured no Americans since 1966. Few knowledgeable Americans believed that a large number of Americans had been captured in Laos. About two-thirds of 1,200 American airmen shot down in Laos were recovered alive through the excellent efforts of the U.S. Air Force search and rescue forces operating from Thailand.[5] Colvin further states in his book that the North Vietnamese held POWs mainly to use them as hostages in negotiations for money reparations. Another theory he advanced was a desire for the technical expertise of people who knew how to handle abandoned military equipment such as helicopters, fighter-interceptors, ground attack tanks, trucks, and weapons. Or they may have wanted to send them to the Soviet Union for interrogation or slave labor. The prisoners might have been reluctant to fix these items.

North Vietnam prison camps never permitted inspections from outside sources, and if any media were allowed in the camps, the Communists would control the situation for propaganda purposes. This was in sharp contrast to South Vietnam prison camps containing Viet Cong and North Vietnam POWs. These camps were open to inspection by the International Committee of the Red Cross and those confined were allowed mail privileges. Mail privileges were denied American POWs. In the Christmas season of 1966, the Communists returned 457 of 467 packages sent by families.

All the POWs captured by U.S. forces, and other Allied forces taken by the South Vietnamese, were turned over to South Vietnam. By 1969 there were more than 33,000 enemy POWs in these camps, about 8,000 North Vietnamese, and the rest South Vietnamese Viet Cong. There were six prison camps in South Vietnam and they were completely inspected by Red Cross representatives who investigated improper treatment, and violators were punished. Visits from families were permitted and writing privileges also were permitted. Some POWs didn't write home for fear that their capture was a disgrace and also that their captors would turn on them.

POW PUBLICITY

Almost all of the 33,000 POWs held by the Army of the Republic of Vietnam were seen by newspaper people and International Red Cross representatives. Ross Perot became a close friend of POW families and tried to bring a film of the camps into Vientene, Laos. He wanted to deliver it to the North Vietnamese Embassy. Perot was accompanied by five POW wives seeking information about their husbands, but the Communists completely disregarded them.[6]

U.S. intelligence sources believed that the Pathet Lao held a small number of Americans and confined them in caves near Viengxay near Samnerce. This was the central headquarters in the mountain wilderness of northeast Laos, and sources placed two American POWs, Captain David Hschlecha and Charles Shelton, and a civilian aviator in these caves. It is unfortunate that Dr. Kissinger chose to wait for a list of POWs before the cease-fire agreement because the problem remained after the cease-fire. No mention was made about any prisoners captured in Laos; the Communists never seemed to supply appropriate lists.

To this day, most POWs held in North Vietnam and released do not think that North Vietnam maintained a secret parallel prison system, and this included Admiral Stockdale and James Warner, both former POWs. Warner firmly believed that the PAVN officers were not smart enough to organize a separate prison system.[7] One person who thought that POWs were held after Operation Homecoming was retired Major-General Secord. More will be said about this issue in the next chapter.

THE GULF OF TONKIN INCIDENT

The Gulf of Tonkin incident involved the capture of Vietnamese naval personnel by the U.S. navy. After four days in office, President Johnson restated U.S. policy that the Vietnamese would have to fight their own war, but he would continue JFK's policy of withdrawing some forces. Johnson asked the Joint Chiefs of Staff about the possibility of a clandestine war against North Vietnam, but a more active, open response was just around the corner that would involve the naval forces of the two countries.

The South Vietnamese navy ordered fast patrol boats into North Vietnamese waters to blow up beach installations and to intercept and destroy North Vietnamese junks and fishing vessels being used to transport arms and equipment to the Viet Cong.[8]

Not far from this area was the *Maddox*, an American destroyer that had been ordered to stay eight miles off the North Vietnamese coast. Captain John Herrick proceeded to investigate the North Vietnamese waters. Three North Vietnamese patrol boats approached the *Maddox* in international waters. When the patrol boats fired on the destroyer, it took evasive action and fired warning shots. These shots were ignored and the *Maddox* returned fire. Herrick sent an urgent appeal to the carrier USS *Ticonderoga* for air support.

Commander Stockdale responded with four fighters, and then one patrol boat lay dead as its crew threw everything overboard and then threw themselves overboard. Stockdale reported one boat was sinking and the remaining two damaged. The nineteen men who dove overboard were picked up by the *Maddox*. These nineteen were all sent back to North Vietnam in 1967 and 1968.[9] Interrogators were able to get useful information from the men.

A second ship, the *C. Turner Joy*, reinforced the *Maddox*, and on August 3 the *Maddox* and *Turner Joy* entered the Tonkin Gulf with orders only to fight in self-defense. Stockdale and other pilots flew back and forth over the ships but saw no torpedo boats. Then the controversy started. Were the torpedo boats really there? Navy officers later said that no attack was made. The end result was the passage of the Tonkin Gulf Resolution, which ignited the war. There was no controversy, however, about the first attack on the patrol boats. The nineteen navy POWs who were seized attested to that. This controversy is described in detail in Moise's book, *The Tonkin Gulf and the Escalation of the Vietnam War*.

The first incident of the Tonkin Gulf controversy took place on August 2 and the second, August 4. On August 4, 1964, Lieutenant (J.G.) Everett Alvarez (later Lieutenant Commander) was shot down. He endured eight and a half years as a POW in Vietnam. His mission had started from the carrier the USS *Constellation*, and he tells the complete story of his captivity in his book *Chained Eagle*. Alvarez became a symbol of strength for all POWs. He never collaborated despite torture, beatings, and starvation. Alvarez and other POWs pronounced Ho Chi Minh's name as Horseshit Min.

When *Life* magazine showed pictures of Dick Stratton bowing to his captors, some Americans thought that he had been drugged or brainwashed. Averell Harriman, in charge of POW affairs for the State Department, replied to *Life:* "From the photographs, videotapes and descriptions by eye-witnesses that I have seen of the so-called news conferences at which Commander Stratton was exhibited, it would appear that the North Vietnamese authorities are using mental or physical pressure on American prisoners of war."[10] He went on to suggest that the brainwashing used in Korea was probably also being used by the North Vietnamese.

Time magazine reported that Lieutenant Commander Charles Tanner said that two fellow pilots were court-martialed for refusal to fly missions, and the names given to Hanoi were Lieutenant Commander Ben Casey and Lieutenant Clark Kent. He made some of his interrogators lose face.

IRRECONCILABLE WAR TACTICS

In his prologue, Alvarez states: "Not a single man I met during all my years in captivity agreed with the conduct of the war. As military men we were told we could not strike certain harbors, airfields, missile sites, and other targets. This was no way to win a war. The lesson we should learn from Vietnam is that if we are going to get involved in a foreign war again, let's make up our minds as a country that the cause is worth fighting for, then let's go in and do it right and win. Otherwise, we shouldn't get involved in the first place."

THE EXPERIENCES OF SOME AMERICAN POWs

Lieutenant Everett Alvarez

When Alvarez knew he was in real trouble, he blew his canopy and ejected. Shortly thereafter he hit the water, not land.[11] Picked up by fishermen, he was ultimately brought to an interrogator to whom he gave his name, rank, and serial number, and date of birth. He gave no information, nor did he identify his squadron or ship.

Colonel Robinson Risner

Robinson Risner, a U.S. Air Force pilot, was shot down on May 16, 1965. He was operating from Korat air base in Thailand and had been a hero in the Korean War. He didn't want to be captured so he decided to stay with his plane until he was over water, but unfortunately he had to eject. He headed for a rice field and saw people running toward him; thus he was captured in enemy territory and became a POW of the Vietnamese. He was stripped down to his flight suit and had his hands tied behind him. His wingman made a pass to capture him but to no avail. Risner's ultimate destination would be downtown Hanoi and then seven and a half years in Hoa Lo prison at the Hanoi Hilton.

About 10:00 P.M. that night he started singing "McNamara's Band" and gave his name, Robbie Risner, to which a voice responded "Hey, Robbie, this is Bob Peel. Where are you?" He told Risner he was with two others—one with broken arms and the other a broken leg. He was their nurse and an air force captain. He gave the names of others in the prison and signed off. Soon Risner would learn of others recently captured and confined there.

Risner learned that the first lesson of life in a Vietnamese prison was to be quiet and started learning the tap code Captain Carlisle (Smitty) Harris had introduced about six months before. He would ultimately be taken to the Zoo and used the tapping code to learn of the presence of other officers. As SRO (senior ranking officer), he tried to get better conditions for POWs. He got some lightbulbs, but this was only a prelude to a period of unmitigated torture and abuse. Risner later was returned to the Hanoi Hilton. A woman guard, Dragon Doll, a civilian, was very mean and had no compassion for the prisoners. Risner did a lot of praying in the stocks. This type of confinement and the denial of food was the closest he came to torture at that time.

Since he had tried to communicate with others, he had to pay the price. Mickey Mouse, a guard, read off to him a list of his alleged crimes. He was in the stocks for thirty-two weeks and tied tighter and tighter with ropes. They pulled his ankles up behind him; he was blindfolded and bound hand and foot. He was on the verge of unconsciousness when someone came and untied the knot and loosened his feet from his neck. Pictures and drawings of other forms of torture are contained in a book by Stockdale. In mid-December a new pilot brought the news that Risner was promoted to full colonel. Risner was brought back to Heartbreak Hotel where his next-door neighbor was Navy Commander Jim Stockdale. Risner's book *The Passing of the Night: My Seven Years As a Prisoner of the North Vietnamese*, details his experiences as a POW.

Commander Stockdale, later Admiral, was shot down on September 1965; Captain Jeremiah Denton (later made an admiral) was shot down in July 1965.

Risner was moved in December 1970 to Camp Unity, where all POWs would be interned together in one place. He had made the rounds at different locations. An important reason for that move was an American commando raid at Sontay camp almost thirty miles away, but unfortunately all POWs had been cleared out. The raid failed in its primary objective because it did not have the proper current intelligence information, but the news of it certainly raised the morale of the prisoners. A decision was made later, when release seemed to be in the near future, that release would be in order of capture.

Commander John McCain

McCain was the son of an admiral and the grandson of an admiral. When offered an early release, he refused it. Commander John McCain was shot down in October 1967, Captain Richard Stratton, U.S. Navy, on January 5, 1967, and Colonel John Dramesi, U.S. Air Force, on April 2, 1967.

Stratton was a junior maintenance officer aboard the *Ticonderoga*. He was flying an A-46 attack plane waiting for his twentieth mission over North Vietnam. Two of his rockets failed and malfunctioned. An explosion caused him to lose altitude and he used his alternate ejection handle and went out head down. The enemy on the ground was waiting for him. He was taken as a POW, marched through a hamlet to his first jail, a small thatched hut, and finally brought to Hoa Lo (the Hanoi Hilton). He gave only his name, rank, serial number, and date of birth.

McCain's story is told in Robert Timberg, *The Nightingale's Song*. On October 26, 1967, McCain was warned by the strike operations officer of the *Oriskany* that he should be careful on the day's mission. McCain's A-4E *Skyhawk* flew through airbursts and past surface-to-air missiles (SAMs). His right wing was shot off, so he blew his canopy and ejected. In the ejection process both his arms and his right knee were broken. He landed in a small lake in central Hanoi and would have drowned but for some soldiers who swam out to get him. His ordeal of terror then began. He was spit on, kicked, and placed (a better term would be thrown) into the back of a truck to be taken to the Hanoi Hilton. He was interrogated for military information that he refused to give. He was informed that he was a war criminal and would not get any medical aid. His wounds were eventually bandaged but he still didn't cooperate.

In a few hours, however, the "Bug" came in and let McCain know that he knew McCain's father was an admiral. McCain was then taken to a hospital. His next destination was the plantation on the outskirts of Hanoi. Of all the POWs shot down, McCain was probably the one in the worst shape. Timberg tells us that another air force pilot was in bad shape when captured in August 1967. This was Bud Day, who would become one of two POWs honored with the Medal of Honor. Stockton, the other, was tortured with ropes and then placed in the Zoo where air force Major Norris Overly began nursing him back to health.[12] Later Colonel Cook of the marines also earned the Medal of Honor. At that time, however, nobody knew about Colonel Cook's courage as a POW. More will be said later about Colonel Cook.

Day and Overly were the first Americans McCain had seen in two months and their discussion taught McCain a great deal. Overly became McCain's nurse and cared for his health. The treatment offered at the Plantation wasn't too bad, which led Day to the conclusion that this was a POW camp the Vietnamese considered for a rumored early release program. McCain, however, wouldn't consider anything like that and strongly believed that the code of conduct for American fighting men governed the actions of the POWs. There was a provision in the code that any release before the war's end would be in order of capture. By early 1968 there were more than 300 Americans in North Vietnam prison camps, dating back to Everett Alvarez, shot down in August 1964. Illness would have been a perfectly valid reason for early release of a POW, but McCain was stubborn and refused early release.

McCain always tried, unsuccessfully, to make contact with other POWs. One night he was taken to an unfamiliar room and questioned by the Cat (Major Bai), the Hanoi prison commander, and the Rabbit (a translator). The Cat said that Overly and some others freed were welcomed home as heroes, but McCain didn't say anything and was returned to his cell, where he tapped his news on the wall to Bob Cramer. McCain's decision was negative. The Cat stated that the president had ordered McCain home but even a letter from his wife could not change him.[13]

McCain was beaten and given the rope treatment. Jeremiah Denton was another POW who was tortured. On Christmas Day 1970, McCain was transferred to Camp Unity. In early 1971 the POWs of Camp Unity defied the North Vietnamese and held a church service, then staged a near riot when three of their leaders were marched off in irons. McCain and Bud Day were sent to Skid Row, a punishment camp where conditions were very poor. McCain was returned briefly to Camp Unity in November 1971 and then was moved to a small camp near the Chinese border called Dogpatch before going back to the Plantation. The POWs coasted through the last year of their captivity. The guards were fairly tolerant, the food was better, and the men rallied physically.

THE PARIS PEACE TALKS

Admiral McCain sent bombers to Hanoi, but President Nixon suspended the bombing at the start of the Paris Peace talks in the fall of 1972; then negotiations broke down and attacks were renewed. The POWs could hear the explosions of the bombs being dropped on Hanoi and cheered them. The cease-fire finally came on January 23.

Henry Kissinger had his hands full with attempted negotiations of secret talks in Paris with Le Duc Tho. He had arranged three secret meetings with this man, who was a member of the North Vietnam Politburo. Negotiations originally got off to a bad start at the Paris Peace Conference when the Communists argued about the shape of the table at which the representatives would sit.[14]

Serious issues that had to be resolved included mutual troop withdrawals, lists of prisoners and their repatriation, and reparations the Communists were seeking. Much had to be agreed on before the war could end. Both Le Duc Tho and Henry Kissinger were awarded the Nobel Peace Prize for their efforts to end the war. Yet Le Duc Tho consistently stood in the way of progress.

Seaman Douglas Hegdahl

On April 6, 1967, an unusual event happened when a seaman, Douglas Hegdahl, was reported missing and presumed lost at sea in the

Gulf of Tonkin. He was a member of the deck crew aboard a missile cruiser, the USS *Canberra*. His absence was discovered when he failed to arrive for his watch. His ship turned about and crisscrossed the waters where he was presumably lost, but no body was found. Four days later a memorial service was held for the sailor, who had been in the service less than six months.

Out on the deck he had been thrown overboard when the concussion of the firing of the guns combined with the ship's turning. Hitting the water revived him, and he swam for nearly five hours in the sea. In the morning he spotted a Vietnamese fishing boat whose men picked him up and treated him well. As he said, "They hadn't got the party line yet."[15]

Unfortunately Hegdahl was turned over to the local militia. The villagers were stirred up, but the crowd was brought under control. He was taken away at night, marched and jogged on foot, placed on a truck and driven to an interrogation center inland. He gave his name, rank, serial number, and date of birth as required. When he did not respond to further questioning, he was hit with a rifle butt. They took away his shoes and forced him to jog in his bare feet. Two days later he arrived at Hanoi and was locked in a cell in the Heartbreak Hotel, part of Hoa Lo. Except for interrogation purposes, he was confined in solitary until May, when he was transferred to the Zoo and into the cell of pilot Charles Stackhouse, a lieutenant commander who had flown an A-4 attack plane off the USS *Bon Homme*. Hegdahl had a very difficult time trying to convince his captors that he wasn't a spy.

Meanwhile, Stratton (see p. 286) was held in a small hut sweatbox under the June sun. Both Stratton and Hegdahl were taken to the Plantation, where Hegdahl was caught tapping to prisoners and had to spend the afternoon with his hands in the air. Hegdahl described a typical day in the late summer of 1967 when he and Stratton were cellmates at the Plantation. The usual procedure was to torture and brutalize POWs.[16]

Stratton was considered a troublemaker and spent a lot of time in solitary confinement. He was still fighting the war as a prisoner of war, hence the title of Blakey's book, *Prisoner at War*. Stratton was winning his war by humiliating the camp commanding officer and his aide, whose careers he jeopardized. Ultimately Hegdahl was persuaded to seek early release if possible, since he had managed to remember hundreds of names of POWs. This would provide invaluable information to the authorities, but this plan was thwarted when two captains, John Dramesi and Edward Atterbury, escaped from the Zoo.[17]

Captain John Dramesi and Captain Edward Atterbury

The escape had been planned for more than a year. Captain (later Colonel) Dramesi was an air force pilot shot down on April 2, 1967. Upon escape, he was quickly recaptured and brutally punished. Dramesi survived, but Atterbury was never seen again. Dramesi dedicated his book to Atterbury. Almost every POW was beaten in retaliation, even Hegdahl, but ultimately Hegdahl was released. In his examination of POWs, John Hubbell wrote, "The speed with which Ho Chi Minh's heir moved to improve the conditions of prisoners seemed to indicate some degree of understanding that the old regime's policies had been counterproductive."[18]

The first black officer to become a POW was air force Major Fred Cherry who, like Risner, was a Korean veteran. He volunteered only what was required: name, rank, serial number, and date of birth.

Some Senate doves were very distressed about the POW situation and demanded trials and executions for the torture of any captured Americans. This list included Senators Fulbright, Morse, McCarthy, and McGovern.[19] No such war crime trials were ever held.

Navy Commander Walter Eugene Wilber and Marine Lieutenant Colonel Edison Wainwright Miller

If you were good, cooperative prisoners like navy Commander Walter Eugene Wilber or marine Lieutenant Colonel Edison Wainwright Miller, you received medical attention constantly.[20] A note at the end of the book mentions that a majority of returned prisoners believed that these two men had willingly collaborated with other captors and had tried to persuade others to do the same, to the extent that they voluntarily wrote and recorded antiwar statements, willingly visited with antiwar delegates, and accepted special treatment, food, and medical care.

After repatriation, both men were charged with mutiny by Rear Admiral James Stockdale, the senior navy POW in Vietnam. The secretary of the navy believed Stockdale's accusations but dropped all charges after investigation because prolonged courts-martial would be injurious to other POWs and their families. Both were officially censured for their actions and retired from the service.

Finally the famous day arrived and Operation Homecoming went smoothly. The media tended to hail all POWs as heroes. Personnel returned from captivity between February and March 1973 included air force, army, navy, and marine members, as well as twenty-four civilians. One of these civilians was Douglas Ramsey, who had an important story to tell.

Douglas Ramsey

Douglas Ramsey was a Foreign Service officer who was fluent in spoken and written Vietnamese. In August 1965, he was transferred temporarily to a heavily populated area on the central coast. His job was to help refugees in Binh Dinh, where thousands of people were fleeing their homes.[21]

Ramsey was ambushed by local guerrillas not far from the U.S. command post. He was taken to the Cambodian border in northeast Vietnam and had a very difficult time trying to persuade his captors that he wasn't working for the CIA. He was a civilian who was carrying a new, fully automatic AR-15 rifle but did not have any infantry training. Nevertheless, he was a prime suspect for being a member of the CIA. He yelled out in Vietnamese "I surrender" and his captors were so happy with their find that "they were almost friendly."[22] Ramsey caught malaria but improved somewhat by the summer of 1967. He was chained to a tree for a few weeks, and his last prison confinement was Kratie in Cambodia.

The real significance of Ramsey's return in Operation Homecoming was the report he gave about the brave and daring conduct of Lieutenant Colonel Donald Cook, a POW who never returned and about whom we knew nothing. Ramsey wrote a letter to General Cushing after Operation Homecoming. Cook was a marine captain who had been considered dead for six years. The letter told the story of Cook, who had been held in different camps in South Vietnam near the Cambodian border.[23]

The Marine Corps headquarters studied carefully the status of captured marines. Melson and Arnold further stated that "as near as could be determined, 48 of all the Americans known to have been captured in Southeast Asia were U.S. Marines. Of these, 9 died in captivity, 10 escaped, 2 were released prior to 1973, 26 returned during Operation Homecoming, and one Private First Class, Robert R. Garwood returned in 1979."[24] Garwood's case will be more fully discussed later in this chapter.

Confinement for marine prisoners and other personnel was often in bamboo "tight cage" enclosures and men were often shackled to their beds.[25]

The first marine to become a POW was Captain Cook, who was promoted to lieutenant colonel while a POW.[26] The U.S. Marine Corps cited the code of conduct in its training and instruction program. Colonel Cook certainly lived up to it, earning him the respect of his fellow POWs as well as his Communist captors (as stated in Melson's account of marine POWs).

Colonel Cook became a Marine Corps reservist as a private and finished OCS at Quantico, Virginia. One assignment he received was as a student in the Chinese Mandarin course at Monterey, California, and then the Army Intelligence School in Maryland. In the ensuing three years he became officer in charge of the first interrogation team with a marine aircraft wing in Hawaii. He authored a pamphlet about experiences of American POWs in Korea that dealt with measures used in Korea. What he learned, he then applied to more realistic training for the marines. Ironically, he himself became a POW of the North Vietnamese.

On the last day of December 1964, Colonel Cook volunteered to join a search and recovery mission for a downed helicopter, but he and the Vietnam marines accompanying him were ambushed. He was wounded in the leg while trying to drag others to safety, taken prisoner, and moved to a Viet Cong camp in southern Vietnam's border near Cambodia.

He was not an SRO but acted like one, which brought harsh treatment on him. The enemy claimed he had bad attitudes, which simply meant he was very uncooperative with his captors. He was confined in a ten-foot square cage and given limited rations but was always ready, willing, and able to help his comrades, even though he himself was not in good health. Through first aid he saved the lives of POWs who had malaria attacks. Cook shared the little food he had with sick and wounded POWs. He refused to obtain his own release.

When he made a vain escape attempt, the North Vietnamese held a gun to his head. His response was to recite the nomenclature of the gun and to show no fear. In November 1967, a fellow prisoner, civilian Douglas Ramsey, saw him on a jungle trail. Cook was never seen again. In 1973, when Ramsey was released in Operation Homecoming, he learned that Colonel Cook had died in captivity on December 8, 1967. Under the Missing Service Persons Act of 1943, Cook was declared dead on February 26, 1980; on May 16, 1980, his wife was presented with his Medal of Honor.

On December 4, 1998, the USS *Donald Cook*, DDC 75, was officially commissioned at Penn's Landing in Philadelphia. The citation for Colonel Cook's Medal of Honor was signed by President Jimmy Carter. Douglas Ramsey claimed he could not have survived without the psychological boost given by Cook.

Present at the commissioning of the navy missile destroyer were Cook's wife and family, a number of high-ranking military and naval personnel, including the chairman of the Joint Chiefs of Staff, who spoke first, about twenty-five of Cook's Xavier classmates and their wives, some faculty members, and a few thousand relatives of the crew of the new destroyer. That day, December 4, 1998, the sun shone down on the ceremony and the temperature was almost ninety degrees. God certainly was showering his magnificence on this memorable day for Colonel Cook.

After the ceremony, a reception was held at the Philadelphia Convention Hall. There I met a marine brigadier general who suggested I write to the director of the Marine History and Museum Division in Washington to learn more about Colonel Cook. I wrote that night and the following week received a phone call from Richard Long, the head of the Oral History Unit. He told me he was forwarding a packet of printed materials and news columns that included an excellent bibliography of marine history books. I am deeply indebted to Mr. Long (a former marine lieutenant who served in Korea) and Colonel Michael Monigan, the director of the museum, for information sent me. The only information that could not be located was the pamphlet Colonel Cook wrote about Korean War prisoners, and as of this writing I am still trying to locate a copy.

Many returning POWs wrote about their experiences, but all of them can't be included in this work. The common denominator in all accounts is the brutality and the poor conditions all of them had to endure.

Marine Private First Class Robert Garwood

Marine PFC Robert Garwood was one marine the Corps would probably want to forget. He was the only member of the military to be seriously disciplined for conduct during the Vietnamese conflict. At first he was considered a captive of the enemy. but he chose to stay with the Communists when he was offered a release in 1967. In this way he was similar to the twenty-one who refused repatriation at the end of the Korean War.

At the time of Operation Homecoming in 1973, Garwood was considered a collaborator, and confirmation of this belief came from POWs held with him. As late as 1975, the DIA learned that Garwood "operated with Command Forces in Eastern Quang Nam and Quang Ngain provinces . . . and had recently been promoted to the rank of Major."[27]

Garwood returned to the United States in 1979 and received a military court-martial during which he was charged with allegedly being an informer and indoctrinator of fellow prisoners. In his defense, some POWs gave testimony that he helped fellow Americans and that his conduct was manipulated by the Communists.

Bill Paul, a *Wall Street Journal* reporter, spoke to Garwood, the returned POW classified as a renegade. He said that there were POW camps at Bat Bat in Sontay province thirty-five miles from Hanoi and eighty miles northeast of Hanoi; warehouses in Gia Lam, an eastern suburb of Hanoi; also a military complex in Ly Nam De Street in Hanoi. Paul knew that Garwood was a collaborator and therefore was not creditable if questioned.

In February 1968, three American pilots were turned over by the North Vietnamese authorities to the U.S. National Mobilization Committee to end the war. This was a propaganda move on the part of the North Vietnamese. Two members of the group were Dr. Howard Zimmer and Daniel Berrigan, S.J. Father Berrigan had participated in the burning of draft records in a government office and was a well-known antiwar activist.

About 90 percent of POWs taken by the enemy were captured within an hour of being shot down. The air force declared that 65 percent of its POWs were captured within two hours. Of 208 air force returnees, only six said that they avoided escape for more than three days.[28]

The next chapter considers POWs not accounted for, MIAs in both Korea and Vietnam, and the efforts (and the lack of government effort) to secure information on MIAs. Both Korean and Vietnam Wars ended with many MIAs unaccounted for, but this issue resulted in great frustration at the end of the Vietnam War.

NOTES

1. Carl Berger, *The United States Air Force in Southeast Asia, 1961–1973* (Washington, D.C.: Office of Air Force History, 1977).

2. Rod Colvin, *First Heroes: The POWs Left Behind in Vietnam* (New York: Irvington, 1987), 161.

3. Mark Sauter and Jim Sanders, *The Men We Left Behind* (Washington, D.C.: National Press Books, 1993).

4. John G. Hubbell, *P.O.W.* (New York: Readers' Digest Press/Thomas Crowell, 1976), 57.

5. Malcolm McConnell, *Inside Hanoi's Secret Archives* (New York: Simon & Schuster, 1995), 43.

6. David Heather, *Operation Rescue* (New York: Pinnacle, 1971).

7. McConnell, *Inside Hanoi's Secret Archives*, 408 n. 8.

8. Wilbur H. Morrison, *The Elephant and the Tiger: The Full Story of the Vietnam War* (New York: Hippocrene, 1990), 138.

9. Edwin E. Moise, *Tonkin Gulf and the Escalation of the Vietnam War* (Chapel Hill: University of North Carolina Press, 1996).

10. Hubbell, *P.O.W.*, 264.

11. Everett Alvarez Jr. and Anthony S. Pitch, *Chained Eagle* (New York: Dell, 1989), 29.

12. Robert Timberg, *The Nightingale's Song* (New York: Simon & Schuster, 1995), 65.

13. Timberg, *Nightingale's Song,* 72.

14. Henry Kissinger, *White House Years* (Boston: Little, Brown, 1979), 237.

15. Scott Blakey, *Prisoner at War: The Survival of Commander Richard A. Stratton* (Garden City, N.Y.: Anchor Press/Doubleday, 1978), 163.

16. Blakey, *Prisoner at War*, 186.

17. John A. Dramesi, *Code of Honor* (New York: Warner Books, 1975), 237.

18. Hubbell, *P.O.W.*, 520.

19. Hubbell, *P.O.W.*, 198.

20. Blakey, *Prisoner at War*, 273.

21. Neil Sheehan, *A Bright Shining Lie* (New York: Vantage, 1988), 541.

22. Sheehan, *Bright Shining Lie,* 560.

23. Charles D. Melson and Curtis G. Arnold, *The U.S. Marines in Vietnam: The War That Would Not End, 1971–1973* (Washington, D.C.: History and Museums Division, Headquarters U.S. Marine Corps, 1991), 233.

24. Melson and Arnold, *U.S. Marines in Vietnam,* 217.

25. Melson and Arnold, *U.S. Marines in Vietnam,* 217.

26. Melson and Arnold, *U.S. Marines in Vietnam*, 232.

27. Melson and Arnold, *U.S. Marines in Vietnam*, 234.

28. Colvin, *First Heroes*, 23.

14

MIAs Unaccounted for in Korea and Vietnam

With little information forthcoming from the U.S. government, many wives of Vietnam MIAs were completely frustrated. They seemed to be getting nowhere. During the Vietnam War many wives kept a low profile at the request of the government, but this couldn't last. Conditions in the Vietnam War were much worse than those in Korea. Sybil Stockdale organized the National League of Families of POWs and MIAs and mobilized it to keep public attention focused on the plight of prisoners.

At a White House social function after Operation Homecoming, Henry Kissinger, when approached and questioned by someone about unaccounted for POWs, stated that he did not want to discuss the matter. Some viewed it as a rather cold response.

The *New York Times* (September 13, 1996) reported that an agreement had been made and that American veterans of the Vietnam War would turn over information about mass graves where 600 North Vietnamese forces were probably buried in return for information from Hanoi about the fate of some missing Americans.

United States officials still listed 2,143 American military personnel and civilians as MIA. Normalized relations between Vietnam and the United States came in July 1985. David Dimas's book *Missing in Action: Prisoners of War* insisted on the existence of definite information indicating some American forces were still alive in Southeast Asia and claimed that the government was not doing anything on their behalf. Lieutenant General Eugene Tighe felt the same way.

The longest held POW was Army Ranger Captain Floyd J. "Jim" Thompson, commander of a Special Forces detachment. This information comes from an excellent article appearing in *Air Force Magazine* (August 1999). The air force lost pilots Lieutenant Hayden and J. Lockhart in early 1965. There were many other cases of downed pilots, too many to discuss here.

In May 1966, Jeremiah Denton was brought before cameras after almost three days of continuous indoctrination and no sleep, but he still outwitted the Communists. He relayed messages to the public in Morse code by blinking his eyelids. The one word he flashed was T-O-R-T-U-R-E. This incident is related by Stewart Powell in *Honor Bound*.

With the publication of Malcolm McConnell's book *Inside Hanoi's Secret Archives* (1995), tremendous progress was made. According to text on the cover of the book, "Here is the key to solving the POW/MIA mystery that has haunted America since the end of the Vietnam War." The *POW/MIA Fact Book* published in October 1995 said that McConnell's book might be "the most significant advancement in the U.S. Government's negotiations with the Socialist Republic of Vietnam" since 1992. Although it did not clear up everything, the book helped solve some of the mysteries.

McConnell, an editor of *Reader's Digest* and author of many fiction and nonfiction books, and Theodore Schweitzer, a field officer of the United Nations High Commission for Refugees, pulled together the material for McConnell to write about.

A total of 2,265 American servicemen were still officially listed as MIAs since the end of the war. Schweitzer had been the principal agent of Operation Swamp Ranger. He was a private researcher under contract as a consultant of the DIA. Hanoi was very cooperative and agreed to give as much information as possible to bring to an end the long POW/MIA issue and stalemate that had caused many in the United States, citizens and government officials, to believe that POWs had been deliberately abandoned after Operation Homecoming.

AMERICAN SERVICEMEN HELD IN RUSSIA

At the end of the Korean conflict, a Pentagon report concluded as follows: "The Soviets transferred several hundred U.S. Korean War POWs to the U.S.S.R. and did not repatriate them. Their transfer was mainly politically motivated with the intent of holding them as political hostages, subjects for intelligence exploitation and skilled labor within the camp system."[1]

To learn about the F-86 Sabre jet fighter, the Koreans attempted to get their hands on captured pilots and bring them to Russia for intense interrogation and information.

McConnell provides some statistics in this area. He reports fifty-six F-86 Sabres and forty-seven pilots were lost, but only fifteen F-86 pilots and the remains of one pilot were turned over during the 1953 prisoner exchanges. He also says that thirty-one F-86 captured pilots disappeared in North Korea. Some might have been from the 80th Fighter-Bomber Squadron stationed at K-13. According to McConnell, a Pentagon report showed that of 200 American POWs sent from Korea to the USSR, thirty-one American pilots were among them. The whole operation, if it actually existed, was naturally kept very quiet and secret. There is no concrete evidence. No information was forthcoming from the KGB, and "to date . . . no reward money has been paid and no surviving American POW has been found on Russian soil."[2] McConnell further states that we might never discover what really happened. How many American POWs were left in Korea will probably never be known. Any who managed to survive would by now probably be deceased or well into their seventies.

There were probably some POWs remaining in Vietnam after Operation Homecoming. Operation Swamp Ranger was Ted Schweitzer's baby. He visited the Hanoi Military Museum and obtained important information that contributed to the success of his dangerous mission. Getting the proper permission from Hanoi was the first problem. His research enabled McConnell to write his book. It is still a mystery why Hanoi officials allowed Schweitzer to examine the Blue Files and the Blue Book, as well as the Red Book, in Hanoi.

SOME BOOKS THAT
SENSATIONALIZED THE PLIGHT OF MIAs

After Operation Homecoming, some people thought captured POWs were still being held. Their ideas were expressed in books that fanned the embers of discontent. *Kiss the Boys Good-bye: How the United States Betrayed Its Own POWs in Vietnam by* Monica Jensen Stevensen and William Stevensen[3] stirred up considerable controversy. The DIA POW/MIA office answered back and gave a well-documented refutation of the book. The agency office said that the book "drew heavily on questionable sources to expand the prevailing conspiracy theory that large members of Americans remained captive in Laos after the war, and that some had been transferred from Indochina to the Soviet Union."[4]

Sanders, Sauter, and Kirkwood presented their ideas in *Soldiers of Misfortune*, which was even more sensational and speculative and also dealt with questionable sources. Hollywood films about attempts to rescue POWs were daring and exciting and featured excellent casts, but they added to the myth that many Americans were still held after the war.

Susan Katz Keating's book *Prisoners of Hope* tried to show what really happened to many of the prisoners as well as expose those who took advantage of the situation to exploit the families of MIAs, including the U.S. government, which she claims lied about the problem for some time. Keating gives credit to returning POW heroes who agreed to be interviewed and helped her considerably, especially Senator John McCain. She claimed that the myth "is so powerful it has spawned round after round of government investigation all leading to the conclusion that there is no solid evidence of live Americans held in Southeast Asia."[5] She rather unfairly singles out the Senate Select Committee on POW/MIA Affairs in 1991. It unearthed considerable information on the problem, and information in McConnell's book bears it out. As of the publication of Keating's book (1994), there were 2,231 names on the government's official Vietnam MIA list.[6] She further states that "the real truth is at least at best, the men on the list are known to be dead."[7]

Admiral Stockdale and General John Vesey Jr. testified before the Kerry Committee and spoke about the problem. Stockdale claimed he had seen a plane crash that surely killed the pilot, but he was not sure how to report the incident. He was told that if he thought the pilot was dead, he should say so and not do an injustice to the family.

McConnell's book helped clear up the mess. Keating in her book identified one senator's great disservice in trying to keep up the hopes of MIA families.[8]

Many MIA wives believed they were being sentenced to silence to prevent the public from becoming too emotional about the war. They felt gagged, and rightly so. The government apparently felt that revealing the truth in the press might harm the POWs.

KISSINGER AND PEROT

Henry Kissinger called Ross Perot from the White House in late 1969 and said that American POWs in Vietnam were suffering. The government could not intervene on their behalf because it would signal weakness. Perot did not hesitate.[9] He headed to Washington and years later recalled his conversation with Kissinger. He quoted intelligence reports for Kissinger indicating that 50 percent of the POWs in Vietnam would die from cruelty or neglect before the war ended.

Perot cleared his mission with Alexander Haig, who was serving as Kissinger's deputy.[10]

Perot had more than a few Annapolis classmates in Vietnam prison camps. He flew 150 relatives of Vietnam prisoners to Paris to be near the Paris talks, where they could be a "haunting presence."[11] Up to this time the State Department had been urging families to play down the problem.[12] The less said the better.

In December 1969, Perot decided to pay a Christmas visit to Hanoi and brought two planeloads of Christmas foods and presents for POWs. North Vietnam kept throwing up obstacles and said that the Christmas packages should go to Moscow.[13] In March 1970, Perot started contacting reporters and getting new gifts. He would try to go to Hanoi again.[14]

Defense Secretary James Schlesinger awarded a medal for public service to Perot at the end of the war, and Perot sponsored a public parade and weekend party in San Francisco for returning POWs. He also invited Bull Simon and his Sontay Raiders to the party.

Fear that revealing the truth could harm the POWs was reminiscent of what happened in the Pacific in World War II. When Dyess came back with his tales of terror about the Death March and the subsequent tortures inflicted on POWs by the Japanese, the first reaction was to suppress any information that could bring harm to the prisoners. The truth, however, eventually came to light.

Mistaken MIA sightings did not help the situation. Although verifying such reports was a delicate issue and many reports could not be confirmed, many believe the government has a responsibility to investigate remains of MIAs. A former DIA director, Lieutenant General Eugene Tighe, believed that Americans were being held against their will, and he said this to Senator John McCain. Tighe had no concrete proof, but McCain said, "When someone like General Tighe speaks you have to listen."[15]

Garwood, the most serious defector of the Vietnam War, claimed he saw American POWs after Operation Homecoming, but his reputation was suspect. He and the activists formed "a perfect partnership."[16]

Other controversial books were Sauter and Sanders's *The Men We Left Behind* and Rod Calvin's *First Heroes*. Calvin advanced the theory that prisoners who had technical expertise in military equipment were sent to the Soviet Union. He also inferred that some might have been used as slave labor, as were POWs held in Japan. Some think this was the fate of many of the men unaccounted for, but do not think that the U.S. government "deliberately" forgot those who were considered not yet returned. Kissinger did his best, but the Communists could not be moved to do anything about the POWs they were still holding.

Private individuals attempted to rescue POWs, but they didn't have the proper intelligence information to carry out successful missions and many never got off the ground because of lack of money and other necessary resources.

During World War II the raids at Los Baños and Cabanatuan were successful. In Vietnam the Sontay raid seemed to be well planned and organized but lacked the proper intelligence. Later it was learned that the POWs had been moved.

After the war Operation Lazarus was designed "specifically to liberate U.S. POWs held captive against their will by Communist forces in Southeast Asia, and return remains of those MIAs that became available for identification."[17] Charles Patterson was involved in the operation. His book, *The Heroes Who Fell from Grace,* faults Nixon and Kissinger for trying to get out of the war but not getting a full account of missing Americans. Patterson faults the U.S. government for the failure of Operation Lazarus, which was based on questionable data.

If the Paris Peace Accords had been executed in good faith by North Vietnam, and if cooperation had been given by Laos and Cambodia, the United States might have achieved a thorough accounting of American MIAs long before Operation Swamp Ranger. The absence of Laos and Cambodia at the peace table in Paris certainly did not alleviate the situation. President Nixon wrote, "Although everyone was aware of the possibility that the peace was incomplete, I had no personal knowledge that any U.S. servicemen still alive had been left behind."[18] Ted Schweitzer, quoted in McConnell's book, said that "nothing in Vietnam is ever straightforward or simple." After two decades of investigation we have been able to determine with some certainty the fates of all but approximately one hundred MIAs in Vietnam."[19]

Former POWs told Keating that visits by Jane Fonda and other antiwar activists caused the torture of POWs to be increased.[20] Many POWs became activists, and some took more dangerous risks—Jeremiah Denton (later Senator Denton) and navy pilot Richard Stratton faked brainwashing by bowing to their captors. Stratton paid the price for his attitude and was worked over for his retaliation. There was some talk about prosecuting Jane Fonda for violation of the Logan Act, but it was thought that this would only make her a martyr.

The peace agreement came on January 23, and the way was paved for Operation Homecoming. The DIA was disturbed that only 91 percent of POWs were repatriated, with 1,321 servicemen still considered MIA. An investigation indicated the possibility that some were deserters and defectors, but this was not a proven fact. The activists did not help the situation with their claims that Kissinger had promised final aid to Vietnam. In the end, the Kerry committee concluded that no one was deliberately left in Southeast Asia and that the government had committed no conspiracy.

With the publication of McConnell's book one year after Keating's, the MIA mystery was almost put to an end. Swamp Ranger had been fairly successful, even though the PAVN had been "a reluctant participant in this effort."[21] When field investigations were conducted, the Vietnamese made sure that they were given maximum publicity to propagandize their attitudes. Crash sites became a "lucrative source of funds for the Vietnamese" before the JTF/FA arrived on the scene. Schweitzer realized after scanning the Red Book how important his examination of PAVN documents was. The 208 handwritten pages contained excellent information. "Schweitzer found his first evidence of holdings on American POWs and two pages later evidence information on our first flying missions after the Tonkin Gulf incident. Schweitzer's visit gave him a wealth of information. Schweitzer sent a coded message of his findings to Washington."[22]

By the end of 1992, McConnell says, more than 300 sets of MIA remains had been repatriated.[23] There were more of course, and General Vesey had estimated the total number in what he called his "sensibility check." There were many more remains in remote crash sites in mountainous areas and along the Ho Chi Minh Trail. There have been several dubious attempts to document the Soviet abduction of American prisoners. This doesn't mean that it actually happened. Chances are that we will never know.

On October 17, a delegation of General Vesey, Deputy Assistant Secretary of State Kenneth Quinn, Brigadier General Thomas Needham ITF/F/A commander, and Senator John McCain reached Hanoi and an agreement was concluded between them and the Vietnamese. Thus American negotiations were accomplished, but Schweitzer's Operation Swamp Ranger had paved the way for them. When President Clinton took over, he told the Vietnamese his administration's position would be the same as President Bush's. He wanted a full resolution of the POW/MIA problem.

The activists rallied with Senator Bob Smith, but when General Vesey's delegation to Hanoi departed from Hanoi, they brought with them many important documents obtained as a result of Operation Swamp Ranger. George Stephanopoulos stated that until the United States had an excellent accounting of the POWs we couldn't really work toward normalization. Vesey commented on the Blue Book facts, which he thought were very valuable.

Clinton followed the advice of General Colin Powell by speaking at the Vietnam Veterans Memorial in Washington. He appealed to a group of people that included activists for unity, and he promised to renew his pledge to families of MIAs. This seemed to pacify some of the crowd and Schweitzer was well aware of this.

The activists did not deter efforts on the part of the DIA's Special Office to complete its work on resolving MIA cases, so some progress continued and McConnell ended his book on a note of hope. The Vietnam War was probably the most controversial war in U.S. history because of the problem of accountability of MIAs. In the Gulf War only one MIA could not be accounted for.

In 1996 construction began on a National Prisoner of War Museum at Andersonville, Georgia. Its dedication in 1998 was highlighted by a talk from Senator John McCain.

NOTES

1. Malcolm McConnell, *Inside Hanoi's Secret Archives* (New York: Simon & Schuster, 1995), 278.

2. McConnell, *Inside Hanoi's Secret Archives*, 283.

3. Monika Jensen Stevensen and William Stevensen, *Kiss the Boys Good-bye: How the United States Betrayed Its Own POWs in Vietnam* (New York: Dutton, 1990).

4. McConnell, *Inside Hanoi's Secret Archives,* 216.

5. Susan Katz Keating, *Prisoners of Hope* (New York: Random House, 1994), xvi.

6. Keating, *Prisoners of Hope*, 19–20.

7. Keating, *Prisoners of Hope,* 20.

8. Keating, *Prisoners of Hope*, 14.

9. Ken Gross and Ross Perot, *The Man behind the Myth* (New York: Random House, 1992), 116–17.

10. Gross and Perot, *Man behind the Myth*, 117.

11. Gross and Perot, *Man behind the Myth*, 126.

12. Gross and Perot, *Man behind the Myth*, 122.

13. Gross and Perot, *Man behind the Myth*, 122.

14. Gross and Perot, *Man behind the Myth*, 120.

15. Keating, *Prisoners of Hope,* 48.

16. Keating, *Prisoners of Hope,* 79.

17. Charles J. Patterson and G. Lee Tippin, *The Heroes Who Fell from Grace* (Canton, Ohio: Daring, 1985), 141–42.

18. U.S. Senate Select Committee, *Report on POW/MIA Affairs,* 1993, 93 n.

19. McConnell, *Inside Hanoi's Secret Archives*, 359, 393.

20. Keating, *Prisoners of Hope*, 83.

21. McConnell, *Inside Hanoi's Secret Archives*, 213.

22. McConnell, *Inside Hanoi's Secret Archives*, 101.

23. McConnell, *Inside Hanoi's Secret Archives*, 247.

15

The Gulf War

The Gulf War was the shortest conflict in which the United States engaged and involved fewer prisoners of war. Michael Gordon described the war as one "without precedent in the annals of warfare."[1]

In the summer of 1990, Saddam Hussein, dictator of Iraq, invaded Kuwait. The reasons he gave for this move were not accepted by President George H. W. Bush. The climax came on January 16, 1991, when U.N. forces attacked Iraqi positions. The Middle East was once again a problem area, but this time the United States was taking a strong stand.[2]

Hussein's main force was his Republican Guard, composed of professional troops whose business was fighting. His remaining soldiers were recruits who were reminiscent of the Chinese troops in Korea. These men were poorly trained and if they died, their religion guaranteed them entrance into paradise. But if they fled and deserted, they would lose paradise forever.[3]

The U.S. Marine commander, Lieutenant General Walter Boomer, was well aware of the possibility of losing pilots as casualties or prisoners of war. He also knew that a dead pilot would certainly be a propaganda factor in Iraq's campaign and that a captured pilot would be a further propaganda factor, as had been the case in Vietnam. Just as navy and air force pilots had been paraded through villages in Vietnam when shot down and captured, so too the Iraqis would treat them as trophies.[4] Hanoi had used American POWs as bargaining agents when negotiating with the Nixon administration, and now President George Bush would be on the firing line.

Special operational bases had to be established across the Saudi Arabian border, which would be convenient for helping downed pilots. Rescue operations in both Korea and Vietnam had excellent results, and it was hoped that search and rescue teams would again be successful ventures. Saudi Arabia did not present any real problem, but the surrounding countries of Jordan, Syria, Turkey, and Iran would be problematic. Egypt agreed to cooperate when President Bush promised to eliminate its multimillion-dollar debt to Washington, a kind of bribe, like the tributes offered against the Barbary nations in the Tripolitan War, but still a very convenient mechanism. The coalition forces joining the United States numbered thirty-two.

As General Horner (and General Boomer) had anticipated, prisoners of war and deaths resulted from the military operations. The numbers, however, were minimal compared with previous wars. Another factor, of great concern in the Korean and Vietnam Wars, as already discussed, was the number of prisoners of war unaccounted for.

NAVY LIEUTENANT COMMANDER MICHAEL SPEICHER

The one pilot shot down, a navy lieutenant commander, who still remains unaccounted for, was Michael Speicher. Speicher's F-18 was shot down two days after the war started. When POWs were released after the war, he was not one of them, and his body was never found. In December 1993, an army general discovered an F-18 and took some pictures of it. The plane had not disintegrated and its canopy was found some distance from the aircraft, which indicated the strong possibility of an ejection.

Permission to visit the crash site was requested in December 1994 but was never received. Nine months later Saddam agreed, but all a day search produced was a flight suit with no blood on it. The pilot had been given a new radio, but there had been no transmission from him nor was any radio found at the site.

No Allied losses happened as a result of air-to-air combat. Thirty-five enemy planes were downed, and the dogfights had been easy ones for Allied pilots. Coalition forces flew a total of 109,876 sorties, and there were downed airmen who became POWs. Interestingly, over ten enemy fighters fled to Iran and Iran refused to return the aircraft.

Several news columns in New York papers covered the missing lieutenant commander. The later mission to try to discover facts about the pilot was under the leadership of the International Committee of the Red Cross and had the support of Saddam Hussein.

Speicher had been a pilot on the aircraft carrier *Saratoga* located in the Red Sea. The U.S. State Department considered Hussein's approval a humanitarian effort.[5] A week earlier on December 6, Tim Weiner wrote an article on the pilot which included a map of the crash site. In that article in *The New York Times*, Weiner cited the Pentagon for its initial refusal to gather information about the crash and the pilot. When the crash site was visited by a search party, there was no ejection seat to be found, the site had been scavenged, no bones were found.

The *New York Daily News*[6] reported that the U.S. Navy changed the status of Lieutenant Commander Michael Speicher. Navy Secretary Richard Danzig did this because there was substantial evidence to indicate that the pilot did not die in his crash. A diplomatic note sent to Baghdad demanded that the Iraqi government tell all it knew about the pilot's fate. His status was changed from KIA to MIA. Several new actions were under way and additional steps under intense review, according to the national security adviser Sandy Berger. Berger's letter, given to the Associated Press, didn't say anything about what some of these steps consisted of.

CHIEF WARRANT OFFICER GUY HUNTER

In the *New York Post*, in a special article, Chief Warrant Officer Guy Hunter of the U.S. Marines recalled his seven weeks as a POW in

Iraq. He had been assigned to a reconnaissance unit that was checking out Iraqi artillery sites for future bombings. Hunter and Lieutenant Colonel Clifford Acree were shot down over southern Iraq on January 18, 1991, by a surface-to-air missile but ejected successfully.

Hunter said that the prison in which he had been confined "was quiet as a tomb." When he heard the noise of rattling keys, it represented a terrifying moment because he knew the guards were probably coming for him. He was only slightly beaten, but many of his fellow prisoners were not as lucky. A further interesting and unusual development for Hunter was receiving a wallet of his about six years after the war. Hunter had buried his wallet in the sand about five minutes before being captured. With the returned wallet was a letter in poor English from a Sri Lanka laborer working in Kuwait. The wallet contained credit cards, $47 in cash, Hunter's military ID, and three family pictures.

OTHER AMERICAN POWs

In the late evening of January 17, Commander Mike Merch, an A-6 Intruder pilot, was given permission for a special attack and chose a dangerous low-level attack. He and three other A-16s were the attackers, but about twenty miles from the target Merch had no trace of his wingman. He immediately suspected the worst—his wingman pilot, Lieutenant Bob Wetzel, and his bombardier, Lieutenant Jeffrey Zaum, had been shot down. Both managed to eject. Wetzel broke both arms and his collarbone; when he regained consciousness, Zaum was trying to get his parachute harness off. The two men were POWs within the hour.[7] Rick Atkinson's book, *Crusade*, includes detailed information on POWs downed in Iraq. Zaum later said that when he ejected he was beaten up by the windblast at 500 knots.

On January 17 a Thunderbird 6 was on its way home and was apparently hit. No wreckage was ever found, but after the war, the bodies of its two crewmen, Lieutenant Colonel Donnie Holland and Major Thomas Koritz, were returned by the Iraqis.

Very disturbed about losing these two men and not knowing what happened to them was Lieutenant Colonel R. E. (Scottie) Scott who had been on a mission two nights before. Before going on his next mission, he complained to Lieutenant Colonel Eberly, who would also be flying on the mission. Bad weather didn't help the situation.

Eberly was flying a Corvette 3 with weapons officer Major Thomas Griffith in the backseat. Eberly never saw the missile that hit his aircraft. The canopy was blown off, but their ejection was triggered by the explosion of two rockets beneath their seats. This was one hell of a way to be ejected! On the ground in a dazed condition, Eberly heard the noise of an approaching truck. He was not seen and the truck drove off.

Eberly headed southwest but wondered about Scottie and suddenly came across an ejection seat. A voice came across from his radio, and about fifteen minutes later the two were together. On January 20, near Al Qaim in Iraq, the two woke up and avoided an oil truck with a car parked behind it. Next they were awakened by the sound of planes overhead. They contacted Major Gary Cole on their radio and told him to hurry up with rescue operations. At least they knew that a search was in progress for them, but their evasion of the enemy was not successful, and they joined the ranks of the POWs.

At the beginning of the war there were seven combat search and rescue bases (CSAR), five in Saudi Arabia and two in Turkey. To frustrate Iraqi efforts to trap downed crews, each airman had a special code word or words to verify his identity.

In Baghdad prison, Eberly had the letters PW on his prison uniform. Treatment was cruel and harsh and he was subjected to frequent interrogation. On February 7 he was removed from his cell, given a razor and small mirror, and soon found himself in a small auditorium in front of a TV camera. He had also been given a flight suit. Eberly wouldn't cooperate, however, so the interview was terminated.[8]

On February 15, two A-10s flew to make an attack on Madinah. The flight leader was Captain Phillis and his wingman, First Lieutenant Robert Sweet. Sweet's plane was hit and he ejected. Phillis called for search and rescue, and then he was hit; his body was recovered in March. Sweet became a POW and spent the rest of the war in prison.[9]

Eberly kept a calendar on the wall of his cell with hatchmarks. His prison was known as the Biltmore. By the end of February, U.S. intelligence had identified three possible prison sites, but the Biltmore was not one of them. These areas had to be off limits to bomber aircraft. Eberly and other POWs were evacuated during a bombing raid, and he met Robert Alvarez from CBS. He was with ten other men who were American fliers, one of whom was Tom Griffith, and the men started memorizing each other's names. Abu Bhurarb prison would soon get the name Joliet prison.

An air force pilot, Captain William Anderson, was shot down during the last week of the war and became a POW. The helicopter sent to rescue him was downed. The pilot, his copilot, and three crew members were killed, but three others managed to survive. What was unusual, however, was that one of the survivors was female flight surgeon Major Rhonda Corman, who suffered two broken arms, a bullet wound, and other injuries.

WOMEN POWs

Among women in the military, nurse officers captured in Bataan became POWs, as well as nurses in MASH units in Korea. These women, however, were not combat personnel. When Major Rhonda Cornum was captured, a woman in a combat situation became a POW for the first time. Major Cornum was a flight surgeon who carried a gun and could fly a helicopter. She told the story of her confinement in her book, *She Went to War: The Rhonda Cornum Story*. When Colonel Eberly was released, he was surprised to meet two women POWs, one of whom was Major Cornum. When the release of U.S. POWs was effected, it was done under the supervision of the International Committee of the Red Cross, which took them into custody, escorted them from Iraq to Riyadh, Saudi Arabia, and finally to the hospital ship USS *Mercy* and then Washington, D.C.[10] One reason for a quick exchange advanced by Michael Gordon was that returned Iraqi POWs would spread the word of Iraqi defeats and might even influence some in not wanting to be repatriated.

In January 1991, the Iraqi government reported that it held an unspecified number of male and female prisoners. Iraq maintained that any females would be given good treatment according to the spirit of Islamic law.[11]

Specialist Melissa Rathburn was the other female POW taken by Iraqi forces. She was one of two army truck drivers listed as MIA. She had the dubious distinction of being the first enlisted woman to be a POW since World War II.[12] On January 30, 1991, Rathburn and Specialist David Lockett were wounded and captured while driving their supply truck.

When Major Cornum was captured, she and her fellow survivors were taken to Baath Party headquarters and then to Baghdad, where they met the third survivor, also injured. Cornum was given medical care but refused necessary surgery. Unfortunately thirteen women did not survive the war.

The helicopter bearing Major Cornum was sent into Iraq to rescue the F-16 pilots, the pilot injured in the crash asked for her. She was well known. When she was brought to a place of confinement, Cornum met Captain Anderson, the pilot she had been sent to rescue.[13] Before meeting him she had come across Sergeant Daniel Stamares, the third member of her crew.

The *American Legion* magazine for September 2001 contains an article, "Sister Soldiers," that discusses the role of women in wars of the United States. It points out that women were "an integral part of Operation Desert Storm both on the ground and in the air." The author of the article is Jay Stuller, but what is missing from the article is anything about Major Cornum. Most of the POWs taken by the Iraqis were American. There was one Italian, one Kuwaiti pilot, and a few British soldiers.

Cornum had logged many combat hours flying search and rescue helicopters during the two weeks prior to her crash and even helped capture a group of Iraqi POWs.[14] Her highlight of the air war was the first time she flew into Iraq and came back with five Iraqi prisoners. That was on February 17. A good indication of the attitude of Iraqi prisoners was demonstrated when a piece of Iraqi currency was shown to one of the Iraqi soldiers (a picture of Saddam was on the money) and he spit on it.[15] Iraqi POWs felt they had been abandoned on the front lines by their officers. A few days later Cornum was called to pick up another Iraqi prisoner whose jeep had been destroyed, and he was very happy to surrender.

Major General Jeanne Holm wrote in *Women in the Military* that women were not permitted to fly the army's Apache or other attack helicopters, but female pilots of the 101st Airborne Division's Screaming Eagles could fly Black Hawk and Chinook helicopters. They usually carried supplies and troops fifty miles into Iraq as part of the largest helicopter assault in military history.[16] The air force planes were less complicated for women, but the navy barred women from serving as crews on combat ships. Holm also said "women's integration into the operational elements of the armed forces could not come without a price."[17] She could foresee the possibility of women POWs just as some of our generals at the outset could have foreseen the seizure of downed airmen.

MILITARY BRIEFINGS

At the first of only three briefings given during the conflict, General Schwartzkopf reported three aircraft lost—one British, one Italian, and one Kuwaiti. On January 20, captured coalition pilots were paraded through Baghdad streets. A videotape of them was broadcast on Iraqi television. Clearly some had been tortured to confess crimes under duress. This violated the principles of the Geneva Convention. A photograph of navy pilot Lieutenant Jeffrey Zaum showed bruising on his face and eyes,[18] although later Zaun said that his bruises resulted from his ejection. There was an outcry after the incident demanding war crime trials for Saddam Hussein and other Iraqi leaders, such as there had been in World War II because of German and Japanese cruelties. This, however, was not to happen, just as nothing happened as the result of Korean, Chinese, and Vietnam cruelties.[19]

American losses were minimal when compared with those of previous conflicts. Air superiority was achieved by Allied forces in the Gulf War and then the ground attack operations began. The ground assault overwhelmed Iraqi forces as coalition forces of army, navy, and marine personnel captured thousands of Iraqi prisoners of war.

THE SURRENDER OF IRAQI FORCES

Entire companies of Saddam's troops—weary, fatigued, and starving—surrendered. There were 300,000 Iraqis in Kuwait and 65,000 were seized, many of whom were wounded, as opposed to 146 of coalition forces KIA and 400 wounded. Many Iraqi officers deserted their men. Of forty-two enemy units, twenty-seven were destroyed and left to die on what came to be called the Highway of Death. Many enemy tanks were destroyed by coalition aircraft, and the captured POWs didn't seem to have any idea of why they were fighting and had no stomach for it. The big battles with Saddam's Republican Army were one-sided, with the enemy being defeated and their officers abandoning their soldiers. Divisions of the enemy were captured and the liberation of Kuwait was accomplished. The U.S. Marine commandant stated that the decisive factor had been air power, but the marines had to do the dirty work afterward, cleaning up the mess. More than 60,000 POWs were taken, a factor that resulted in the enemy's agreeing to almost every demand.

The U.S. Navy also took POWs. On January 24, 2001,[20] the guided missile frigate USS *Curtis* seized the island of Kura, a mine-laying ship, and fifty-one POWs as they were capturing enemy equipment and supplies. It should be mentioned that U.S. Army helicopters supported the operation. Kura is an island about fourteen miles off the Kuwaiti coast. It was used by the Iraqis as an intelligence-gathering site.[21]

At the battle of Khafji coalition forces defeated the Iraqis, and subsequent POW interrogations revealed that Iraqi troops balked at fighting when they were ordered to attack. They were threatened with execution by their officers if they refused to fight, much like the so called Chinese volunteers in Korea who were forced to advance against U.N. forces on the battlefield. A Qatari battalion and two Saudi Arabian national guard battalions attacked the city on December 31. When the last enemy unit surrendered, the Arab forces had seized 463 POWs while only eight of their own men were taken as prisoners.

On January 24, the battleships *Wisconsin* and *Missouri* fired on the Kuwaiti shoreline; the marines landed on the beach and received the surrender of many Iraqis. As dusk began to settle, many more gave up, so many that marines had to give them food and water and then send them south on foot to be picked up by others following them. This was necessary so that the advance of the marines would not be delayed.[22]

A very impressive sight was the surrender of hundreds of Iraqis to French forces. The commander of the U.S. Airborne Brigade said, "Every soldier I saw, surrendered."[23] The French commander called on American engineers to clear the road. Over 2,100 POWs had been captured.

At the battle of Burgan oil field, the captured POWs were in poor condition. They were happy to be taken because their own army officers had treated them so poorly. The number of POWs began to grow, and by the evening of January 25, the marines had their work cut out for them with the processing of 2,200 POWs.

At the battle of Busayya the British took 5,000 prisoners, and at the battle of Bloody Heels, about a hundred Iraqis surrendered to the 24th Infantry Division. The Iraqis' feet were bare and bloody because their officers had sliced their tendons so they could not move quickly in any direction. The officers then fled north. This was an indication of the cruel culture of Saddam's officers. The battle of As Salman on January 25 took over 2,900 POWs, while coalition forces suffered only three killed and fifty wounded.

The war, called the 100 hours war, was basically over as of February 27, 2001. It started on January 16, 2001.

THE END OF THE WAR

President George Bush ordered the fighting to cease, stating that coalition forces had won. Some feel the only mistake he made was not bringing justice to Iraq dictator Saddam Hussein. As Everett Alvarez, the first naval officer downed in Vietnam, commented, if we are going to fight a war we must go all the way.

One of the first objectives of the Allies' high technology in this conflict was to take out the Iraqi command and control centers. This had to be accomplished before the ground attack would start. This war also introduced a clear view of the role that well-trained women of the U.S. military service can play, from flying transports to loading bombs to servicing radars. The best example was offered by flight surgeon Major Rhonda Cornum. Women in the military had close proximity to the battlefield and they proved themselves.

Coalition forces put forth a five-week demonstration of air power, but the ground forces took only four days. Coalition tanks destroyed many Iraqi tanks from long range, and the infantry was exceptional. Coalition aircraft, of course, helped considerably to destroy enemy tanks. It was no wonder that so many Iraqis were eager to surrender.

NOTES

1. Michael Gordon and Bernard Trainor, *The Generals' War* (New York: Little, Brown, 1995), x.

2. Walter Boyne, *Gulf War* (Lincolnwood, Ill.: Publications International, 1991), 24.

3. Boyne, *Gulf War*, 28.

4. Gordon and Trainor, *The Generals' War*, 249.

5. Tim Weiner, "With Iraqi's O.K. a U.S. Team Seeks War Pilot's Body," *New York Times*, December 14, 1995, A3.

6. Thursday, January 11, 2001, 25.

7. Rick Atkinson, *Crusade: The Untold Story of the Gulf War* (New York: Houghton Mifflin, 1993), 101.

8. Atkinson, *Crusade*, 243.

9. Atkinson, *Crusade*, 313.

10. Rhonda Cornum, *She Went to War: The Rhonda Cornum Story* (Novato, Calif: Presidio, 1992), 487.

11. E. A. Blacksmith, ed., *Women in the Military,* The Reference Shelf, vol. 64, no. 5 (New York: H.W. Wilson, 1992), 74.

12. Blacksmith, *Women in the Military*, 75.

13. Cornum, *She Went to War*, 108.

14. Cornum, *She Went to War*, 4.

15. Cornum, *She Went to War*, 66.

16. Blacksmith, *Women in the Military*, 447.

17. Blacksmith, *Women in the Military*, 455.

18. James Blackwell, *Thunder in the Desert* (New York: Bantam, 1991), 146.

19. Blackwell, *Thunder in the Desert*, 146.

20. Blackwell, *Thunder in the Desert*, 149.

21. Blackwell, *Thunder in the Desert*.

22. Blackwell, *Thunder in the Desert*, 196.

23. Boyne, *Gulf War*, 32.

16

The War against Terrorism

It is very difficult to write about a war and its prisoners before it has ended, but it would be inappropriate not to say something about the current war against terrorism. Before this war was proclaimed, the United States had a confrontation with China involving a navy EP-3 reconnaissance aircraft that was monitoring the Chinese coastline. This came about as a result of what can be described as a Chinese Communist MIG "hot-shot pilot." The newly elected U.S. president was presented with this situation.

Thanks to the expertise of the pilot, his plane crash-landed in Communist China without casualties, and no one was injured seriously. The crew of twenty-three, which included two women, was taken into custody. All were released after a short detention period. Were they prisoners of war or simply people being held in detention?

Before granting permission to retrieve the aircraft (in parts), many people think that the Chinese made a thorough examination of the plane and its equipment. Then came the real confrontation. The United States had not gone to war over the Chinese incident, nor over the terrorist attack on the USS *Cole*, but the question would have been: against whom?

The leader of the terrorists responsible for the *Cole* attack, as was later learned, was Osama bin Laden. When the United States went to war in Afghanistan, it was not against the country of Afghanistan, but against the terrorists of the Taliban. Also opposing the Taliban government was the Northern Alliance. The country is basically a tribal one with few major cities.

SEPTEMBER 11, 2001

On September 11, 2001, the war against terrorism began in earnest. Four commercial jets were highjacked by terrorist pilots who used the planes as weapons of war. The first two jets crashed into the Twin Towers in New York City, a nonmilitary target; the third plane attacked the Pentagon in Washington, D.C., a military target, but more civilians were killed than military personnel. The fourth plane never reached its original target, which may have been the White House. This plane crashed into a field in Pennsylvania when the passengers resisted the terrorists. The *New York Times* summarized of the tragedy of 9/11:

> Official estimates are that 3,117 people died or are missing and presumed dead as a result of the attack on September 11, not including 17 hijackers.
>
> At the World Trade Center, 2,893 dead or missing, with 147 dead on two hijacked planes; 309 missing, 637 death certificates issued by medical examiner's office. 1,947 death certificates issued at request of families.
>
> At the Pentagon, 181 dead or missing, with 59 dead on hijacked plane.

Following this tragedy, the FBI conducted an intensive investigation of many suspicious Arabs residing in the United States, both permanently and on temporary visas. Many of those detained (almost 1,000) were not officially charged with anything. This stirred up sad remembrances of what Americans did to Italians and Japanese during World War II.

Some weaknesses that contributed to this tragedy were poor airport security, inadequate immigration laws, and probably the lack of serious efforts to investigate some of the previous confrontations in this country, as well as in other countries. The president called reservists into active service for airport security and announced a build-up of reservists for foreign duty. A more controversial action was an increase in wire-tapping and other surveillance measures.

The USS *Cole*

Little did anyone know that all the previous attempts against the United States were links in a chain that would culminate with the Twin Towers massacre. Attacks had occurred in February 1993, October 1995, June 1996, and November 1996. A real blow came on October 12, 2000, when a ship carrying explosives crashed into the USS *Cole* at Aden, Yemen. Seventeen sailors were killed and more than thirty wounded. Bin Laden was associated with the event. The final blow came on September 11, 2001, a date that will rank with the infamous attack on Pearl Harbor.

Should the internees associated with the crackdown on terrorism be considered prisoners of war? Perhaps some should be, but not all. As already noted, some were probably in violation of the immigration laws, which means that they should be under the jurisdiction of that federal agency. That decision remains undecided at this time. Once made, other decisions must follow.

Does military jurisdiction ultimately mean military court-martial or a specially established war crimes trial? Here again a decision must be made.

PRISONERS OF WAR

Finally, what about POWs taken on land by Afghan forces? These people deserve consideration because the Northern Alliance may not act kindly to their prisoners. In a newspaper report on November 29, 2001, a tribal chief openly admitted that his fighters had executed 160 POWs.

A report on November 26 stated that about 1,000 fighters surrendered when they were surrounded by Northern Alliance forces, and on December 2, 2001, more than eighty Taliban fighters reported that thirteen soldiers, weak and suffering from the cold, surrendered. They claimed that two days previously they had been prevented from surrendering by a group of seven Arab fighters.

In the *New York Times*, a picture of a new prison camp appeared. It showed about 4,000 Taliban fighters who surrendered at Kurduz, including some Pakistanis and other volunteers. They had been moved by truck to a prison hundreds of miles to the west in Sheblurghan.

Captured fighting for the Taliban was John Walker, an American who had fought in northern Afghanistan. More will be said about him in the closing pages of this chapter.

One week after September 11, U.S. and British bombers struck Taliban targets to prepare for the entrance of soldiers and marines, and in a short while marines were on the scene.

THE INTERIM GOVERNMENT

An interim government was agreed to on December 6, 2001, which was quite an accomplishment, despite the Northern Alliance and the different tribes.

On the evening of December 8, 2001, an ex-colonel of the Taliban who had defected stated on TV that there would still be trouble because of factions within the country. Even at the beginning of this conflict President Bush recognized the possibility that this war could last several years.

Early on, Secretary of Defense Donald Rumsfeld indicated he opposed the detention of large numbers of Taliban and Al Qaeda prisoners, except for the top leaders. Later Rumsfeld changed his mind.

As mentioned previously, in all likelihood prisoners held by Afghan forces (chiefly the Northern Alliance) would not be humanely treated. Al Qaeda prisoners were taken in the intense fighting near Tora Bora, the last location of Osama bin Laden's forces, which were trapped in the White Mountains.

PRISON CAMPS FOR AL QAEDA AND TALIBAN POWS

The actual number of prisoners held by anti-Taliban forces is not known and almost impossible to determine. Holding pens built by the marines housed many of the prisoners. Camp Rhino, the confinement center, had a remote location, ideal for POWs.

New developments concerning POWs took place almost daily. In the last three weeks of January 2002 this was especially true. On December 28, 2001, the three major newspapers in New York City, the *Post*, *Times*, and *News* (as well as many papers throughout the country), reported that Secretary of Defense Donald Rumsfeld announced that Al Qaeda and Taliban prisoners would be transported to Guantanamo naval base on Cuba. This base, a forty-five-square-mile area on the southeastern tip of the island, represented another excellent choice because of the location and the security that it provides. Rumsfeld felt that Fidel Castro would not be a problem, but anyone who managed to escape from the compound might receive aid from Castro's regime. This was the only flaw in the plan, but the security measures imposed on the POWs made escape nearly impossible.

In early December 2001, the marines had forty-five captive POWs classified as "battlefield detainees" at Kandahar and on board the USS *Peleliu* in the Arabian Sea. John Walker Lindh was temporarily held on this ship. Walker Lindh made the rounds as a prisoner. The confinement center in Cuba took several weeks to build and was called Camp X-Ray.

Rumsfeld did not indicate where Osama bin Laden or Mohammed Omar, if captured, would be confined. At the end of 2001, the enemy leaders had not been caught. For the last two weeks of January 2002, the main news topic was the POWs at Camp X-Ray and John Walker.

TREATMENT OF TALIBAN POWs

On January 13, 2002, a news article in the *New York Post* showed a picture of a soldier and his attack dog at the Guantanamo prison. Twenty Taliban POWs were confined there.

Other security measures included tying a POW's hands behind his back on exercise walks and during the medical exam on his first day. POWs who didn't have a Koran were provided with one, and other necessary supplies were given them. Also assigned to Camp X-Ray was a special Islamic chaplain.

All POWs were adequately fed, but some critics criticized their conditions and the treatment they received. Those who criticized U.S. treatment of POWs were politicians from Britain, Germany, and the Netherlands, as well as some U.S. civil rights groups. They resented the fact that Taliban and Al Qaeda POWs were bound and shackled; that they were kept in open six-by-eight-foot cells. Rumsfeld said they were dangerous, and some of them actually threatened their guards. He fired back at these critics and said that the charges of cruelty were false. Tony Blair, the British prime minister, supported the U.S. position.

One group in California tried to bring suit in a federal court over the conditions at Camp X-Ray. Even former Attorney General Ramsey Clark got involved as a civilian civil rights attorney. Clark had also opposed the U.S. role in the Vietnamese conflict. Those who claimed the United States was not officially at war deplored the imprisonment of Taliban and Al Qaeda fighters.

JOHN WALKER LINDH

Controversy erupted over the case of John Walker Lindh, a twenty-year-old civilian who chose to fight with the Taliban against his own country. As indicated previously, he was a POW at Camp Rhino, was temporarily held on the USS *Peleliu*, and was also aboard the USS *Bataan,* from which he was sent to the detention camp at Kandahar.

His final trip was in a C-141 cargo transport plane to the United States, where he was charged in a federal court in Virginia. He arrived by helicopter at Dulles International Airport and was turned over to the Justice Department.

The only reason the leader of the San Patrícios avoided the death penalty was that General Winfield Scott decided that his desertion preceded the actual declaration of war. Lindh was spared because of plea bargaining. This was done with the approval of Attorney General Ashcroft and Defense Secretary Donald Rumsfeld. Walker received a twenty-year sentence; defense lawyers and prosecutors spent fifty-seven hours negotiating. On July 15 the final decision was made. Lindh's lawyer called him a kid who thought he was doing the right thing. Other prisoners held by our government for alleged crimes still await trials. Some of them are U.S. citizens as well.

On January 24, a raid on a Taliban lair captured twenty-seven prisoners. A Green Beret was wounded, while many of the enemy were killed. The twenty-seven enemy POWs were taken to the makeshift prison at Kandahar. According to General Myers, this meant the United States had a total of 297 POWs. A Pentagon briefing pledged to eliminate all pockets of resistance. On January 24 shipment of POWs to Camp X-Ray stopped. More temporary holding pens had to be built, and the plan was to move all POWs into cells with solid walls to take care of POWs already held and an expected influx of more. Such an arrangement was more likely to pass visits from the International Red Cross, which already had been there.

While all these developments were taking place, Tom Ridge, Pennsylvania governor, was assigned by President Bush to head the newly created Office of Homeland Security. This was a new cabinet agency position concerned with security within the United States.

The FBI was digging deep for information to find conspirators. This was the biggest criminal investigation it had ever conducted. Airport security was greatly improved and many jet fighters were patrolling the skies. Many problems, however, remained to be solved and answered.

CIVILIAN PRISONERS

What is the United States going to do with civilian internees seized by the FBI? Should they be charged in the federal courts or should they be handed over to the jurisdiction of the military for courts-martial or military tribunals? Or should they be held for war crimes trials? If there are proceedings by the military, should they be held in secret? No matter what court they are finally tried in, many people believe nothing should be done in secret.

Then there are the military prisoners being held at Camp X-Ray. Should they be repatriated to their original countries according to the principles of the Geneva Convention? That might be a problem if they do not wish repatriation or if their original countries do not want them, which is a good possibility.

Throughout the Afghan war General Myers and Secretary of Defense Donald Rumsfeld gave daily briefings on TV, something rarely done in previous conflicts.

As of January 2002, no American pilot has been shot down and captured as a POW, nor has any member of the military become a POW of the Taliban or Al Qaeda forces. But the United States must expect some casualties. Whether or not the government will be able to capture Osama bin Laden, and the outcome for prisoners are events that only the future will reveal.

As of January 28, 2002, the detainees in Cuba, according to President Bush, would not be considered POWs. They would, of course, be afforded humane treatment and probably receive much better treatment than they would receive in Afghanistan or their country of origin.

The president called them parasites and terrorists, not soldiers. Not having POW status meant that they would not receive any stipends and that they would be fully interrogated for information on other terrorists and their activities, which would be helpful perhaps in saving many lives, both military and civilian. This last point concerning interrogation was specifically mentioned by columnist William Safire in the *New York Times* (January 28, 2002).

In an article published in the *New York Times* (January 29, 2002) Nicholas D. Kristoff differed slightly. He argued that the Geneva Convention principles apply to the detainees, that interrogators can ask them anything, that no force should be used against them in interrogations, and that they can be tried for crimes of terrorism. Another point is that the United States must return POWs at the conclusion of the war. The U.S. government did not press Chinese POWs in Korea for repatriation because many did not desire it, and President Truman refused to see anyone repatriated against his will. The controversy over POW status for the detainees continues.

On the evening of January 29, 2002, President George W. Bush delivered his second State of the Union message and briefly reiterated his position on POW status, assuring the American people that ultimately the United States will prevail and destroy the enemy.

Will there be war crimes trials? No one knows. Once again, history will tell the tale.

Glossary

AEF   American expeditionary forces that fought in World War I in France under the leadership of General John Pershing

ARVN   Army of the Republic of South Vietnam

Afrika Korps   German unit that fought in North Africa under the leadership of General Erwin Rommel

Al Qaeda   terrorist group working for the Taliban government in Afghanistan as well as Arab, European, and American countries

Alamo Scouts   unit created in World War II in the Philippines to fight against the Japanese

Amnesty   general pardon of the offences of subjects against the government or the proclamation of such pardon

Annexation   act by which sovereignty is formally extended over territory acquired by discovery, occupation, or absorption of the territory of another state

Armistice   temporary suspension of hostilities by agreement of parties; a truce

Arraignment   the legal procedure by which a prisoner is called to a court to be identified, to hear the charge brought against him, and to make an appropriate plea

Articles of Confederation   the first written national constitution of the United States; later replaced by the Constitution

BNR   body not recovered

Bastinado method of torture used against U.S. prisoners in the Tripolitan War. It involved beating a prisoner on the soles of his feet with a stick called a bastinado. It was also used by the Communists in Vietnam against American POWs.

Blue Book central list of American POWs registered at Hoa Lo Prison in Hanoi between 1964 and 1972

Blue Files individual personnel records of American POWs held by the Vietnamese at Hoa Lo Prison in Hanoi

Bomb-Ketch also known as a mortar boat or bombard; a small ship mounting one or two heavy mortars and several light cannons

Brainwashing indoctrination technique used extensively by the Chinese Communists during the Korean War. Employed mental and physical measures to change a person's mind about what he thought of his country and perhaps to effect a decision not to be repatriated

Brig two-masted, square-rigged vessel

Bush Road Map process and plan leading to normalization between the United States and North Vietnam to effect rapid repatriation of American POWs

CIA Central Intelligence Agency

CPV Chinese People's Volunteers; Chinese troops in Korea

Camp X-Ray POW camp on Guantanamo Naval Base in Cuba for Taliban and Al Qaeda detainees of the U.S. war against terrorism

Cartel agreement between belligerents for the purpose of a POW exchange

Cartel ships ships carrying POWs

***Chesapeake* Incident, 1807** A British ship, *The Leopard*, demanded to search an American ship, the *Chesapeake*. The captain refused and was fired on and the ship boarded. Four seamen taken as deserters were American citizens.

Code of chivalry code of honor that emphasized loyalty to God and to the knight's lord and included protecting the oppressed and helpless, supporting justice, defending Christianity, and encouraging courtesy, gallantry, and generosity during feudal times

Code of conduct   military action developed to regulate behavior of American POWs in the Vietnam War and all succeeding conflicts

Colditz prison   Nazi POW camp that Germans considered escape-proof. Housed prisoners who were difficult or considered troublemakers.

Colis   a common name for packages of food and clothing for a POW

Collier   small vessel used for carrying coal in the Spanish-American War

Cooler   confinement cell where a POW received little food and was often harassed

Corvette   a war vessel ranking in the old sailing navies, next below a frigate and having usually only one tier of guns

Croix de Guerre (Cross of War)   French decoration awarded to military personnel, French and American, for deeds of valor and courage

DAC (Department of the Army)   civilians hired by the United States in most cases to serve as interpreters in Korea for repatriation sessions

DIA   Defense Intelligence Agency

DPRK   People's Democratic Republic of North Korea

DRV   Democratic Republic of North Vietnam

Dalag   German POW airmen's transit camp; also called Dalag Luft

Dawes Mission   failed OSS operation to rescue prisoners or aid downed airmen in Europe during World War II

Death March   route from Bataan and Corregidor taken by American prisoners, many of whom succumbed to lack of food and medicine

Death Ships (Hell Ships)   designation given to Japanese ships that transported POWs to Japan. Many died on these ships as a result of crowded conditions, scarcity of food, and poor sanitary conditions

Demilitarized Zone (DMZ)   heavily fortified frontier between North and South Vietnam during the war (same term designates the line between North and South Korea)

Desert Shield   Iraq invaded Kuwait on August 2, 1990. The U.N. General Assembly voted unanimously for economic sanctions on

Iraq, and the United States began a military buildup code-named Desert Shield. It ended on January 16, 1991, when Iraq was attacked by coalition forces in an operation called Desert Storm

Dodd Incident Communist seizure of General Dodd on Koje-do during the Korean war

Doolittle Raid special bombing attempt on Japan itself led by Jimmy Doolittle

Emancipation Proclamation declaration of freedom for all slaves under Confederate control by President Abraham Lincoln

Encarnacion prisoners American military taken as prisoners during the Mexican War at the Encarnation plantation

Escadrille (French) unit of combat pilots in World War II that consisted of French and Americans, later the Americans were absorbed into the U.S. Army Air Force

Exchange trading private for private, sergeant for sergeant, lieutenant for lieutenant, and so on. This was the system carried over to the United States in the Revolutionary War and other subsequent wars. During wars, exchanges were made on both sides with commanding officers, and after the wars official treaties governed such exchanges. Operations Little Switch and Big Switch in Korea were exchanges in which rank was essential.

Executive Order 9006 presidential order curtailing the rights and privileges of Italians and Japanese in the United States, many of whom were American citizens, who during World War II were considered security risks

Explanation session method used to persuade POWs in the Korean War to seek repatriation or not to seek it. Many prisoners who were anti-Communist chose not to go back to Communist control and twenty-one Americans refused to be repatriated to the U.S

Feldivebel German noncommissioned officer assigned as an overseer of working commandos in World War I

Final Solution Hitler's policy of extermination and elimination of the Jewish race

Freedom Valley   place where U.S. POWs from Korea were released and given their repatriation and freedom at the end of the Korean War

French Directory   five-man group that was formed by the National Convention in France to rule the country; lasted four years and gave way to one-man rule under Napoleon Bonaparte

Frigate   originally a light vessel propelled by sails and by oars, later a ship-rigged war vessel, intermediate between a corvette and a ship of the line

Geneva Convention   an international agreement for the conduct of belligerents drafted in 1864 and ratified by nearly every country

Gestapo   German secret police during World War II

Great Escape   escape of British airmen who tunneled out of Stalag 13, many of whom were recaptured and executed by the Germans

Green Berets   American special military forces unit used in tactical operations against the enemy

Guerrillas   people who engage in irregular warfare, especially as members of an independent unit carrying out harassment and sabotage

Gulf of Tonkin incident   attacks on two U.S. Navy ships that escalated the Vietnam War

Hague Convention (Court of Arbitration)   tribunal (1899) that tried to settle international disputes peacefully

Hanoi Hilton   name given by American prisoners to the prison in which they were confined in Hanoi, Vietnam

Hessians   German mercenary troops hired by England to fight against American forces in the Revolutionary War

Highway of Death   name given to the route of enemy tanks in Iraq during the Gulf War; destroyed by U.S. aircraft and many Iraqis killed

Houseboat mission   OSS operation to rescue prisoners and/or downed airmen in Europe during World War II

Impressment   seizure of American seamen on the high seas by Britain to serve in the British service; used by Chinese Communists to force Chinese to fight against their will in Korea

KIA/BNR   killed in action/body not recovered

Karbrriche Hotel   place of confinement for American military POWs when they were questioned by German intelligence officers in World War II

Know-Nothing Party   political party founded around the time of the Civil War that opposed immigrants and Catholics

Kommandantur   German government officer in charge of a prison camp

Kriegsgefangener   American POW

Lao Patriotic Front   Communist Laotian government; also known as Pathet Lao

Legion of the Lafayette   American pilots who flew combat missons in the French air force in World War II and who were later absorbed into the U.S. Army Air Force

Leiber Code   code of war guiding how an army treated POWs; first comprehensive codification of international law issued by any government

Letters of marque   empowered receivers to cross the boundaries or marches of an enemy; a license granted to a private ship to make attacks on the belongings of a public enemy, usually in the phrase *letters of marque and reprisal* which constitute a vessel privateer

Logan Act   a controversial act that fines or imprisons any American who attempts to deal with a foreign government in opposition to U.S. foreign policy

Luftlager or Luftwaffelager   camp for captured airmen in World War II run by the Germans; known as Stalags

Luftwaffe   German air force

Malmedy massacre   the merciless World War II killing of American soldiers who were German POWs in Belgium; led by an SS officer

McGregor project   failed OSS operation to rescue prisoners and/or downed airmen in Europe (World War II)

NKPA North Korean People's Army

NVA North Vietnamese Army

National League of Families of POWs and MIAs organized by Sybil Stockdale to keep public attention on POWs in Vietnam

Nisei second-generation Japanese Americans

Nuremberg war crimes trials military trials of Germans who allegedly committed crimes against humanity during World War II

OCS Officer Candidate School

OSS Office of Strategic Services created in World War II; predecessor of the Central Intelligence Agency (CIA)

Oflag a permanent officers camp for POWs

Op persuasion attempted repatriation of chiefly Chinese and North Korean prisoners who claimed to be anti-Communist

Operation Attila planned capture of North Africa

Operation Avalanche planned invasion of Italy

Operation Big Switch POW exchange between the United Nations and North Korea at the end of the Korean War

Operation Cartwheel island-hopping tactic, planned by General Douglas MacArthur in World War II, to recapture islands that had fallen into the hands of the Japanese; combined army–navy effort

Operation Homecoming return of U.S. military POWs in 1973

Operation Husky planned invasion of Sicily

Operation Lazarus failed mission to liberate U.S. POWs in Southeast Asia and return the remains of MIAs

Operation Little Switch POW exchange between the United Nations and North Korea during the Korean War

Operation Overlord Normandy invasion, World War II

Operation Shingle Anzio beach invasion, World War II

Operation Swamp Rangers covert mission to find unaccounted POWs of the Vietnam War; designed by Theodore Schwartzer

Operation Torch three landings planned by different task forces in North Africa, World War II

PAVN People's Army of Vietnam

PBY   Patrol Bomber, consolidated aircraft corporation. Designated a general class of amphibious patrol bombers. These planes were used mostly in the Pacific to conduct anti-submarine patrols.

Papago Park escape   escape from a POW camp in the United States by twenty-five German officers and sailors during World War II; all were recaptured

Paris Peace Talks, 1972   joint attempt to end the Vietnam War and settle difficulties between the United States and North Vietnam

Parole   system of freeing POWs and giving them a limited amount of territory within which they can live and take care of themselves; those who participate in acts of war forfeit their parole

Pathet Lao   Laotian Patriotic Front—the Communist Laotian government

Peace of God   a decree instituted to protect women, children, clergy, and other noncombatants in medieval times

Persona non grata   personally unacceptable or unwelcome

Philippine insurrection   revolution that occurred at the end of the Spanish-American War in the Philippines; directed against the United States in retaliation for its attempted control of the country; started on February 4, 1901, by Emilio Aquinalda

Postliminy   principle by which people and things seized by an enemy in war are restored to their former state when peace returns

Press gang   kidnapping of Americans in the United States by the British to serve on British ships, used largely in the War of 1812

Presumptive finding of death   U.S. Department of Defense legal procedure of declaring missing casualty dead

Prigioniere de guerre   Italian term for prisoner of war

Primitive tribes   tribes that make little or no provision for unproductive days and make little or no use of writing (according to historian Will Durant)

Prisoner of war   member of the military captured in a war or battle

Privateers   armed ships privately owned and commissioned by the government by letters of marque and reprisal to make war on enemy vessels. During the American Revolution more than 2,000

were commissioned and in the War of 1812, American privateers captured hundreds of British ships. Privateers were abolished by common agreement of the great powers by the Declaration of Paris (1856)

Pueblo incident   capture of a U.S. ship, the *Pueblo,* and its crew off the coast of North Korea in the absence of a state of war

Quasi-war   unofficial war; not officially declared by the Congress, for example, the war with France in 1798–1799; could also be applied to Korea and Vietnam and even the current war against terrorism

ROK   Republic of Korea (South Korea)

Raiders   a group of renegade prisoners of war held at Andersonville during the Civil War

Rangers   special military forces used in certain military situations against the enemy

Ransom   payment that a country makes to the enemy for the release of prisoners

Razeé   ship with its upper deck cut away and thus reduced to the next inferior class

Red Book   index of holdings of the Central Military Museum in Hanoi

Relocation center   designated area detaining and confining Japanese nationals and some U.S. citizens of Japanese ancestry. Such areas were spread out in the United States during World War II. Italians were also gathered in relocation centers but in lower numbers.

Repatriation   return of a POW to his country after the end of hostilities

Reprisal camp   place of confinement for troublesome or difficult prisoners

Retaliation   principle by which mistreatment of prisoners by one side triggers mistreatment of prisoners by the other side

SAM   surface-to-air missile

SRO   senior ranking officer in a prison camp

Salutary neglect   a period in American colonial history when England did not enforce its laws against the colonies

San Patrício Battalion   group of renegade U.S. Army soldiers in the Mexican War who deserted and fought for Mexico

Scalawags   white Southerners, many pro-Union, during the Civil War. They cooperated with the carpetbaggers—Northerners who went south after the Civil War in the reconstruction period to further their own fortunes.

Schooner   fore-and-aft rigged vessel, typically having two masts, with the smaller sail in the foremast and the main mast slipped amidships

Slidell case   refusal of the Mexican government to accept American negotiator John Slidell and his proposals that the United States buy the New Mexico and California territories and assume Mexico's debts to Americans in exchange for the Rio Grande boundary

Sloop of war   fore-and-aft vessel with one mast and a single headsail jib, usually between 110 and 122 feet in length; drew 15 feet of water

Sontay raid   attempt to free Vietnam War POWs that failed because all POWs had been cleared out

Sparrow mission   failed OSS operation to rescue prisoners or aid downed airmen in Europe during World War II

Taliban   Islamic government in Afghanistan defeated by U.S. and coalition forces in October 2001

Tarleton's quarter   killing captured soldiers instead of taking them prisoner

Tories   American colonists who supported England during the Revolutionary War

Torpedo   any one of a variety of explosive devices; now usually called free-floating or drifting mines. Fulton tested their use. Known in the Civil War as "spar torpedos."

Treaty of Ghent, 1814   treaty that officially ended the War of 1812. It established the prewar boundaries of the United States but did not mention impressment and the seizure of American ships

Treaty of Guadalupe-Hidalgo   treaty that officially ended the Mexican War

Treaty of Montefontaine   final negotiations between France and the United States that ended the quasi-undeclared naval war

Treaty of Versailles   treaty that ended World War I but was not ratified by the U.S. Senate

Tribute   sum of money and/or supplies; a bribe to persuade a hostile force to cease its attacks

Truce of God   decree that prohibited fighting and warfare on certain days of the week and special holidays in medieval times

Turtle boat   invented by Robert Fulton to submerge and attach torpedoes to ships' bottoms

Tuskegee airmen   African American pilots in World War II who distinguished themselves in aerial combat

UNCRC   United Nations Repatriation Commission

UNCRG   United Nations Command Repatriation Group

VC   South Vietnamese Committee military forces

War crimes tribunal   court specially created to deal with military who allegedly committed serious crimes in war. These were created during World War II to deal with the Germans and Japanese. No such courts were created after the Korean, Vietnam, and Gulf Wars

Wehrmacht   German army in World War II

Woodstock Letters   collection of material supplying primary sources of information on Jesuit history from its beginning. These papers were once kept at Woodstock College in Maryland, which is no longer in existence, but complete copies are maintained in the libraries or archives of most Jesuit communities today.

Working commandos   work parties sent out from the main POW camps (sometimes just one person) to work on a farm, on a highway, or in a factory or mine during World War II

XYZ Affair   In 1797 President John Adams sent negotiators to Paris. The delegation was insulted by French agents who demanded that Americans pay off a large debt. The three French agents were identified only as X, Y, and Z

Yellow fever   disease contracted in damp, hot regions, usually transmitted by mosquitoes. It killed many Americans in the Spanish-American War and also in the jungle areas of Korea and Vietnam.

Yellow journalism   media propaganda that promoted U.S. involvement in the Spanish-American War

Zimmerman telegram   German plot to draw Mexico into World War I against the United States, suggesting that Mexico could regain some of its territories. The telegram was intercepted and decoded by the British, and it aroused American war sentiment.

Bibliography

Acheson, Dean. *Present at the Creation.* New York: Norton, 1973.

Adams, Henry. *The War of 1812.* 9 vols. Washington, D.C.: Infantry Journal Press, 1944.

Albion, Robert, and Jennie Pope. *Sea Lanes in Wartime, The American Experience, 1775–1942.* New York: Norton, 1942.

Alcaraz, Ramon. *The Other Side: or Notes for the History of the War between Mexico and the United States.* New York: Wiley, 1850. Translated from the Spanish and edited by Albert C. Ramsey.

Alexander, Bevin. *Korea: The First War We Lost.* New York: Hippocrene, 1986.

Alger, Russell A. *The Spanish-American War.* 1901. Freeport, N.Y.: Books for Libraries Press, 1971.

Allen, Ethan. *A Narrative of Colonel Ethan Allen's Captivity from the Time of His Being Taken by the British: Written by Himself and Now Published for the Information of the Curious in All Nations.* Newburg, Mass.: John Mycall, 1799.

Alvarez, Everett, Jr., and Anthony S. Pitch. *Chained Eagle.* New York: Dell, 1989.

Alvarez, Ramon, et al. *The Other Side.* Translated by Albert Ramsey. New York: Wiley, 1850. First published in Mexico in 1848.

Ambrose, Stephen. *The Victors: Eisenhower and His Boys: The Men of World War II.* New York: Simon & Schuster, 1998.

Andersen, Bern. *By Sea and by Rivers: The Naval History of the Civil War.* New York: Knopf, 1962.

Andros, Thomas. *The Old Jersey Captive: Or a Narrative of the Captivity of Thomas Andros*. Boston: William Peirce, 1833.

Appleman, Roy E. *South to the Nakong: North to the Yalu. United States Army in Korea War*. Washington, D.C.: Office of the Chief of Military History, U.S. Government Printing Office, 1961. Reprinted in 1975.

Appleman, Roy E., et al. *Okinawa: The Last Battle*. Rutland, Vt.: Tuttle, 1960

Arthur, Anthony. *Deliverance at Los Baños*. New York: St. Martin's, 1985.

Ashe, S. W. *The Trial and Death of Henry Wirz*. Raleigh, N.C.: Uzell, 1908. Available through University Microfilms, Ann Arbor, Michigan.

Atkinson, Rick. *Crusade: The Untold Story of the Gulf War*. New York: Houghton Mifflin, 1993.

Bailey, Ronald H. *Prisoners of War*. Alexandria, Va.: Time and Life Books, 1981.

Baldwin, Hanson. *World War I*. New York: Harper & Row, 1962.

Barker, A. J. *Behind Barbed Wire*. London: B. T. Batsford, 1974.

Barnes, James. *Naval Actions of the War of 1812*. New York: Harper, 1896.

Bauer, K. Jack. *Surfboats and Horse Marines: U.S. Naval Operations in the Mexican War, 1846–1849*. Annapolis, Md.: U.S. Naval Institute, 1969.

Bemis, Samuel Flagg. *A Diplomatic History of the United States*. Rev. ed. New York: Holt, 1942.

Berger, Carl. *The United States Air Force in Southeast Asia, 1961–1973*. Washington, D.C.: Office of Air Force History, 1977.

Biderman, Albert. *March to Calumny*. New York: Macmillan, 1963.

Bill, Alfred Hoyt. *Rehearsal for Conflict: The War with Mexico, 1846–1838*. New York: Cooper Square, 1969.

Blacksmith, E. A., ed. *Women in the Military*. The Reference Shelf, vol. 64, no. 5. New York: H. W. Wilson, 1992.

Blackwell, James. *Thunder in the Desert*. New York: Bantam, 1991.

Blair, Clay. *The Forgotten War: America in Korea, 1950–1953*. New York: Time Books, 1987.

Blakey, Scott. *Prisoner at War: The Survival of Commander Richard A. Stratton*. Garden City, N.Y.: Anchor Press/Doubleday, 1978.

Blumenthal, Walter Hart. *Women Camp Followers of the American Revolution*. New York: Arno, 1974.

Bosworth, Allan R. *America's Concentration Camps*. New York: Norton, 1967.

Bowman, Larry G. *Captive Americans during the American Revolution.* Athens, Ohio: Ohio University Press, 1976.

Boyington, Gregory. *Baa Baa, Black Sheep.* New York: Arno, 1958.

Boyne, Walter. *Gulf War.* Lincolnwood, Ill.: Publications International, 1991.

Brady,William C. *The Hard War Home.* Washington, D.C.: Infantry Journal Press, 1947.

Brainard, Dyer. *Francis Leiber and the American Civil War.* Huntington Library, Quarterly II, 1939.

Breasted, James Henry. *The Conquest of Civilization.* New York: Harper, 1926.

Bristol, Frank Milton. *The Life of Chaplain McCabe.* 2d ed. New York: Fleming H. Revell, 1908.

Brougher, W. E. *South to Bataan, North to Mukden.* Athens: University of Georgia Press, 1972.

Brown, Bernard Edward. *American Conservatives: The Political Thought of Francis Lieber and John W. Burgess.* New York: AMS Press, 1951. Reprinted in 1967.

Brown, Charles H. *The Correspondents' War.* New York: Scribner's, 1967.

Brown, Daniel Patrick. *The Tragedy of Libby and Andersonville Prison Camps.* Ventura, Calif.: Golden West Historical Publications, 1980.

Brown, William Wells. *The Negro in the American Revolution.* Miami: Mnemosyne, 1969.

Bruer, William B. *Retaking the Philippines.* New York: St. Martin's, 1986.
———. *The Great Raid on Cabanatuan: Rescuing the Doomed Ghosts of Bataan and Corregidor.* New York: Wiley, 1994.

Burchett, W., and Alan Winnington. *Koje Unscreened.* Peking, China: W. Burchett and Alan Winnington, 1953.

Byers, Edward. *The Nation of Nantucket.* Boston: Northeastern University Press, 1987.

Caffrey, Kate. *The Twilight's Last Gleaming: Britain versus America, 1812–1815.* New York: Stein & Day, 1977.

Caraccilo, Dominic, J., ed. *Surviving Bataan and Beyond.* Mechanicsburg, Pa.: Stackpole, 1999.

Cartwright, H. A., and M. C. C. Harrison. *Within Four Walls.* London: E. Arnold, 1930.

Cavada, Frederick F. *Libby Life: Experiences of a Prisoner of War in Richmond, Virginia 1863–64.* Philadelphia: Lippincott, 1865.

Chadwick, Frank E. *The Relations of the United States and Spain: The Spanish-American War*. Vols. 1–2. New York: Scribner's, 1911.

Chesley, Larry. *Seven Years in Hanoi*. Salt Lake City: Bookcraft, 1973.

Chidsey, Donald Barr. *The War with Mexico*. New York: Crown, 1968.

Churchill, Sir Winston. *The Second World War*. 6 vols. London: Cassell, 1948–1954.

Clark, Mark W. *From the Danube to the Yalu*. New York: Harper, 1954.

Coffman, Edward M. *The War to End All Wars: The American Military Experience in World War I*. New York: Oxford University Press, 1968.

Cohen, Bernard M., and Maurice Z. Cooper. *A Follow-Up Study of World War II Prisoners of War*. Washington, D.C.: U.S. Government Printing Office, 1954.

Coles, Harry L. *The War of 1812*. Chicago: University of Chicago Press, 1965.

Colvin, Rod. *First Heroes: The POWs Left behind in Vietnam*. New York: Irvington, 1987.

Commager, Henry Steele, and Richard Morris. Editors. *The Spirit of '76*. 2 vols. Indianapolis: Bobbs-Merrill, 1958.

Cook, Graeme. *In and Out of Rebel Prisons*. Oswego, N.Y.: R. J. Oliphant, 1888.

Cornum, Rhonda. *She Went to War: The Rhonda Cornum Story*. Novato, Calif.: Presidio, 1992.

Crane, Stephen. *Wounds in the Rain*. Freeport, N.Y.: Books for Libraries Press, 1900. Reprinted in 1972.

Crowl, Philip. *Campaign in the Marianas*. Washington, D.C.: Office of the Chief of Military History, Department of the Army, 1960.

Crowl, Philip, and Edward Love. *Seizure of the Gilberts and Marshalls*. Washington, D.C.: Office of the Chief of Military History, Department of the Army, 1955

Dandridge, Danske. *American Prisoners of the Revolution*. Charlottesville, Va.: Michie, 1911.

Daniels, Roger. *Concentration Camps USA: Japanese Americans and World War II*. Hinsdale, Ill.: Dryden, 1971.

——. *The Decision to Relocate the Japanese Americans*. Malabar, Fla.: Krieger, 1975.

David, Heather. *Operation Rescue*. New York: Pinnacle , 1971.

Davis, Jefferson. *The Rise and Fall of the Confederate Government*. 2 vols. New York: Appleton, 1881.

———. *Andersonville and Other War Prisons*. New York: Belford, 1890.

Davis, Samuel. *Escape of a Confederate Officer from Prison*. Norfolk, Va.: Landmark, 1892.

Daws, Gavan. *Prisoners of the Japanese: POWs of World War II in the Pacific*. New York: Morrow, 1994.

De Conde, Alexander. *The Quasi-War*. New York: Scribner's, 1966.

De Kay, James Tertius. *The Battle of Stonington: Torpedoes, Submarines, and Rockets in the War of 1812*. Annapolis, Md.: Naval Institute Press, 1990.

De Voto, Bernard. *Year of Decision 1846*. Boston: Little, Brown, 1943.

Dean, William F. *General Dean's Story*. New York: Viking, 1954.

Del Castillo, Richard Griswold. *The Treaty of Guadalupe Hidalgo*. Norman: University of Oklahoma Press, 1990.

Dennett, Carl P. *Prisoners of the Great War*. Boston: Houghton Mifflin, 1919.

Denney, Robert E. *Civil War Prisons and Escapes, A Day-by-Day Chronicle*. New York: Sterling, 1993.

Dillard, Walter Scott. *Sixty Days to Peace: Implementing the Paris Peace Accords in Vietnam*. Washington, D.C.: National Defense University, 1982.

Dimas, David D. *Missing in Action/Prisoner of War: A Report to the American People*. La Mirada, Calif.: Orion, 1987.

Dower, John W. *War without Mercy*. New York: Pantheon, 1986.

Downey, Fairfax. *Texas and the War with Mexico*. New York: Harper & Row, 1961.

Dramesi, John A. *Code of Honor*. New York: Warner Books, 1975.

Draper, G. I. A. D. *The Red Cross Conventions*. New York: Praeger, 1958.

Dring, Thomas. *Recollections of the Jersey Prison-Ship*. Providence: H. H. Brown, 1829.

Dufour, Charles L. *The Mexican War: A Compact History, 1846–1848*. New York: Hawthorn, 1968.

Dupuy, R. Ernest, and William H. Baumer. *The Little Wars of the United States*. New York: Hawthorn, 1968

Durand, Arthur A. *Stalag Luft III*. Baton Rouge: Louisiana State University Press, 1988.

Durant, Will. *Our Oriental Heritage. The Story of Civilization: Part 1*. New York: Simon & Schuster, 1954.

Dyess, William E. *The Dyess Story: The Eye-Witness Account of the Death March and the Narrative of the Experiences in Japanese Prison Camps and of Eventual Escape*. Edited by Charles Leavelle. New York: Putnam's, 1944.

Eaton, Clement. *A History of the Southern Confederacy*. New York: Macmillan, 1954.

Eisenhower, Dwight. *Crusade in Europe*. New York, 1948.

Eisenhower, John R. *So Far from God: The U.S. War with Mexico*. New York: Random House, 1989.

Elting, John R. *Amateurs to Arms! A Military History of the War of 1812*. Chapel Hill, Md.: Algonquin Books of Chapel Hill, 1991.

Engleman, Fred. *The Peace of Christmas Eve*. New York: Harcourt Brace, 1962.

Evans, A. J. *The Escaping Club*. 6th ed. London: John Lane, 1921.

Falls, Cyril. *The Great War*. New York: Putnam's, 1959.

Farwell, Byron. *Over There: The United States in the Great War, 1917–1918*. New York: Norton, 1999.

Flanagan, E. M., Jr. *The Los Baños Raid. The 11th Airborne Jumps at Dawn*. Novato, Calif.: Presidio, 1986.

Fooks, Herbert C. *Prisoners of War*. Fredericksburg, Md.: Stowell, 1924.

Foote, Shelby. *The Civil War: A Narrative*. Vols. 1–3. New York: Random House, 1958, 1974, 1991.

Foss, John. *A Journal of the Captivity and Sufferings of John Foss, Several Years a Prisoner at Algiers: Together with Some Account of the Treatment of Christian Slaves When Sick, and Observations on the Manners and Customs of the Algerines*. Newburyport, Mass.: Printed by Angier March, 1798.

Fowler, William M., Jr. *Jack Tars and Commodores: The American Navy, 1783–1815*. Boston: Houghton Mifflin, 1984.

Foy, David A. *For You the War Is Over*. New York: Stein & Day, 1984.

Fredericks, Pierce G. *The Great Adventure: America in the First World War*. New York: Dutton, 1960.

Freidel, Frank. *The Splendid Little War*. Boston: Little, Brown, 1958.

French, Allen. *First Year of the American Revolution*. Boston, 1934.

Fujita, Frank. "Foo": *A Japanese-American Prisoner of the Rising Sun*. Denton: University of North Texas Press, 1993.

Fuller, J. F. C. *The Second World War*. New York, 1949.

Futch, Ovid L. *History of Andersonville Prison*. Gainesville: University of Florida Press, 1968.

Futrell, Robert Frank. *The United States Air Force in Korea, 1950–1953*. New York: USAF Historical Division, Research Studies Institute, 1961.

Gansberg, Judith. *Stalag U.S.A*. New York: Crowell, 1971.

Gardner, W. Allen. *Our Navy and the Barbary Corsairs*. Boston: Houghton Mifflin, 1905.

———. *Our Naval War with France*. Boston: Houghton Mifflin, 1909.

Gareth, Porter. *A Peace Denied: The U.S., Vietnam, and the Paris Agreement*. Bloomington: Indiana University Press, 1976.

Garland, Albert N., and Howard McGraw Smith. *Sicily and the Surrender of Italy*. Washington, D.C.: Office of the Chief of Military History, Department of the Army, 1965.

Gibbs, D. L. A. *Apennine Journey*. Gale & Polden.

Gilbert, Martin. *The First World War*. New York: Holt, 1994.

Gillmer, Thomas. *Old Ironsides*. Camden, Maine: International Marine, 1993.

Gilpin, Alex. R. *The War of 1812 in the Old Northwest*. East Lansing: Michigan State University Press, 1958.

Glatthaar, Joseph T. *Forged in Battle: The Civil War Alliance of Black Soldiers and White Officers*. New York: Free Press, 1990.

Gordon, Michael R. and Bernard Trainor. *The Generals' War*. New York: Little, Brown, 1995.

Greene, Bob. *Homecoming*. New York: Putnam's, 1989.

Gross, Ken, and Ross Perot. *The Man behind the Myth*. New York: Random House, 1992.

Hansen, K. K. *Heroes behind Barbed Wire*. Princeton, N.J.: D. Van Nostrand, 1957.

Harbord, James G. *The American Army in France, 1917–1919*. Boston: Little, Brown, 1936.

Hargrove, Hondon B. *Black Union Soldiers in the Civil War*. Jefferson, N.C.: McFarland, 1988.

Harrison, M. C. C., and H. A. Cartwright. *Within Four Walls*. London: E. Arnold, 1930.

Hart, B. H. Liddell. *History of the Second World War*. New York: Putnam's, 1970.

Hastings, Max. *The Korean War*. New York: Simon & Schuster, 1987.

Hemmerline, Richard E. *Prisons and Prisoners of the Civil War.* Boston: Christopher, 1934.

Henry, Robert Selph. *The Story of the Mexican War.* New York: Dc Capo, 1961.

Hermes, Walter G. *Truce, Tent, and Fighting Front.* Vol. 2. Washington, D.C.: Office of the Chief of Military History, United States Army, 1966.

Hesseltine William Best. *Civil War Prison: A Study in War Psychology.* New York: Frederick Ungar, 1930.

Hickey, Donald R. *The War of 1812: A Forgotten Conflict.* Urbana: University of Illinois Press, 1989.

Hobson, Richard Pearson. *The Sinking of the Merrimac.* Annapolis, Md.: Naval Institute Press, 1987. Originally published in 1899 by the Century Co., New York.

Hoffman, Ronald, and Peter J. Albert, eds.. *Peace and the Peacemakers: The Treaty of 1783.* Charlottesville: University Press of Virginia, 1983.

Holm, Jeanne. *Women in the Military: An Unfinished Revolution.* Rev. ed. Novato, Calif.: Presidio, 1992.

Holmes, Clay W. *The Elmira Prison Camp: History of the Military Prison at Elmira, NY July 6, 1864 to July 10, 1865.* New York: Putnam's, 1912.

Horsman, Reginald. *The Causes of the War of 1812.* New York: Knopf, 1969.

——. "The Paradox of Dartmoor Prison." *American Heritage*, February 1975, 13–17, 85.

Hougland, Vern. *Caged Eagles.* Blue Ridge Summit, Pa.: Tab Aero, 1992.

Hoyt, Edwin P. *Guadalcanal.* New York: Stein & Day, 1982.

——. *The Pusan Perimeter.* New York: Stein & Day, 1985.

Hubbell, John G. *P.O.W.* New York: Crowell, 1976.

Hyde, Solon. *A Captive of War.* Shippensburg, Pa.: Burd Street Press, 1996.

Hymoff, Edward. *The O.S.S. in World War II.* New York: Ballantine, 1972.

If You Should Be Captured, These Are Your Rights. War Department Pamphlet no. 21-7. Washington, D.C.: War Department, U.S. Government Printing Office, May 16, 1944.

Israel, Fred. L., ed. *Major Peace Treaties of Modern History, 1648–1967.* 4 vols. New York: Chelsea House, 1967.

Jackson, W. G. F. *The Battle for Italy.* New York: Harper & Row, 1967.

——. *The Battle for North Africa, 1949–1953.* New York: Mason/Charter, 1967.

Jenson-Stevenson, Monika, and William Stevenson. *Kiss the Boys Goodbye.* Toronto: McClelland & Stewart, 1990.

Johnson, Forrest Bryant. *Hour of Redemption: The Ranger Raid on Cabanatuan.* New York: Manor, 1978.

Jolidan, Laurence. *Last Seen Alive.* Austin, Tex.: Ink Slinger, 1995.

Jones, E. H. *The Road to Endor.* 4th ed. London: John Lane, 1920.

Joy, C. Turner. *How Communists Negotiate.* New York: Macmillan, 1955.

Kalb, Marvin, and Bernard Kalb. *Kissinger.* Boston: Little, Brown, 1974.

Karnow, Stanley. *Vietnam, a History: The First Complete Account of Vietnam at War.* New York: Penguin, 1984.

Keating, Susan Katz. *Prisoners of Hope.* New York: Random House, 1994.

Keegan, John. *The First World War.* New York: Knopf, 1998.

Kellogg, Robert H. *Life and Death in Rebel Prisons.* Freeport, N.Y.: Books for Libraries Press, 1971. First published in 1865.

Kennan, George. *Campaigning in Cuba.* Port Washington, N.Y.: Kennikat, 1977. First published in 1899.

Kerr, E. Bartlett. *Surrender and Survival: The Experience of American POWs in the Pacific, 1941–1945.* New York: Morrow, 1985.

King, John H., *Three Hundred Days in a Yankee Prison.* Kennesaw, Ga.: Continental, 1959.

Kinkead, Eugene. *In Every War but One.* New York: Norton, 1959.

Kissinger, Henry. *White House Years.* Boston: Little, Brown, 1979.

Knightly, Philip. *The First Casualty.* New York: Harcourt Brace Jovanovich, 1975.

Knox, Donald. *Death March.* New York: Harcourt Brace Jovanovich, 1981.

Knox, Dudley W. *A History of the United States Navy.* New York: Putnam's, 1936.

———. ed. *Naval Documents Related to the Quasi-War between the United States and France, 1797–1801.* 7 vols. Washington, D.C.: U.S. Government Printing Office, 1935–1938.

Krammer, Arnold. *Nazi Prisoners of War in America.* New York: Stein & Day, 1979.

Kurzman, Dan. *The Race for Rome.* Garden City, N.Y.: Doubleday, 1975.

Lane-Poole, Stanley. *The Barbary Corsairs.* Westport, Conn.: Negro Universities Press, 1970. First published in 1901.

Lavender, David. *Climax at Buena Vista.* Philadelphia: Lippincott, 1966.

Leckie, Robert. *The Wars of America.* Vol. 1, *Quebec to Appomattox.* New York: Bantam, 1968.

———. *The Wars of America.* Vol. 2, *San Juan Hill to Tonkin.* New York: Bantam, 1968.

——. *The Wars of America.* Rev. ed. New York: Harper & Row, 1981.

Lesinski, Jeanne M. *MIAs: A Reference Handbook.* Santa Barbara, Calif.: ABC-CLIO, 1998.

Lewis, George, and John Mewha. *History of Prisoner of War Utilization by the United States Army, 1776–1945.* Pamphlet no. 20-213. Washington, D.C.: Department of the Army, 1955.

Lewis, John H. *Recollections from 1860 to 1865.* Washington, D.C.: Peake, 1895. Reprinted in 1983 by Morningside House, Dayton, Ohio.

Lewy, Guenter. *America in Vietnam.* New York: Oxford University Press, 1978.

Linklater, Eric. *The Campaign in Italy.* London: H.M. Stationery off., 1951.

Lonn, Ella. *Desertion during the Civil War.* Gloucester, Mass.: Peter Smith, 1966. First published in 1928.

Lord, Walter. *The Dawn's Early Light.* New York: Norton, 1972.

Lowell, Edward J. *The Hessians and the Other German Auxillaries of Great Britain in the Revolutionary War.* New York: Harper Brothers, 1884.

MacDonald, Callum A. *Korea: The War before Vietnam.* New York: Free Press, 1987.

MacDonald, James Angus. *The Problems of U.S. Marine Corps Prisoners of War in Korea.* Washington, D.C.: History and Museum Divisions, Headquarters U.S. Marine Corps, 1961.

Mahan, A. T. *Sea Power in Its Relations to the War of 1812.* Vols. 1–2. Boston: Little, Brown, 1918.

Mahon, John K. *The War of 1812.* Gainesville: University of Florida Press, 1972.

Manchester, William. *American Caesar.* Boston: Little, Brown, 1978.

Markle, Clifford Milton. *A Yankee Prisoner in Hunland.* New Haven, Conn.: Yale University Press, 1922.

Marshall, Samuel L. A. *The Military History of the Korean War.* New York: F. Watts, 1963.

Marvel, William. *Andersonville, the Last Depot.* Chapel Hill: University of North Carolina Press, 1994.

McCarthy, W. *The Angels Came at Seven.* New York: Maryknoll Fathers, 1980.

McConnell, Malcolm. *Inside Hanoi's Secret Archives.* New York: Simon & Schuster, 1995.

McElroy. "Chaplains of the Mexican War, 1846." *Woodstock Letters* 15 (1886): 201.

McGrath, John M. *Prisoner of War: Six Years in Hanoi.* Annapolis, Md.: Naval Institute Press, 1975.

McWhiney, Grady, and Sue McWhiney, eds. *To Mexico with Taylor and Scott, 1845–1847.* Waltham Mass.: Blaisdell, 1969.

Meaney, Peter. "The Prison Ministry of Father Peter Whelan, Georgia Priest, and Confederate Chaplain." *Georgia Historical Quarterly,* Spring 1987, 1–24.

Melson, Charles D., and Curtis G. Arnold. *The U.S. Marines in Vietnam, the War That Would Not End, 1971–1973.* Washington, D.C.: History and Museums Division, Headquarters U.S. Marine Corps, 1991.

Merrill, James M. *The Rebel Shore: The Story of Union Sea Power in the Civil War.* Boston: Little, Brown, 1957.

Metzger, Charles. *The Prisoner in the American Revolution.* Chicago: Loyola University Press, 1971.

Miller, John C. *The Triumph of Freedom, 1775–1783.* Boston: Little, Brown, 1948.

Miller, John, Jr. *Cartwheel: The Reduction of Rabaul.* Washington, D.C.: Office of the Chief of Military History, Department of the Army, 1960.

Miller, Robert Ryal. *Shamrock and Sword: The Saint Patrick's Battalion in the Mexican War.* Norman: University of Oklahoma Press, 1989.

Millis, Walter. *The Martial Spirit: A Study of the War with Spain.* 1931. Chicago: Ivan R. Dee, 1989.

Minear, Richard. *Victors' Justice: The Tokyo War Crimes Trial.* Princeton, N.J.: Princeton University Press, 1972.

Moise, Edwin E. *Tonkin Gulf and the Escalation of the Vietnam War.* Chapel Hill: University of North Carolina Press, 1996.

Moorehead, Alan. *The March to Tunisia: The North African War, 1940–1943.* New York: Harper & Row, 1967.

Morison, Samuel Eliot. *The Rising Sun in the Pacific.* Vol. 3, *History of the U.S. Naval Operations in World War II.* Boston: Little, Brown, 1948.

Morrison, Wilbur H. *The Elephant and the Tiger: The Full Story of the Vietnam War.* New York: Hippocrene, 1990.

Moss, George Donelson et al., eds. *Vietnam: An American Ordeal.* Englewood Cliffs, N.J.: Prentice Hall, 1990.

Murphy, Edward F. *Vietnam Medal of Honor Heroes.* New York: Ballantine, 1987.

———. *Korean War Heroes.* Novato, Calif.: Presidio, 1992.

Murray, J. Ogden. *The Immortal Six Hundred.* Winchester, Va.: Eddy, 1905.

Musicant, Ivan. *Empire by Default: The Spanish-American War and the Dawn of the American Century.* New York: Holt, 1998.

Nash, Howard P., Jr. *A Naval History of the Civil War.* South Brunswick: Barnes, 1972.

Norman, Elizabeth M. *We Band of Angels.* New York: Random House, 1999.

Olmstead, A. T. *History of Assyria.* Chicago: University of Chicago Press, 1951. First published 1923.

Olsen, Jack. *Aphrodite: Desperate Mission.* New York: Putnam's, 1970.

Partridge, William Ordway. *Nathan Hale: The Ideal Patriot.* New York: Funk & Wagnalls, 1902.

Pasley, Virginia. *21 Stayed: The Story of the American GIs Who Chose Communist China: Who They Were and Why They Stayed.* New York: Farrar, Straus & Cudahy, 1955.

Patterson, Charles J., and G. Lee Tippin. *The Heroes Who Fell from Grace.* Canton, Ohio: Daring, 1985.

Paullin, Charles Oscar. *The Navy of the American Revolution.* New York: Haskell House, 1971.

Peele, Margaret W. *Letters from Libby Prison.* New York: Greenwich, 1956.

Perkins, Bradford. *Prologue to War: England and the United States, 1805–1812.* Berkeley, Calif.: University of California Press, 1961.

Perret, Geoffrey. *A Country Made by War.* New York: Random House, 1989.

Physick, Syng. *The Home Squadron under Commodore Conner in the War with Mexico.* Philadelphia, 1896.

Playfair, I. S. O. *The Mediterranean and the Middle East.* Vol. 2, *The Germans Came to Help Their Allies.* London: H.M. Stationery Off., 1956.

———. *The Mediterranean and the Middle East.* Vol. 3, *September 1941 to September 1942.* London: H.M. Stationery Off., 1960.

Porter, David. D. *The Naval History of the Civil War.* Glendale, N.Y.: Benchmark, 1970.

Porter, Gareth. *A Peace Denied: The United States, Vietnam, and the Paris Agreement.* Bloomington: Indiana University Press, 1975.

Poulos, Paula Nassen. *A Woman's War Too.* Washington, D.C.: National Archives and Records Administration, 1996.

Prados, John. *The Hidden History of the Vietnam War.* Chicago: Ivan R. Dee, 1995.

Prago, Louis. *The Battles of San Juan and El Caney, or The Siege of Santiago.* Santiago, Cuba: E. Betran, 1911.

Prange, Gordon. *Miracle at Midway.* New York: McGraw-Hill, 1982.

Pratt, Fletcher. *The Navy: A History.* Garden City, N.Y.: Doubleday, Doran, 1938.

Quarles, Benjamin. *The Negroes in the Civil War.* Boston: Little, Brown, 1953.

Records Relating to American Prisoners of War and Missing in Action from Vietnam War in 1960–1994. Reference Information Paper 90. Washington, D.C.: National Archives and Records Administration, 1995.

Records Relating to Personal Participation in World War II: American Prisoners of War and Civilian Internees. Reference Information Paper 80. Washington, D.C.: National Archives and Records Administration, 1992.

Reed, Paul, and Ted Schwarz. *Kontum Diary: Captive Writings Bring Peace to a Vietnam Veteran.* Arlington, Tex.: Summit, 1996.

Reid, P. R. *The Colditz Story.* Philadelphia: Lippincott, 1953.

Ridgway, Matthew B. *The Korean War.* Garden City, N.Y.: Doubleday and Company, Inc., 1967.

Risner, Robinson. *The Passing of the Night.* New York: Random House, 1973.

Rives, George Lockhart. *The United States and Mexico 1821–1848. Volumes I and II.* New York: Charles Scribner's Sons, 1913.

Robertson, Chimp. *POW/MIA: America's Missing Men.* Lancaster, Pa.: Starburst Publisher, P.O. Box 4123, 1995.

Robinson, Ralph. "Retaliation for the Treatment of Prisoners in the War of 1812." *American Historical Review,* October 1943, 65–70.

Rochester, Stuart, and Frederick Kiley. *Honor Bound: American Prisoners of War in Southeast Asia, 1961–1973.* Annapolis, Md.: Naval Institute Press, 1999.

Roosevelt, Theodore. *The Naval War of 1812.* 3d ed. New York: Putnam's, 1882.

Sakaida, Henry. *The Siege of Rabaul.* St. Paul, Minn.: Phalanx, 1996.

Sakamada, Kazuo. *I Attacked Pearl Harbor.* New York: Association Press, 1949.

Sauter, Mark, and Jim Sanders. *The Men We Left Behind.* Washington, D.C.: National Press Books, 1993.

Schear, George F., and Hugh F. Rankin. *Rebels and Redcoats.* Cleveland: World, 1957.

Schnabel, James F., and Robert J. Watson. *The History of the Joint Chiefs of Staff: The Joint Chiefs of Staff and National Policy.* Vol. 3, *The Korean War,* pt. 1 (1978) and pt. 2, (1979). Washington, D.C.: Government Printing Office.

Scott, John A. *Encarnacion Prisoners: Comprising an Account of the March of the Kentucky Cavalry from Louisville to the Rio Grande, together with an Authentic History of the Captivity of the American Prisoners, Including Incidents and Sketches of Men and Things on the Route and in Mexico.* Louisville: Prentice & Weissenger, 1848. Signed "A Prisoner."

Semmes, Raphael. *Service Afloat and Ashore during the Mexican War.* Cincinnati: Moore, 1851.

——. *Memoirs of Service Afloat, during the War between the States.* Baltimore: Kelly, Piet, 1899.

——. *The Confederate Raider Alabama.* Civil War Centennial Series Bloomington: Indiana University Press, 1962.

Shawson, John. *The Battle for North Africa.* New York: Bonanza, 1969.

Sheehen, Neil. *A Bright Shining Lie.* New York: Random House, 1988.

Sheppard, G. A. *The Italian Campaign, 1943–1945.* New York: Praeger, 1968.

Shultz, Duane. *Hero of Bataan: The Story of General Jonathan M. Wainwright.* New York: St. Martin's, 1981.

Sides, Hampton. *Ghost Soldiers.* New York: Doubleday, 2001.

Singletary, Otis A. *The Mexican War.* Chicago: University of Chicago Press, 1960.

Smith, Daniel M. *The Great Departure: The United States and World War I.* New York: Wiley, 1965.

Smith, George Winston, and Charles Judah. *Chronicles of the Gringos: The U.S. Army in the Mexican War, 1846–1848.* Albuquerque: University of New Mexico Press, 1968.

Smith, Joseph. *The Spanish-American War: Conflict in the Caribbean and the Pacific, 1895–1902.* New York: Longman, 1995.

Smith, Justin H. *The War with Mexico.* 2 vols. Gloucester, Mass.: Peter Smith, 1963.

Smith, Page. *John Adams, 1784–1826.* Garden City, N.Y.: Doubleday, 1962.

Smith, Robert Ross. *Triumph in the Philippines.* Washington, D.C.: Office of the Chief of Military History, Department of the Army, 1963.

Smythe, Howard. *The United States Army in World War II: Sicily and the Surrender of Italy.* Washington, D.C.: Government Printing Office, 1962.

Sotham, John. "The Heroes." *Air and Space Smithsonian,* July 2000.

Spector, Ronald H. *Eagle against the Sun.* New York: Free Press, 1985.

Speer, Lonnie R. *Portal to Hell: Military Prisons of the Civil War.* Mechanicsburg, Pa.: Stackpole, 1997.

Stagg, J. C. A. *Mr. Madison's War.* Princeton, N.J.: Princeton University Press, 1983.

Stern, Lewis M. *Imprisoned or Missing in Vietnam.* Jefferson, N.C.: McFarland, 1995.

Stevens, Frederic H. *Santo Tomas Internment Camp.* New York: Stratford, 1946.

Stevensen, Monika Jensen, and William Stevensen. *Kiss the Boys Goodbye.* New York: Dutton, 1990.

Stewart, Rochester, and Frederick Kiley. *Home Bound: The History of American Prisoners of War in Southeast Asia, 1961–1973.* Washington, D.C.: Office of the Secretary of Defense, Historical Office, 1998.

Stewart, Sidney. *Give Us This Day.* New York: Norton, 1957.

Stokesbury, James. *A Short History of the Korean War.* New York: Morrow, 1988.

Stone, Isidor F. *Hidden History of Korean War, 1950–1951.* New York: Monthly Review Press, 1952.

Strawson, John. *The Battle for North Africa.* New York: Bonanza, 1969.

Sugarmen, Joe. "Breakout from Chosen." *Air and Space Smithsonian,* July 2000.

Thomson, Basil. *The Story of Dartmoor Prison.* London: William Heinemann, 1907.

Timberg, Robert. *The Nightingale's Song.* New York: Simon & Schuster, 1995.

Titherington, Richard H. *A History of the Spanish-American War.* 1900 Freeport N.Y.: Books for Libraries Press, 1971.

Toland, John. *The Rising Sun: Decline and Fall of the Japanese Empire.* New York: Random House, 1976.

——. *In Mortal Combat: Korea, 1950–1953.* New York: Quill, 1991.

Trask, David E. *The War with Spain in 1898.* New York: Macmillan, 1981.

Tucker, Glenn. *Poltrons and Patriots.* Vols. 1–2. Indianapolis: Bobbs Merril, 1954.

——. *Dawn Like Thunder.* Indianapolis: Bobbs-Merrill, 1963.

Tutorow, Norman, ed. *The Mexican-American War: An Annotated Bibliography.* Westport, Conn.: Greenwood, 1981.

Two Historic Days: Snapshots of Spanish Prisoners from Cervera's Ships Landing at Seavey's Island. Portsmouth Harbor Pamphlet. Portsmouth, N.H.: Preston, 1898.

The U.N.C. REG Story, Munsan-ni Korea, September 1, 1953 to December 31, 1953. Pamphlet issued at Munsan-ni to all participating in the operation concerning repatriation of POWs.

Updyke, Frank A. *The Diplomacy of the War of 1812.* Baltimore: John Hopkins University Press, 1915.

U.S. Army in the World War, 1917–1919. Vols. 4–9. Washington, D.C.: Historical Division, Department of the Army, 1948.

U.S. Army in World War II: Mediterranean Theater of Operations. Northwest Africa: Seizing the Initiative in the West. Washington, D.C.: Office of the Chief of Military History, Department of the Army.

U.S. Army in World War II: War in the Pacific. Washington, D.C.: Office of the Chief of Military History, Department of the Army.

U.S. Department of Defense. *POW/MIA Fact Book.* 3 vols. Washington, D.C., 1983–1992.

U.S. House of Representatives. *Hostilities with Mexico, 1847.* 29th Congress, 2d sess. Document no. 119.

U.S. Navy. *Navy Documents Related to the U.S. Wars with the Barbary Pirates.* 6 vols. Washington, D.C.: U.S. Government Printing Office, 1939–1944.

U.S. Senate. *Report of the Select Committee on POW/MIA Affairs.* 103d Congress, 1st sess. Senate Report 103-1. Washington, D.C.: U.S. Government Printing Office, 1993.

U.S. Senate Committee on Foreign Relations. *An Examination of U.S. Policy Toward POW/MIAs.* 3d printing, November 1991. European theater only.

Vatcher, Hal. *Mutiny on Koje Island.* Rutland, Vt.: Tuttle, 1965.

Victor, John A. *Time Out: American Airmen at Stalag Luft 1.* New York: R. R. Smith, 1951.

Wainwright, Jonathan. *General Wainwright's Story.* Westport, Conn.: Greenwood, 1945.

Weems, John Edward. *To Conquer a Peace.* Garden City, N.Y.: Doubleday, 1974.

Weglyn, Michi. *Years of Infamy: The Untold Story of America's Concentration Camps.* New York: Morrow, 1976.

Weingartner, James. *Crossroads of Death: The Story of the Malmedy Massacre and Trial.* Berkeley: University of California Press, 1979.

Werstein, Irving. *1886: The Spanish-American War.* New York: Cooper Square, 1966.

———. *1898: The Spanish-American War Told with Pictures.* New York: Macmillan, 1981.

West, Richard S., Jr. *Mr. Lincoln's Navy.* New York: Longman, Green, 1958.

Westheimer, David. *Sitting It Out: A World War II POW Memoir.* Houston: Rice University Press, 1992.

Wheeler, Richard. *A Rising Thunder.* New York: HarperCollins, 1994.

Whipple, A. B. C. *Vintage Nantucket.* New York: Dodd, Mead, 1978.

———. *To the Shores of Tripoli.* New York: Morrow, 1991.

White, William L. *The Captives of Korea: An Unofficial White Paper of the Treatment of War Prisoners.* New York: Scribner's, 1957.

Whitehouse, Archibald. *Legion of the Lafayette.* Garden City, N.Y.: Doubleday, 1962.

Whiting, Charles. *Massacre at Malmedy.* New York: Stein & Day, 1971.

Whitlow, Robert H. *U.S. Marines in Vietnam, 1954–1964.* Washington, D.C.: History and Museums Division, Headquarters, U.S. Marine Corps, 1977.

Wilson, Joseph T. *The Black Phalanx: A History of the Negro Soldiers of the United States in the Wars of 1775, 1812, 1861–1865.* Hartford, Conn.: American, 1890.

Winnington, Allen, and Wilfred Burchett. *Plain Perfidy.* Peking, China, 1954.

Woodstock Letters 15, no. 2 (1886): 198–202.

Woodstock Letters 70 (1941): 46–47, 466–67.

Young, Kenneth T. *Negotiating with the Chinese Communists, 1953–1967.* New York: McGraw-Hill, 1968.

Zimmerman, James F. *Impressment of American Seamen.* New York: Columbia University Press, 1925.

About the Author

Harry P. Riconda graduated from Xavier High School, a Jesuit junior army ROTC high school in Manhattan. He then attended Fordham University in the Bronx, receiving a B.A. in government. Completing the ROTC program, he received a commission in the air force.

He worked as an assistant dean and taught one class at Xavier High School for three years as he studied for an M.A. degree in educational administration at Columbia Teachers College. His commission was activated in June 1952, and he served as an intelligence officer for about eighteen months, including one year in Korea.

His main duties were briefing and debriefing F-86 fighter-bomber pilots, as well as serving as group historian for the 8th Fighter-Bomber Wing. When the war ended, he was assigned to the army prisoner of war command and acted as an observer at the explanation sessions at Munsan-ni for the Chinese prisoners of war who claimed to be anti-Communist.

He was discharged as a first lieutenant in late January 1954 and returned to Xavier as a high school teacher of history and English. He studied for an M.A. in English at Lehman College in the Bronx. He also taught as an English adjunct at Touro College for four years and on retirement taught as an English adjunct at Westchester Community College for four years.

He resides in the Bronx with his wife, Kathleen. He has five sons, two grandsons, and five granddaughters.

Publisher's note: Sadly, Harry P. Riconda passed away in April 2003, during the production of this book.